A DIGITAL GUIDE

WEB
DESIGN

This is a Starfire Book
First Published in 2002

02 04 05 03

1 3 5 7 9 10 8 6 4 2

Starfire is part of
The Foundry Creative Media Company Limited
Crabtree Hall, Crabtree Lane, Fulham, London SW6 6TY

Visit the Foundry website: www.foundry.co.uk

Copyright © 2002 The Foundry

ISBN 1 903817 92 7

A copy of the CIP data for this book is available from the British Library

Printed in China

Special thanks to: Karen Fitzpatrick, Vicky Garrard, Michael Janes, Julia Rolf, Colin Rudderham and Tom Worsley

A DIGITAL GUIDE

WEB
DESIGN

ROGER LAING & RHYS LEWIS

CONSULTANT EDITOR: PRIYA RAVEENDRAN

STAR
FIRE

CONTENTS

HOW TO USE THIS BOOK

This book covers all aspects of web design and aims to give readers a wider practical and theoretical knowledge of the field. Readers are introduced to the design process and shown how to carry a web site project through from concept to completion, as well as learning the basics of web terminology. The book outlines design principles for crafting effective web pages and explains the different types of graphic formats, together with their use and how to optimize them for web delivery. There is also deeper discussion of graphic techniques, explaining the use of graphic tools and various image enhancement and manipulation techniques.

Readers are introduced to the myriad of software packages that are on the market. The major graphic programs such as Adobe Photoshop, Macromedia Fireworks and JASC Paint Shop Pro are covered, as well as the leading web-authoring programs Macromedia Dreamweaver, Macromedia Homesite and Microsoft FrontPage. There is also information on the major web browsers and their roles in successful web design.

Readers are shown how to create web pages to professional standards, employing user interface and usability principles. The book explains the Web's technical limitations, such as bandwidth and browser compatibility, and outlines measures that can be taken to manage and overcome them.

Tutorials are offered on creating effective web pages for both personal and commercial purposes, with explanations of HTML, style sheets and the inclusion of tables and frames. The book also covers animation and shows how to add dynamic factors and interactivity to web pages.

Dozens of tips are provided, helping readers to make informed decisions and to avoid common pitfalls that some beginners experience. Also included are a number of excellent sources where readers can obtain additional information, free software, graphics and fonts.

Importantly, the book gives an insight into more advanced techniques and technologies so that readers can understand and be aware of the Web's potential capabilities. Basic JavaScript is covered and the use of CGI, ASP, XML and Java in web pages is explained.

This book offers sound and thorough coverage of the fundamentals of web design and is suitable for both beginners and more advanced web designers. It successfully identifies the different facets of effective web design and gives readers a broader understanding of the field from a visual, a technological and a user-friendly point of view.

Each A–Z entry is tagged by themes which can be followed as threads throughout the book

Advanced	Software	Hot Websites
Intermediate	Hot Tips	Web Terminology
Basic	Technical	Web Theory

There are two types of pages throughout the book: the main A–Z entries and feature spreads (within the A–Z order), which focus on major topics and often present step-by-step information:

Main A–Z entries

Feature Spreads

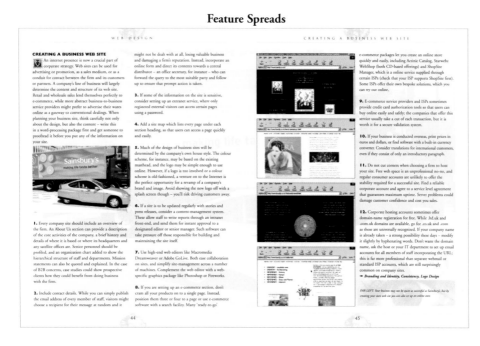

INTRODUCTION

With the World Wide Web being one of the fastest growing areas on the Internet, an increasing number of people want to take advantage of this new interactive and dynamic communications medium.

Web site design has made a significant impact on the Web. It is essentially information design and is a means of communicating information to your audience. Designing web sites is undeniably fun and exciting, but it is important to understand that web design is a multi-faceted field, encompassing a mixture of artistic and technological disciplines which range from graphic and user interface design to programming and client/server technology.

Most people have some idea of what they want their web site to communicate. The difficulty comes in knowing how to effectively present that idea. It is a common misconception that style is all that matters in web design, but this is not the case. What happens behind the scenes in creating a web site is just as important as how it looks up front and it is essential to understand the theory and practice behind why a site works. Knowing your design and technological options means you will be conscious of their potential, regardless of whether or not you decide to use them in your pages.

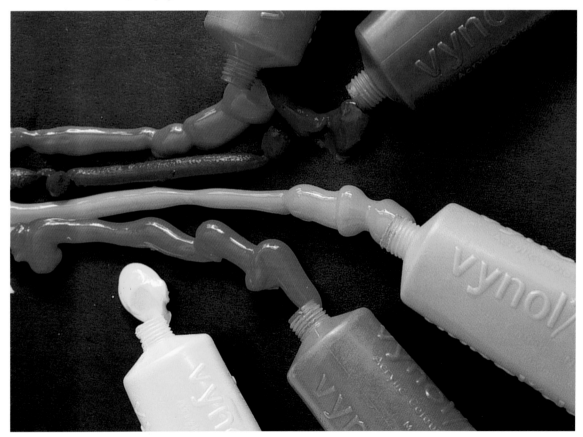

Good web design is hard to define, but there is an understanding of what you should and should not do. Guidelines and standards have been developed to assist web designers in creating more user-friendly pages. It is imperative to understand the motivation behind such rules rather than blindly applying them.

Web sites are often developed from one particular angle or another. Some are technology-oriented (which can result in the exclusion of users who do not have the most up-to-date browsers or plug-ins), others are content-oriented (which may result in a dull, boring site) and many more are visually oriented (which can result in the overuse of graphics, leading to higher file sizes and slower page-loading times).

The real emphasis, however, should be on the user, without losing sight of the technological and visual factors. Usability plays an integral part in the effectiveness of a web site and is directly related to user satisfaction. Meeting user needs and expectations is the key focus of user-oriented design, although it can be difficult to achieve a fine balance between designer wants and user needs. It is always important to remember that designers are not users and that users are not designers; progressive web designers need to have a solid understanding of their medium and their users.

The key to creating a successful web site lies in having a sound knowledge of all the factors influencing web design and in understanding how to achieve an effective balance between them.

ROGER LAING

1001FREEFONTS.COM

Free fonts site. This site has exactly what it says in the URL, if not more. As new fonts are regularly added, it is the fount of all free fonts – some 10,000 at the last count (notwithstanding that a few are shareware,

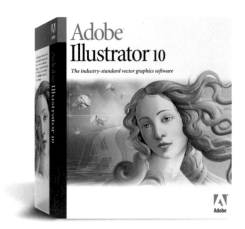

which have to be paid for if you decide to keep them). The site is boldly designed to give a clear view of how the fonts look and also divides up the fonts available for PC and those for the Mac. The splash page link to the Top 20 fonts is a bit misleading: it's not a countdown of the most popular hits on the site, but a completely different freeware site. This also happens elsewhere on the site – what appears to be part of the site's navigation is really an external link. There are, however, links to tools that enable you to create your own fonts, together with some useful tutorials guiding you through the pitfalls of Type 1 font management etc. If you send a sample of your handwriting with the appropriate fee, it can be made into a font – just keep it away from anyone with access to your chequebook.

➡ *Free Web Extras, Font, Dingbat, Fontfreak.com*

ACROBAT (ADOBE)

Cross-platform document writer and reader. Adobe's Acrobat lets publishers distribute documents originally created for print-based publication over the Web, without compromising the design and without relying on the recipient having a copy of the software application that created the original. Documents created in common office applications such as Word, Excel or desktop-publishing program QuarkXPress can be converted into Adobe's portable document format (PDF)

using Acrobat. Anyone with a copy of Acrobat Reader, available free from www.adobe.com, can view the file. Browsers will open a hyperlinked PDF file within the main browser window just like any other web page. Files can be saved to the hard disk and printed, and documents can be read on Windows and Macintosh computers. Because it compresses large documents into convenient, platform-independent files, Acrobat is commonly used to distribute longer, design-led publications such as company reports or brochures. Acrobat users can also create interactive online application forms, called eForms, which recipients can complete and return using their browsers.

Users of the full Acrobat program can add comments and virtual sticky notes to a PDF file of a draft document using a browser. A third Acrobat product – Approval – lets managers approve documents or forms using an encrypted digital signature.

➡ *Adobe, PDF, Plug-In*

ACTIVEX CONTROL

Web page technology. ActiveX controls can add greater interactivity to web pages than other technologies, but you should bear in mind that they also carry greater risks. ActiveX is the brand name of a group of technologies developed by Microsoft, which sets down rules for how applications share information. ActiveX programs – called controls – are reusable bits of software that add interactivity to a web page. These mini programs, similar to Java applets, can be as complex as a video player or as simple as a highlighting button.

The controls are downloaded to your hard drive where they are saved; this means that if you visit a page which needs the same control it won't be downloaded again. This is the notable advantage of ActiveX over Java applets, which are not cached and have to be downloaded each time you visit a page. Once downloaded, ActiveX controls can access all parts of your computer. Consequently, they carry a greater security risk than Java applets, which only interact with your machine within a specified area (sandbox). Accordingly, you can set different levels of security within your browser, to warn you every time an ActiveX control is encountered.

➠ *Applet, Functionality, Java*

ADOBE

Design software specialist. The long-time favourite developer of the design community, Adobe has eased its proponents' journey to the Internet by adding web-specific features to its set of established design programs, producing a web site creation tool and creating the Acrobat portable document format (PDF).

High-end image editing package Photoshop includes tools to optimize and compress graphics for web use, as does Adobe's vector-based drawing application, Illustrator. Both programs simplify the creation of dynamic buttons and animations, while LiveMotion combines Photoshop

and Illustrator images into complex, full-screen animated sequences.

GoLive is the company's fully featured professional web-authoring package, while the Acrobat system lets publishers distribute desktop-publishing files and forms across the Internet, regardless of the recipient's operating system or hardware and software setups.

➠ *Acrobat, Graphic Design Package, Illustrator, Macromedia, PDF, Photoshop*

ABOVE: Adobe's Illustrator allows artists, graphic designers and even beginners to approach art in a different way.

ALIGNMENT

Positioning text and graphics. In print layout, programs such as QuarkXPress let you put text and images where you want, with pixel precision. On the Web it is a much more tortuous process, in part because little on a web page is fixed. There are a number of alignment tags used within HTML. For basic text, line breaks <BR> will wrap text to the next line. If you want to add extra space, use the paragraph break instead <P>. To align text next to an image use the <IMG> tag with the ALIGN attribute. The text can be aligned to the top, middle, bottom, left or right of the image. If you want to put more space between the text and graphic, use the HSPACE and VSPACE attributes.

For better control of alignment, however, it is best to use tables; it is also possible to use cascading style sheets for pixel-perfect alignment, but browser support is patchy. The same HTML tags work within the individual cells of the table, but by using tables to create a design grid it is possible to achieve much more.

➡ *HTML Tags, Spacing, Spacing Using the Single Pixel, Page Layout*

ANCHOR

In HTML an Anchor is the target of a hypertext link within a document, or a reference to such a target. They are the tags that form the basis of the links set up between web pages, or to different sections of the same page.

The coding:

<a name="name"></a>

creates a target location within a document, and:

<a href="name"></a>

links to that target location from elsewhere in the document.

The anchor tag is perhaps the most fundamental of all for the Web, as it is the one that makes linking possible. The start and end tags wrap around the text or graphic you want linked. Whatever is within the anchor tag shows up as a link in the browser. Conventionally, a linked text or graphic is shown as blue and underlined, although this styling can be changed.

To tell the browser where to link to the attribute, HREF (hypertext reference) is added with the URL of the page. Usually the HREF points to a web page, but it can also be used to link to images or sound or video files. The URL can be absolute, usually when pointing to a document on the Web, such as <A HREF=http://www.bbc.co.uk>The BBC</A>. Alternatively, it is a relative URL if it is linked to a page on your own site or server, e.g. <A HREF="about.html">Information about our company</A>.

You can also use the anchor tag together with the name attribute to create a point on the page which can be linked to or from another spot on the same document. This is useful for finding a specific section on long, scrolling pages, or for getting back to the top of the page with a single click.

➡ *Link, HTML, Target*

ANGELFIRE (www.angelfire.com)

Web site hosting service. The slightly ethereal name comes from the founder's ex-girlfriend who believed in Angel power. Thankfully, the resulting site is more down-to-earth. Part of the giant Lycos network, this is a personal web site builder that offers free graphics, template designs and a personalized URL. The easy-to-use building tools provide access to cut-and-paste JavaScript and CGI scripts and the service also supports sites created in Microsoft's FrontPage. The only drawback is that the free service places ads on your site; however, you get a reasonable 20 MB of space and free games that you can add to your web page. What's more, if those ads become too annoying, you can pay a small monthly fee to get rid of them. The Angelfire Plus service also lets you add more

space – up to 250 MB – if you're feeling popular, and up to 2.5 GB extra bandwidth. The extra web space can be used for other purposes if your PC is getting cluttered or you need remote access to files, you can store them in the web folders that can be accessed from any PC.

➠ *Free Web Hosting, Tripod, Geocities*

ANIMATED GIF

Graphics file format; a simple but effective way to bring some action to your web pages. Animated GIFs work in much the same way as flipping through a cartoon book: several images are combined into a single GIF file and the animation effect is produced by rotating through them in sequence.

The compact GIF file can be put on your web page like any other graphics file. The original images can be composed in your regular graphics program. It is advisable to restrict the number of images – or frames – you use, as the more there are, the bigger the file size and the longer the download time. The individual frames are put together in sequence in an animation program, such

as GIFmation on the Apple Macintosh or GIF Animator on the PC. Here, you set such features as the delay between frames and the number of times you want the animation to repeat (loop).

While animated GIFs aren't as smooth or clever as animations produced in other formats, they are extremely popular because of their low file-size and the fact they can be viewed in nearly all browsers without the need for any additional viewer or plug-in.

➠ *Animation*

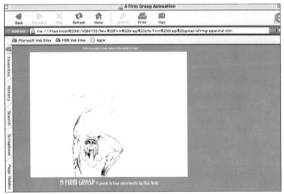

TOP: Animated GIFs work in much the same way as flipping through a cartoon book.

ANIMATION

Interactivity on the Web. Animation on the Web is becoming increasingly sophisticated, thanks to multimedia tools like Flash and Shockwave. While animated GIFs have been a popular way to add action to a web page, they do not allow any interaction. Another problem with these is that they are bitmaps (in the raster format), where each dot of the image is made up on screen from coloured pixels. A lot of information is needed to describe each pixel in the file, with the result that if more than a few frames are used, or the animation is used full screen, the file size is excessively large.

Macromedia's Flash will give you full-screen, fully-interactive streaming animation with sound. This uses a vector instead of raster format, where shapes, objects and colours are described mathematically rather than being mapped to individual pixels. This data is stored in a simple plain text file and it takes relatively little text to describe a full-blown animation. There are a number of advantages to Flash: it is scalable, so images can be resized with no loss of detail; it uses streaming technology, so animations start playing as soon as enough data is downloaded and carry on while the rest of the file is transferred; image quality is high; and it is a good way to add user-triggered sound effects to the Web, as animations can be synchronized with high-quality streaming audio.

Flash will also do a lot of the work for you. If you make the first and last 'keyframes', Flash will build all the frames in between and even include actions such as rotating or fading the image. Inevitably, there is one main drawback. Flash files (which have the SWF extension) need to be viewed through a special plug-in or player, although both are readily available from the Macromedia site. Flash is both a product and an open file format, so Adobe also have a tool – LiveMotion – that creates interactive buttons and animated objects and saves them in the Flash format.

Macromedia's Shockwave for Director is another technology for creating complex interactive presentations to run on the Web. It does so by synchronizing sound, video and animation. While more sophisticated and versatile than Flash, Shockwave file sizes tend to be much bigger, so they are not as good for delivery over the Web.

➡ *Animated GIF, Macromedia Flash, Macromedia Fireworks, Raster, Vector*

ANIMATION PRINCIPLES

Creating and using inline animations. Colourful graphics set the Web apart from its text-based precursors, but animation really brought the new medium to life.

Movement can entertain, engage and inform, and has been used on the web for everything from eye-catching advertising banners and buttons to corporate presentations.

Most of the animations you will see on the Web are simple animated GIFs. An animated GIF is merely a series of small images strung together using a graphics package such Fireworks or Photoshop, or a separate dedicated application such as Jasc Software's Animation Shop for PC or GIF Builder for the Mac. Each frame can be set to appear for a set time, but no music can be attached to the animation and interactivity extends only as far as a simple hyperlink or image map. However, all the major browsers can display animated GIFs – a universality that makes the format appealing.

Designers seeking more complex and interactive animations should investigate Macromedia's Flash format. Flash lets users combine imported images and their own vector-graphic creations into small animations, full-screen presentations or even broadcast-quality animated movies. Flash animations are also scaleable, so a user could view your work full-screen with very little of the ugly pixel break-up evident when animated GIFs are increased in size. Flash's advanced features mean that interactivity can be built into each frame, so for instance you could display a Flash animation of floating hyperlinks each of which links to a different destination.

The flexibility of Flash comes at a price, however. Unlike the universally accepted GIF, Flash technology requires that the end user has the latest Flash Player plug-in installed. This is available from Macromedia's web

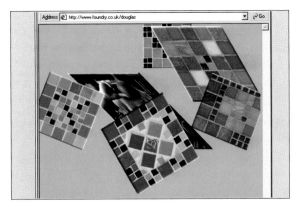

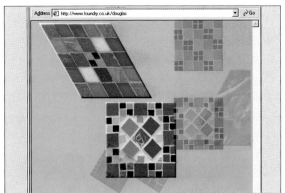

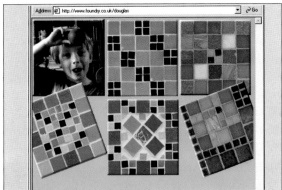

If you can't create the images yourself, you might find images or effects you like at online GIF libraries, but be careful what you use; 'Email Us' buttons showing a letter posting itself are so hackneyed they could turn some visitors away. Consider the overall design and colour scheme of your site – if a graphic clashes with your design, it is probably better to produce your own animation or use a static image instead.

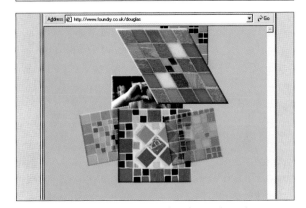

Finally, don't loop an animation continuously, as this is more likely to annoy readers than prompt them to click on the link. A good idea is to set the last frame of the animation to pause for around 10 seconds before it repeats, then set it to repeat just three or four times.

➡ *Animated GIF, Animation, Non-Linear Animation, Macromedia Flash*

FAR LEFT: Create a soundtrack for your animation; use Macromedia's Shockwave for Director to synchronise sound and images.

site and, at around 200 KB, makes for a relatively small download, but some users could view the wait as an inconvenience.

Just because packages such as Flash, Fireworks and Photoshop make animating easy by performing tricks, like adding intermediate frames between your start and finish points, doesn't mean you should plaster your site with movement, so use sparingly.

ANIMATION USING FLASH

Interactive, scalable animated sequences. Macromedia Flash has become the industry standard format for compact, interactive animations. Their small size makes them ideal for distribution over the Internet, and the powerful Flash application lets developers create everything from two-frame animations and drop-down menus to broadcast-quality movies and entire e-commerce sites offering links into server-side databases.

Creating a simple animation using Flash is based around two main windows: the Timeline and the Stage. Like the main window of any graphics package, the Stage is where you place the elements of your animation, and as with Photoshop and Fireworks can be built up in layers to give accurate control over each element. Vector elements like circles, rectangles or irregular shapes can be created and edited using the program's comprehensive toolset, or existing images can be imported from other graphics applications including Macromedia's own FreeHand.

Audrey Hepburn

Elements can also be dragged and dropped from libraries.

Where the Flash Stage differs from the main window of a regular graphics package is that what you see on the Stage represents only one frame of the animation, with all the objects in their positions at a particular point in time, indicated in the Timeline window. This point can be changed by dragging the indicator across the Timeline to the desired frame.

Among the frames will be several Keyframes. These mark the points where a new element – image or sound – enters or exits an animation, or begins and ends a pre-determined path or sequence. These sequences are the key to the simple creation of smooth animations in Flash. Simply convert the element from a graphic to a symbol, position it where you want it to be at the beginning and end of the sequence, and Flash will chart the symbol's movement, adding the frames in between using what Macromedia terms 'Tweening'.

As well as moving an object across the screen, Tweening can be used to change the size, shape and

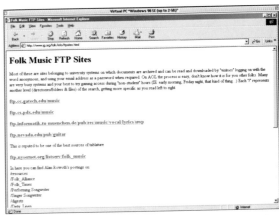

colour of an object as it moves. Simply double the size and alter the colour of the graphic in the first and last frames, specify a path by clicking and dragging your mouse and the object will appear to zoom towards the viewer and across the screen. Similarly, a Shape Tween can morph one image into another, to eye-catching effect.

By adding audio tracks to the Timeline and spreading elements across several independent layers, Flash can be used to create simple, small and effective animations.

➥ *Animation, Animation Principles, Macromedia Flash, Non-Linear Animation*

ANONYMOUS FTP

System on FTP archive sites where users can log on anonymously in order to download the files they want. This is not quite the cloak-and-dagger operation its name suggests, and there are many sites on the Web where files can be downloaded through anonymous FTP. In practice, it simply means you can log on to the server without having your own personal account on that machine. Usually the login ID is 'anonymous' and the password will typically be your email address. Some FTP client software, such as LapLinkFTP, will automatically enter this information for you.

Archive sites that let anyone enter and download files in this way are known as anonymous FTP servers. By contrast, some FTP sites where files are stored are only accessible by authorized users. They will have to enter a previously arranged username and password to connect to the server.

Anonymous FTP sites make an enormous amount of information available to anyone who wants it, from archives of mailing lists to software, MP3 and other audio files. There are also several sites that offer free graphics, clip art and images for use on web pages. Most files will be need to be decompressed before use.

➥ *FTP, CuteFTP, LaplinkFTP, Uploading a Web Site*

FAR LEFT: *Bring the glamour and style of the movies to your site using Macromedia Flash.*

ANTI-ALIASING

Method of smoothing over the jagged effect of low-resolution images on screen. Because everything shown on screen is mapped to square pixels, the edges of curved lines in images and text will have a block effect; an effect sometimes referred to as having the 'jaggies'. In technical terms, images like this are said to be aliased. Many imaging programs, such as Adobe Photoshop and Jasc's Paint Shop Pro, enable you to

anti-alias low-resolution graphics by blending the edges with tints of the next colour to smooth over the jagged lines. This has the effect of blurring the edges, which with smaller images may be worse than the jaggedness itself; it is particularly noticeable with small type. While anti-aliasing can improve the look of large headings used in graphics it makes smaller text more difficult to read. As a result, it is generally accepted that type 12 points or under should not be anti-aliased. There are also problems if an anti-aliased graphic with a transparent background is put on a web page that has a different background colour. One way around this problem is to anti-alias the graphic using the colour of the background on to which it will eventually be placed.

➠ *Graphic Design Package, Image Enhancement Techniques*

APPLET

Miniature programs, designed to run within another application, which can add interaction to your web site. Before the coming of the World Wide Web, the terms applets mainly referred to the small programs that came as part of the Windows package, such as Calculator and Character Map, which could be accessed from many different applications. In the internet age, however, this has changed. Now applet more commonly refers to any small program sent to a user with a web page. By downloading the applet the user can run programs from the Internet that they do not have on their machine. In particular, applets are associated with the Java programming language. Java programs can be run on a computer like any other application. When they are run from the Internet, within a browser, they are called applets. The range of what they can do is limitless – from providing interactivity, database connectivity or doing computations in real-time.

As they are generally quite small, applets download quickly, are cross-platform compatible and secure. The programs can be placed directly on the web page by using the <applet> tag. Although this tag is deprecated in HTML 4.01 in favour of the <object> tag, it is currently more widely supported and reliable.

➠ *Java, ActiveX Control, Script, Functionality*

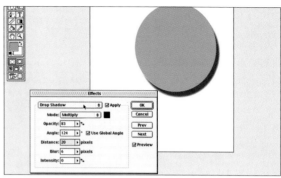

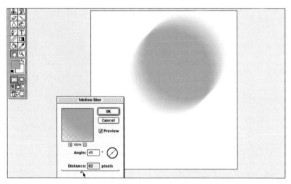

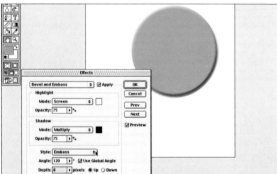

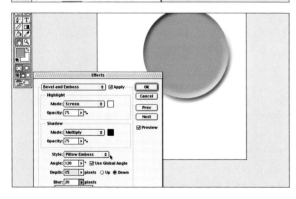

ARTFUL DISTORTION

Using graphics filters and special effects. Every good graphics software application boasts a myriad of distortion filters, and while many of these special effects are actually little more than novelty tools to entertain and impress, some of them can add a professional touch to your site.

The simplest distortion filters alter the brightness and contrast settings. These can be used to rectify scanning errors, but also allow you to convert a full-colour image into a light-saturated background image for a web page. Similarly, filters can convert an image to greyscale or render a whole picture in shades of a single colour to achieve an eye-catching effect.

Applying a blur filter also helps to take the emphasis off an image, and is best used to create an abstract background image, over which solid blocks of text become even more visible. The common motion blur effect gives the appearance of movement, while the drop shadow brings depth to a page. Likewise, bevel tools cleverly give the impression of raised or indented buttons on the flat computer screen.

Despite the plethora of distortion tools on offer, avoid the temptation to turn all your images into mosaics or pointillist works of art. Used wisely, such tools can help enhance the appearance of your site.

➡ *Graphic Design Package, Image Enhancement Techniques, Image Manipulation*

FAR LEFT: Imaging programs blend the edges of images with tints of the next colour, smoothing away any jagged lines.

ASP

Active Server Pages; server-side scripting. Microsoft's framework for server-side scripting can handle major e-commerce sites or simple form-processing for those working with windows-based web servers. It can be used to construct major e-commerce web sites but is also useful for anyone with a Windows-based web server. ASP enables you to process and store information – such as from a form – in a database. It also allows you to personalize content according to users' preferences, or to vary the web page layout for different browsers.

ASPs have the extension .asp instead of .html. This indicates that it is a text file with HTML and scripting (usually it is written in VBScript). When your browser requests an .asp file from the server, the web server calls ASP, which processes the file from top to bottom and runs any scripts commands before sending the results as a web page to the browser.

As the scripts run on the server rather than the client the process is faster than client-side processing. In addition, scripts cannot be easily copied as the commands used to create the page run server-side and are not viewable within the page they generate.

➥ *Script, Functionality, VBScript*

ASSET MANAGEMENT

Web-site organization. Even a small web site can amass an amazing number of different files, including HTML pages, graphics files, 3D images, flash buttons, a database and so on. Just as it is important to have a clear navigation structure for the site as a whole, it is also important to organize the files that make up the site. The easiest way is to create a directory structure to hold the different categories of material. The first directory, or folder, you create is the root directory, which typically carries the name of the site (e.g. mycompany). The HTML files are usually held directly in this root

folder, but it is a good idea to create six further folders to hold other types of material e.g. 'Images' to hold graphics files; 'Media' to handle flash, audio and video files; 'Database' to cover any database-held material, such as a catalogue or membership information; 'Resources' containing original vector images or shared media; a 'Library' for commonly used HTML-based objects; and 'Templates'as a standard layout pattern for HTML pages. On bigger sites, sub-sections would go within their own folders or directories.

➥ *File Organization*

BACKGROUND COLOUR

Colour on the page. Solid colour backgrounds can be used with graphic images to set the tone while the rest of the page downloads. By default a web page is fairly colourless – plain white or grey. Yet, it is a simple matter to add some colour. To put a solid colour in the background of the page we use the <BODY> tag. This is the tag that determines what we see in the visible part of a web document. With the attribute BGCOLOR you can add a splash of interest to the background, but be careful which colours you choose. For example, <BODY BGCOLOR="dodgerblue"> might brighten up the day, but it might also clash with the text and graphics you have used. A paler background is 'aliceblue'. You can specify colours by their name or hexadecimal value, but

be warned that they will not always look the same to your users as they do to you. The colours they see will depend on how their monitor is set up – the number of colours it can display and the brightness.

The BGCOLOR attribute can also be used in tandem with the BACKGROUND attribute, which is used to add a graphic as a background image. By making the background colour the same as the main colour in the graphic, the page will load the main colour immediately while the rest of the graphic is downloading.

➡ *Colour, Colour Combinations, HTML*

BACKGROUND IMAGE

Visual backdrop to a web page. Using a background image can add a lot of interest to a page for relatively little overhead. A background graphic can fill the browser screen without taking up all the bandwidth, although it will load slower than one with just a solid background colour. The reason for this is that the image does not need to be the size of the space it will

eventually fill. The graphic file (or tile) which is downloaded is automatically repeated by the browser to fill the page.

Images can be any web graphic as long as it is correctly formatted – whether a picture, a textured pattern, or a piece of clip art. However, while textured backgrounds are good because they add a bit of depth to your web page, remember that they can make the text very difficult to read if they are too obtrusive. Watermark backgrounds work slightly differently in that the image does not move when you scroll the page. When using an image as a background it is also worth specifying a background colour. This way the colour appears while the image is downloading. It also provides a background if users have turned off image viewing in their browsers.

➡ *Image Use, HTML, Watermark, Tiling Background Images*

ABOVE: Use a striking background image to add interest to an otherwise dull page.

BANDWIDTH

Data transmission measure; designing for the Web is limited by the amount of bandwidth available to the average user. Bandwidth is the great constraining factor on web design: there could certainly be more fantastic works of art on the Web but for the fact that it all has to be delivered through a noisy connection at an average speed of 56 Kbps or less. Technically, bandwidth is a measure of the amount of data that can be transmitted in a fixed amount of time. It is usually shown as bits per second (bps). The greater the bandwidth the faster data can be sent. The new broadband connections, such as ADSL, offer much faster speeds than a typical modem connection. They are therefore ideal for viewing multimedia sites, but they have not yet been widely adopted. For the designer, the typical user is still more likely to be using a standard 56 Kbps modem on a dial-up connection. While text does not carry any great payload on a page, graphics and video files do. Superfluous images are only likely to annoy users who have to wait for them to download. Generally, it is best to limit the total size of files on web pages to a maximum of 30 KB.

➠ *Page Loading Time, Technical Limitations*

BANNER

Advertisement usually placed at the top of a web page. As essential to commercial web sites as the ads on television, the banner ad isn't going to go away soon. While advertising spend is not sufficient to support most web operations it is still a crucial part. Typically, clicking on a link within the banner ad will launch the advertiser's website in a new page. Originally, the cost of such ads was based on page impressions (the number of people who could potentially see it) but now it is usually linked to the number of people who click through to the advertiser's site. As part of the continuing battle to catch the user's attention, banner ads have gone from plain text and pictures to all-dancing animations. The downside of this is that it is proving increasingly annoying to many users, leading to a demand for software that kills the ads.

There are several 'standard' banner-ad sizes, of which the most common is 468 x 60 pixels. Advertisers are always keen to be placed in a prominent position –

usually as close to the top of the page as possible – while designers are keen to differentiate banner ads from content by adding rules, borders and spaces.

➠ *Animation, Promoting a Web Site, ImageReady (Adobe), Flash (MacroMedia)*

BEVEL AND EMBOSS

Special effects for graphics. Whether you want a ready-made set of 3D-style rollover buttons or a smoothly embossed company name, there are tools to make the process as effortless as possible. A bevel effect can be used to give a 3D appearance to buttons or letters.

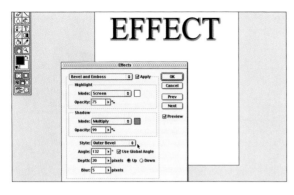

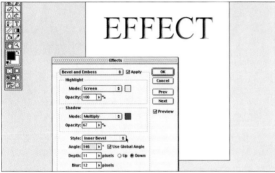

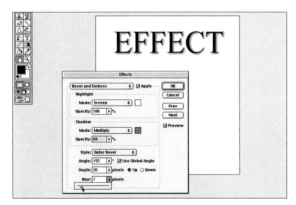

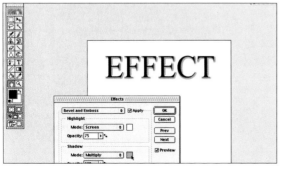

Different looks can be created by using an outer bevel (which makes the whole object look raised) or inner (which gives the impression of a raised rim). Having selected the bevel effect, there are a number of options to set. If you chose an outer bevel you can select the colour of the bevel (if you chose an inner bevel it takes its colour from the original object). If the bevel appears a bit blocky around curved objects, use the softness control to alter the severity of the edges.

Some graphics editors, such as Macromedia's Fireworks, come with a number of preset bevel shapes. The bevel effect can be flat, sloped, smooth, like a frame, or a ring. To change the size of the effect, you alter the pixel size of the bevel. Fireworks also comes with four button presets to apply special effects to the bevels, which can be handy for setting up rollover buttons. The four states are the default, 'raised' button; the 'highlighted' look, which applies a 25 per cent white tint to the object; 'inset', which changes the lighting to invert the 3D effect; and 'inverted', which reverses the lighting and applies a tint to lighten the object. The four different states can be applied to rollovers so that, for example, 'raised' is used for the Up state graphic, 'highlighted' for the Over state, and 'inset' for the Down state.

The emboss effect pushes the shape of an object out from its background (raised emboss) or down into the object (inset emboss). Again the effect can be varied using a set of controls. The width control alters the size of the embossed edge; the contrast control changes the light to create highlights and shadows; while the softness control alters the sharpness of the embossed edge.

Bear in mind that most graphics editors will let you apply several effects to the same object, but the order in which you apply them will change the final look of the graphic. For example, if you create a button and add a bevel effect after a drop shadow, it does not appear as raised as if you apply the bevel effect before adding the drop shadow.

➡ *Graphic Design Package, Fireworks (Macromedia), Image Enhancement Techniques*

FAR LEFT: Apply special effects to any bevels using Macromedia's graphic design package, Fireworks.

BITMAP

Graphics file format. Bitmapped images are represented by pixels rather than mathematical formulas and are often compressed to reduce file size. There are two basic kinds of computer graphics – bitmapped (also known as rasterized) and vector (also known as object-oriented). Bitmapped graphics come in many file formats including GIF, JPEG, and TIFF as well as BMP (which has the filename extension .bmp).

Bitmapped images are made up of rows and columns of dots. Each dot of the image is created on screen by individual pixels, that is the bits of information are mapped to the pixels. The number of colours in a bitmapped image is determined by the bit depth. With black-and-white images, one bit equals one dot, but for colours each dot is represented by several bits of data. For example, a GIF file can save up to 8 bits per pixel, which is 256 colours. Reducing the number of colours can lower the file size. Equally, bitmap files can be compressed, but the advantages of this have to be weighed against the reduction in picture quality.

Vector graphics are generally smoother, because shapes are mathematically defined instead of being mapped to individual pixels. Most drawing or illustration programs, such as Freehand or Illustrator, produce vector graphics. However, they need to be turned into bitmaps in a program such as Photoshop before being posted to the Web.
➠ *Pixel, Vector, Raster, GIF, JPEG*

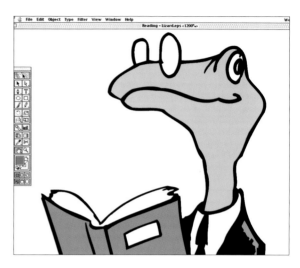

BMP

Graphics file format; filename extension .bmp (bitmapped). This is the file extension that marks the standard Windows graphic file in its uncompressed form. In a bitmapped graphic, the image is made up of dots. The density of the dots (measured as dots per inch or dpi) shows the resolution, or sharpness of the image. On screen the images are mapped to the pixels. The number of colours in the image is determined by the bit depth. A 24-bit BMP would represent 16.7 million colours and would be a much larger file than the same image saved as a 256-colour bitmap.

If you create a picture in Paint, the graphics program that comes with Windows, it will be saved in the BMP file format by default. However, like many similar applications, it is possible to save files in an alternative format to the native file format. In fact, for use on the Web BMP files should be saved as either JPEGs or GIFs as both these formats involve compressing the image files to make them much smaller, so they download more quickly.
➠ *File Type, Bitmap, Pixel*

BRANDING AND IDENTITY

Creating a recognizable company image. Although it is the primary visual representative of a company, a brand is more than just a smart logo and a catchy slogan; it encompasses the message and the emotion that comes to mind when people think of a company or a

product. For web-based companies, the branding and identity will involve everything from the logo and site design to the usability of a site and the levels of service they claim – and manage – to offer. For traditional 'bricks-and-mortar' firms, a web site might simply be a brand extension that offers another way of dealing with the company. If a web site is slow and difficult to use, however, visitors will perceive the whole company in the same way.

The first step to achieving a strong brand is to combine a simple, eye-catching logo with a tagline that puts your company's main concerns – be it customer care, low-cost products or quick service – into four or five words.

On the Web, a domain name becomes as important as a company name. When choosing a domain, if your company name has already been registered, why not incorporate the brand message into the URL? Analysts claim that all the words in the English language have already been registered, so www.furniture.com is certainly out of the question. Avoid using the tagline as a sole domain as it may be difficult to remember (though it may be worth registering and redirecting to your primary URL).

Unless your business is going to be wholly web-based, do not incorporate 'net' into the domain or begin an URL with a gratuitous 'e'; this already looks a little out of

date. Sometimes unconnected words can make good domain names (think of Yahoo, Egg or Cahoot) provided the tagline and brand are strong enough to support it.

The growth of the Internet has led to many companies rebranding as web concerns. Budget airline Ryanair moved almost all of its sales operations over to the Web and since rebranding itself as 'Ryanair.com – The Low Fares Airline', has seen passenger numbers skyrocket. This has much to do with the combination of a reliable, no-nonsense web storefront and its clear and recognizable brand message. There is little point of rebranding fully as a dotcom, however, if high-street sales are going to continue to be the main conduits for business. One high-street store that rebranded all its outlets with a .co.uk suffix to coincide with the launch of a web-based shopping service saw sales fall as customers thought that it had closed down its regular stores.

➡ *Colour Combinations, Consistency, Creating a Business Web Site, Logo Design*

TOP LEFT: The Foundry's logo. A logo is an important aspect of company branding and therefore must be simple, yet eye-catching.

BROWSER

Web page viewer. Designing a magical shop window display can be difficult enough. But imagine the problems if you don't know what size window the display will be viewed through, whether the colours will show up, whether the exhibits will stay in the position they were put, or whether they can be seen at all. Yet that is the problem in designing for the Web. Not only are there differences in the way the browsers see each page and deal with the HTML, there are also differences between the same browsers on different platforms. The designer's challenge is to make the page as interesting as possible, making full use of the technological advances each new version of a browser brings, without alienating the audience with older browsers.

The standard compromise is to assume the majority of your users will have a version 4.0 browser or above. Consequently, tables, frames and most JavaScript functions are well supported, but the more sophisticated DHTML effects won't be.

By far the most popular browsers are Internet Explorer and Netscape Navigator (more commonly called Netscape 6.0 in the latest version), with surveys showing that 75% of people use Internet Explorer, 24% use Netscape Navigator and 1% use other browsers. Mini-browsers are also being built into other non-PC devices, such as PDAs, mobile phones and WebTV.

➠ *Microsoft Internet Explorer, Netscape Navigator, Netscape Communicator, Cross-Browser Compatibility*

BULLETS

Add emphasis to lists. It can be easier to read a list of items if they are separated as bullet points. Using the <UL>…</UL> container tag for unordered lists, the bullets are added automatically for each list item, marked with the <LI> tag.

You can change the bullet type using the TYPE attribute from the default black dot <UL TYPE="disc"> to a circle <UL TYPE="circle"> or a square <UL TYPE="square">. However, these can be a bit plain. You might want to jazz these up with your own bulleted lists – such as an anchor or a smiley face. To do so you don't use the list tags, as these would automatically insert the default bullets. First create

your graphic, which is usually best saved as a GIF. To make sure the bullet flows with the text without forcing extra space, keep the height to 10 or 12 pixels. For a short list, separate the entries with line or paragraph breaks. To create an indent, add space to the left and right of the graphic use the HSPACE attribute. For longer entries it is more accurate to use a table to control the alignment of the bullets with the text.

➡ *Lists, Links, Site Layout*

BYTE

Basic unit of storage, used as a measure of file size and, more generally, a computer's capacity. The term 'byte' comes from the phrase binary term. A byte is the smallest unit of storage on a computer that can hold a single character, such as a number, letter or symbol.

Under the binary system, it is made up from eight bits where each bit can have one of just two values: 0 or 1.

In graphics files, the number of colours is shown by its bit depth – that is, the number of bits used to represent each pixel of information in a file. For example, a one-bit image is monochrome; an 8-bit image supports 256 colours or shades of grey; and a 24-bit image includes 16.7 million colours. The higher the bit depth, the larger the file size.

The file size itself is measured in bytes. For example, a Word file that took up 1 MB of space would be able to store just over a million individual characters, roughly equivalent to 2,100 pages of information. More generally, a computer's capacity, such as its memory and disk space, is measured in bytes.

➡ *File Size*

FAR LEFT: A wizard would find designing his magic shop window display extra tricky if he didn't know what size window it would be viewed through.

CACHING IMAGES

Store for downloaded images. In the battle to minimize download time, the browser cache is very useful. When any graphics are downloaded they are automatically stored in the cache, saved to the web visitor's hard drive or memory so that if they are needed again they can be displayed pretty much instantly. As a result, if you use the same graphic – such as an icon or part of a navigation bar – several times, it costs nothing in download time after the first use.

The cache can also be used to download large image files and store them until they need to be displayed. Preloading images is done quite simply, by putting the graphic on an early page (such as the homepage) that is likely to be accessed and read first. But the trick is to set the width and height attributes to one pixel, such as <IMG SRC="largepic.gif" WIDTH="1" Height="1">. This way, the image will only appear as a one dot pixel (which can be placed somewhere unobtrusive) but will download with the rest of the page. When the user then goes to the page where the image is positioned full size, it will be loaded instantly from the cache.

➠ *Page Loading Time*

CGI

Common Gateway Interface; server-side processing. CGI is a simple standard for linking programs and Web servers, to provide server-side processing to web sites. It is a simple protocol for communication between a web server and an external program. CGI handles the flow of information between the two, in the same way as HTTP regulates the transfer of data between the server and the browser.

CGI applications, sometimes called scripts, work in a different way. They receive the data from the server and return it via the Common Gateway Interface. These programs are the most popular way for users to interact dynamically with the site – such as connecting to a database, sending information via email or processing information from a form. They can be written in any programming language, but are typically in C, C++, Perl, AppleScript or Visual Basic.

Unlike Java Applets and ActiveX controls, which run on the client machine, CGI programs run on the web server. Although the CGI protocol is easy to use, it can slow performance on the web server when a large number of people use an application at the same time.

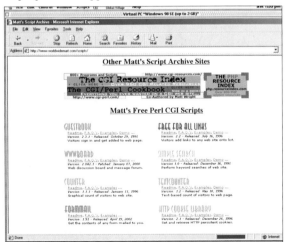

There are many CGI scripts and applications, covering everything from loan calculators to logging the number of visitors to your site, freely available for download from a number of sites. Among them is Matt's Script Archive at www.worldwidemart.com/scripts.

➡ *Script, Functionality, Form Handler*

CLIENT

Server-linked PC or program. Clients can either be the PCs themselves or the programs on them that rely on servers to carry out certain services for them. Typically, a client PC is linked, either through a physical network or, in the case of the Internet, over phone lines to a server. The 'back-end' server – also called the host computer – carries out certain services for the 'front-end'

client program, which runs on the PC. For example, a mail server delivers or sends messages that have been written in a client program, such as Outlook.

Another client program is your browser. Type in a URL in the address bar of the browser and the request goes first to a DNS server the translates that address into a network location. It then goes to the web server, which processes the request and returns the page.

Web servers can also run a number of other server-side scripts and programs, such as querying a database, and return the results, together with the HTML page, for viewing through a browser. Clients are part of a client/server architecture that runs applications by combining the performance of standalone PCs with the data management, information sharing, security features and processing power of servers.

➡ *Browser*

FAR LEFT: CGI is easy to use, but be warned: it could slow down your web performance.

CLIENT-SIDE

On the Web, client-side programs are those run by the browser or client PC. Typically, web programs come in two types: those on the client-side, such as JavaScript, which are run by the browser (the client); and those that run on the server computer – server-side programs. For client-side programs, the information is available through the client and there is no need to access the server for any data. Client-side scripts are written directly within the HTML code, embedded between the <script> and </script> tags in the head of the document. Putting them here ensures that the scripts are read before the rest of the HTML page. The scripts carry out the actions requested. So, for example, in rollovers, the script enables the colour of the background to change when a mouse moves across it. Client-side scripts can also swap one image for another, validate form data before it is sent to the server, or 'sniff' for which type of browser is accessing the site and show different content accordingly.

Most scripts are written in JavaScript, although Microsoft browsers also support Visual Basic Script. Some Java applets also work client-side. JavaScript support is variable in browsers and can be turned off altogether by users, so it is a good idea to embed alternate content between the <noscript>…</noscript> tags for browsers that do not understand scripting.

➠ *Browser, Server*

CLIP ART

Ready-to-use art. Not all of us are great at drawing, yet even simple graphics such as buttons, icons or backgrounds can really lift the look of a web page. While drawing programs and photo-editing applications aim to make the creative process as simple as possible, there is plenty of ready-made art available online. Clip art collections offer all sorts of graphics. Most are web-ready, but you may want to import them into a graphics editor to customize the image, such as changing the colours or cropping out part of the picture.

Clip art is handy for providing ready-made navigation icons or for graphics to illustrate links, such as an envelope illustrating an email address. Used sparingly, the images can help break up pages of unappealing text and illustrate abstract ideas.

There are a number of freeware clip art collections (such as the Absolute Web Graphics Archive at www.grsites.com/webgraphics/) or paid-for collections where you can purchase clip art either by the graphic, or by different packages and themes (www.eyewire.com). Most clip art sites offer other graphics such as decorative fonts for web site headlines and royalty free photographs.
➠ *Illustration, Illustrator (Adobe), Free Web Graphics*

CLIPART-GRAPHICS.NET
(www.clipart-graphics.net)

Online clip art directory. This site is a kind of graphics co-operative. It does not hold any free clip art itself, but instead it links through to a host of sites that do – some 290 sites at the last count. It ranks those sites in order of the amount of traffic they bring to the main directory site. The more traffic they bring, the more they get. Alongside each entry in the directory is a measure of the traffic flow, so you can see which sites are proving popular.

Besides being a useful resource, the directory also has the advantage of being relatively restrained in its advertising. It is, for the moment, refreshingly pop-up, so there's no chance of being lured away to an online casino.

Clipart-graphics.net lists other sites that are useful to the aspiring webmaster, including free font sites. But it is predominantly a guide to free graphics and links to an amazing hoard of free animations, backgrounds, rules, buttons and general graphics. Although most of the artwork is royalty free, it is largely restricted to personal use.
➠ *Animated GIF, Background Image, Clip Art, Free-clipart.net*

FAR LEFT: To help you find the best clip art images, clipart-graphics.net lists its featured sites by rate of traffic flow.

CLOSING BROWSER WINDOWS WITH JAVASCRIPT

Any browser window can be closed via the File menu or by clicking the exit button (the X in the top right-hand corner on PCs, or the box in the top left-hand corner on the Mac). But if your web site regularly calls up new pop-up windows (for displaying full-sized versions of photos indexed as thumbnails, for instance), you can make your readers' browsing experience easier by offering a link or a button which they can click to close the new window. This is best done using JavaScript routines. Simple lines of code can be added to your pages so that windows can be closed from hyperlinks or buttons. You can add the lines to your page as you would any line of HTML and, in some web-editing applications, store them in a JavaScript library and simply drag and drop them into place on the page.

To create a simple Close hyperlink, insert the following code:

```
<a href="javascript:window.close()">Close</a>
```

Where we have written 'Close', you can write anything, or even add an image – an 'X' in a circle or 'Close' in your house style are good examples. To insert an image, use this code, calling your chosen image 'closeimage.gif':

```
<a href="javascript:window.close()">
<img border="0" src="closeimage.gif">
</a>
```

A Close button can add a professional touch to your window. The 'value' parameter in the following code represents the text that appears in the button.

```
<form>
<input type="button" value="Close"
onClick="window.close()">
</form>
```

> Functionality, JavaScript, Pop-up

An image can also be used for the button instead of the 'Default' button:

```
<input type="image" alt="xx" src="image-path"
```

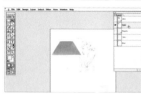

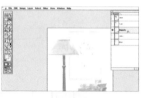

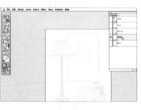

CMYK

 Colour model. In the print world, graphics are often dealt with in CMYK mode. This is where all colours are described as a mixture of the four process colours that make up its name: Cyan (a type of blue); Magenta (close to red); Yellow; and blacK. In high-end printing the colour images are separated into different plates, each plate for one of the CMYK colours. Consequently, the process is also known as four-colour printing. Another feature of CMYK is that it is a reflective colour model, i.e. the light source, whether the Sun, electric light, etc., is bounced off the object, such as the page you are looking at.

In contrast, when we look at the computer monitor the light source is directly behind the screen and comes straight at us. In fact, each pixel colour is created from a mixture of Red, Green and Blue lights shone directly at it. Because the monitor uses the RGB model it is difficult to match how colours on screen will look when converted into CMYK and printed. For viewing web pages it is less of an issue, as online graphics should normally be saved in RGB mode.

➡ *Colour, RGB*

CMYK CONVERSION

Colour format conversion; graphics programs allow you to specify how the RGB colours seen on the monitor are converted to CMYK for high-end printing.

Images for the Web are saved in RGB (Red, Green, and Blue) mode, the same system used by the monitor for displaying colours. But while it is the standard way to view on-screen images, if you are intending to use the same graphic for a printed brochure or other publication it needs to be converted to CMYK. This is the standard file mode for high-end printing, also known as four-colour printing.

Each image is split into its four constituent colours – Cyan, Magenta, Yellow and blacK. In fact, mixing cyan, magenta and black together will produce black, but the addition of a separate black ink gives richer tones and deeper colours. In publishing it has always been difficult to reconcile the colours seen on screen in RGB mode with those printed in CYMK mode. Most graphics programs do allow you to convert RGB images to CMYK for printing. For example, in Paint Shop Pro you can create your own profile – or preferences – which determine how images are converted. In the profile you can adjust how black ink is used, how greys are handled and alter the lightness or darkness of tone before separating the graphic into its CMYK elements.

➡ *Colour, Graphic Design Package, RGB*

TOP LEFT: If an image used on the Web, for example a fine art image, is going to be used in a printed publication, it will need to be converted from RGB to CMYK.

CODESWEEPER

The codesweeper feature in Macromedia's HTML editing program HomeSite automatically checks to make sure your code is properly formatted. It is a useful tool if several developers are working on the same site, as the final code will conform to the same codesweeper options. It is also an advantage if your pages have been developed in a visual authoring tool such as Dreamweaver, which might follow a different set of rules.

There are several codesweepers packaged with HomeSite that can be edited, or new ones created to conform to newer specifications, such as XHTML. Included with the program are an HTML codesweeper, one for JSP and HTML Tidy. This was originally designed for W3C, the web standards body, and has features for line wrapping, tag conversions and working in XML that are not covered by the other codesweepers.

The HTML codesweeper can be set to apply rules for tags and to trim white space by deleting extra spacing that some visual tools introduce. It also applies a particular format for quote marks around an attribute and for changing the case of characters to mixed, lowercase or uppercase as wanted.

➡ *Dreamweaver (Macromedia), FrontPage (Microsoft), HTML, HTML Editor*

COLOUR

The personality of a site is reflected by its use of colour, which need not be totally constrained by the technical limitations of the Web. Colour on the Web is very different to printed colour, because ultimately the pages will be viewed on screen in RGB mode. The colours on a page are also affected by the browser and platform on which they are viewed. There are ways to compensate for this, such as by using a web-safe palette; this is a selection of 216 colours that are common to all browsers and operating systems. The problem with these is that they are not very exciting or attractive.

However, some graphics programs, such as Macromedia's Fireworks, will convert any colour within an image to the nearest web-safe colour. Other programs like Photoshop have a Dither box where you can create your own hybrid web-safe colour by combining several web-safe colours together.

Ultimately, it is the colour of the site that provides the personality. It is often a process of trial and error to get the right balance between a colourful site and one that looks like a paint-mixer's worktop. Using a limited range of colours can make the pages look stunning and well-organized. It does not exclude using pictures or the odd extra colour for special emphasis. Colours can be high contrast, or similar, but keeping them consistent on the site makes it easier for users to navigate.

➥ *Colour Code, Colour Combinations, Colour Wheel, CMYK, Hex Code, RGB*

COLOUR CODE

Specifying colours for use in HTML. In converting their talents to the Web, designers accustomed to the four-colour CMYK print process have to get to grips with the three-colour RGB (red, green, blue) concept used by computers.

Specifying the red, green and blue values of on-screen colours works the opposite way to picking a CMYK colour.

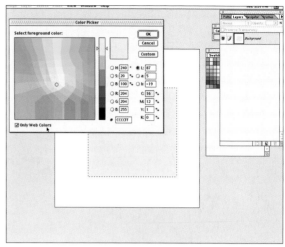

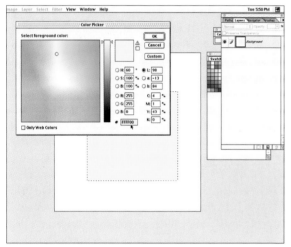

The cyan, magenta, yellow and black values represent the amount of ink on a page, so 100 per cent magenta and 100 per cent yellow produces a warm red, with no cyan or black ink on the page. With the RGB mode, however, you have to specify the amount of red, green and blue light that is projected on-screen. Thus a warm red would require a maximum red value of 255, and green and blue values of zero.

Colours within HTML pages or cascading style sheets (CSS) have to be specified not by their RGB values, but in hexadecimal code. Hex code, or base-16, runs from 00 (zero) to FF (255), and the Calculator accessory on the Windows Start Menu will convert these values for you. Alternatively, several design web sites, including the Web Building section at www.builder.com, have colour code converters. You simply type in the decimal value of each

element of the colour and the converter displays the hex code, along with a panel which fills with your chosen colour – a useful precaution in case you should get a number wrong.

When specifying a colour in HTML, you need to include the hash sign in front of the six-character value. For instance, if you were specifying a bright yellow background for a page, the code <body bgcolor="#FFFF00"> tells the browser that it should mix maximum red and green (FF) with no blue (00). Note that there are no spaces or commas between the three colour values.

Fortunately, Netscape Navigator and Internet Explorer also allow you to specify colours by name, and some 140 named colours – all of which are web-safe – have been specified. These run from the basic red, green, blue, black and white through simple variations such as navy blue and sky blue to almost abstract shades like 'peru' and 'papayawhip'. Our example, then, would read <body bgcolor="yellow">.

If you do use named colours rather than hex RGB code, make a note of its RGB values as you may want to replicate the colour in an inline graphic where you will need to enter the RGB values into your graphics package.

➥ *CMYK, Colour, Hex Code, RGB, Web-Safe Colours*

FAR LEFT: Although the nature of the Web limits the range of colours that can be used, web-safe palettes provide a rainbow of web-safe colours.

COLOUR COMBINATIONS

Almost all printed documents use dark text on a white background, but just because the Web gives easy access to thousands of colours, do not try to use as many as you can all at once. Web designers understand this, and more sensible, legible, colour combinations have replaced the somewhat garish designs witnessed during

the early days of the Web. When choosing a colour scheme for the text-heavy areas of your site, contrast is crucial. Black on white is the obvious solution, but if you want to add colour, dark blues, greens or reds make for legible text on white or light backgrounds. Combining dark and light shades of the same colour is a common solution. But while they make good headline colours, resist the temptation to use bright colours for text, as this could be hard to read continuously for any length of time. Avoid light text on dark backgrounds as again this can be difficult to read for more than a paragraph. Even where light on dark is acceptable, for example for menu panels, straplines or boxouts, use a bold typeface to make the text stand out.

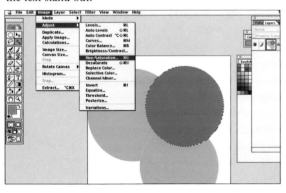

The fashion for loud, tiled backgrounds has eased of late, but if you must use a mottled background for your page, choose a text colour that will read well over it. With pictorial backgrounds, try to lighten the background image so that text is still legible over the top of it. Black text is often your only option here. For graphics, legibility will be less important, but the dangers of mismatching

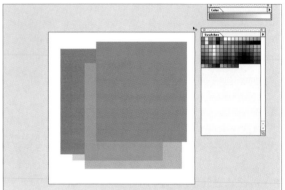

colours are no less prevalent. The eye is a good indicator of which colours complement each other and which clash, but you can get a fair idea by using a colour wheel. Using an RGB colour wheel, adjacent colours, for instance red and yellow or green and light blue, are said to be complementary and can offer a good contrast between light and dark.

Another good way of creating effective colour combinations is to select a fully saturated colour, and combine it with a variety of tints, tones and shades by adding more white, grey or black to the original hue. Specifying three hues that are side-by-side on a colour wheel is good for creating a thematic effect. A saturated red, orange and yellow, for instance, presents a sunny disposition, while shades of these three colours adds an earthy feel. Tints of blue, green and light blue, meanwhile, create a cold but calming effect.

Three colours that are equidistant on a wheel, or their tints, tones and shades, work surprisingly well together. Generally, a good rule of thumb when specifying colour schemes using a colour wheel is to keep two of the hue, saturation and light settings constant across the three or four colours you select.

When combining colours, however, do consider colour-blind PC users. Do not combine any two of red, green, brown, grey or purple in an image, and insist on a strong contrast between foreground and background colours. If possible, switch to a greyscale setting and see how legible your web site is. If it proves difficult to read, try a more contrasting combination.

➥ *Colour, Colour Wheel, RGB*

COLOUR WHEEL

A colour wheel gives designers a visual representation of the colours available to them. All graphics design packages let you access colour wheels to select a colour, and while they should be combined with a web-safe colour palette to make sure you pick suitable colours, wheels expose relationships between colours that can be used to enhance the design of your site.

Wheels come in both RGB and CMYK models, but for web design you will be using the RGB/HSL model. A

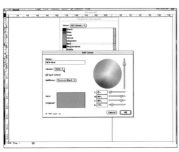

colour wheel is essentially a spectrum wrapped into a circle, with the primary colours – red, green and blue – set every 120 degrees on the perimeter of that circle. In between the primary colours are the secondary colours, produced when the primaries are combined (red and green producing yellow, blue and red making violet and green and blue combining to form light blue). The outside of the wheel is completed by the tertiary colours, produced by combining each

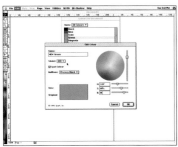

primary colour with its adjacent secondary colours.

These 12 basic colours are called the hues and form the basic colour wheel. In the more complex wheels found in graphics packages, the amount of white added to each hue increases towards the centre of the wheel. By adding more white, the hue's saturation decreases to create tints of the original colour.

Independent to the colour wheel is the brightness (or luminosity) setting. By decreasing the brightness of a hue, you are effectively adding degrees of grey and then black to the original, to create tones and shades. Good colour combinations can be created by combining a tint, a tone and a shade of a hue with the original.

As well as an RGB reading, good colour wheels will also display a reading for the hue, saturation and luminosity/brightness (HSL or HSB). Hue is valued between zero and 0.999, while saturation and luminosity are rated between zero and 1.000. While you will only need to make a note of this if you are adding colours to Java applets, understanding how altering hue, saturation and light can affect a colour is the key to selecting suitable and complementary colours for your site.

➥ *Colour, Colour Combinations, RGB*

ABOVE: The colours used on your web site can greatly affect the impact it has, for example a combination of oranges and yellows will convey a warm and sunny mood.

COMMENTS IN HTML

Tags to help explain how the page was built or how to navigate the HTML. There is nothing worse than going through someone else's web pages, trying to fathom out why they coded them the way they did – or for that matter going back to pages you did yourself a long time ago. Some notes would be useful. There is an oft-overlooked feature in HTML that provides exactly this function. The Comment tags <!– Your comments go here –> enable you to put notes on your page that don't show up in the browser (although they will if users view the source code). Anything within the tags is excluded.

You can use the comments to provide information about the code itself; or to temporarily exclude code that is not yet ready, without deleting it; or to communicate with clients. For example, if the clients are going to add or change content themselves, once the site is up and running, comment tags are a useful way to show them where to do it. A comment, such as <!– Title text goes here –>, makes it easier for them to navigate the HTML and also makes it less likely that they will alter code they shouldn't. Note that you must include spaces between the initial tag and the first letter and before the end tag.

➤ *HTML*

CONFIRMATION PAGE

To encourage response from users it is good practice to set up a confirmation page that loads once they have submitted a form, or order. While it's good to give your users a voice, they also like to know that their comments have been heard. HTML forms make it easy for users to send feedback or to fill in information for products they want to purchase. But when they submit the form it is important they get some response that shows them the data was safely sent and that it has been successfully received. For an online store it is imperative that users get that feedback so they can feel confident in buying over the Internet. But the two-way interaction also enhances the user's experience and creates an element of trust between the two parties.

The easiest response is to create a confirmationpage to which users are directed once the form has been submitted. For a feedback form this could just be a

general note of thanks with a link back to the main site. For online purchases any confirmation page should contain the relevant details of the transaction, including what has been ordered, the amount paid and delivery method. The same confirmation may also be sent by email.

➤ *HTML, Form Handler*

CONTENT

What to put on your site. There is such a mass of information on the Web that most people simply scan until they find something they want to investigate further; reading from the screen is slower than from the page – up to 25 per cent slower according to studies by usability expert Jakob Nielsen. For this reason it is important to have clear headlines and introductory paragraphs to draw readers in. There are ways to maximize the impact of this 'microcontent', as it is also called. First, keep it short: the headline should sum up what follows rather than be a clever pun – content should not tease the reader; if they go for it and download something they didn't really want to read, it destroys all trust for the future.

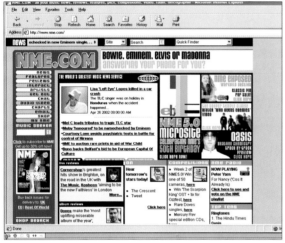

Similarly the text itself should be sharp and concise. Generally, readers do not like to scroll, so it is advisable to keep pages down to about 400–500 words. Copy should also be broken into more digestible chunks of information in much the same way as a tabloid newspaper does. Important elements can be emphasized by being put in a separate bullet-pointed list or set in a sidebar. An eye-catching phrase can be picked out in a Quotebox.

Content should also be structured – or weighted – by its importance. The main news story should have more space than the date of the next board meeting. Readers should be able to see at a glance the main items.

There are specific web devices to catch the readers' interest, in particular hypertext links which are

fundamental to the Web's philosophy of interconnection. Hyperlinks can help break content into logical elements. For example, one page can give an overview of a topic, or deal with just one particular aspect. For more detailed information, or an article on a related issue, or previous stories on the same subject, the readers can follow the hypertext links. As links are typically blue and underlined, they also provide a visual 'chain' that encourages readers to scan down the page. A similar emphasis can be used by applying colour to keywords or phrases. However, these should be a different colour to the hyperlinks so the two do not get confused. There is nothing more irritating to the reader than clicking on what they think is a link only to discover it goes nowhere.

➡ *Maintaining Web Site Interest, Readability, Image Usage, Web Design Process*

FAR LEFT: A confirmation page provides essential security for online shoppers, as well as an opportunity for them to ensure that they get the exact product they require.

CONTRAST

On a web page, contrast helps provide visual clues to what is important. Applying a contrast filter to photos can improve the image. The Web thrives on differences and web sites are no exception. For effective design there needs to be strong contrast on a page, to draw the viewer's eye to what's there. The contrast can be achieved through a variety of effects – bolder text, different typefaces, contrasting colours, rules, emphatic graphics. Contrast can provide an important focal point on the page. If everything was the same size it would seem to have the same importance. By giving major headings a different size, by creating a logo for the company name, by making sure the navigation buttons do not dwarf everything else, you can provide clues as to the relative importance of the material on the page.

More technically, most photo editors have a brightness and contrast filter for enhancing pictures. By modifying these, you alter the highlights, shadows and midtones of an image. Most have a slider control which will boost contrast (i.e. make dark pixels darker and light pixels lighter) when moved one way, or will lessen the contrast when moved the other way.

➡ *Graphic Design Package, Image Enhancement Techniques*

CONVERTING GRAPHIC FORMATS

Image file conversion. There are many file formats used for storing information about an image: some are platform-specific and some are program-specific. Generally, though, the main ways images are saved on a computer are as raster (bitmap) files, used in painting programs, and vector files, used by drawing programs.

Vector images create pictures using simple lines and curves that are described by mathematical formulas. Bitmaps use screen pixels to represent the image, rather like tiles in a mosaic. For the Web, images are saved as bitmaps in the GIF or JPEG file formats; a few use the

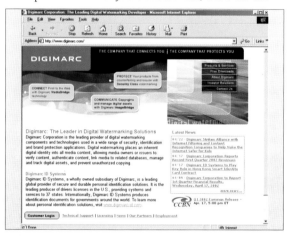

PNG format but this is not supported by all browsers.

Most drawing programs will be able to save images you created with them as bitmaps as well as vector graphics. However, the compression is handled better if it is opened in a bitmap graphics program and saved there.

Bitmap editors, such as Photoshop and Fireworks, enable you to preview the same image in the three different formats – GIF, JPEG and PNG. At a glance you can compare picture quality, file size and estimated download time, allowing you to alter the degree of compression, the number of colours used and the amount of dither, until you achieve the look you want.
➡ *Graphic Design Package*

COPYRIGHT IMAGES

Graphics for which license is needed for reproduction. As images can easily be downloaded from any web page there is the temptation to borrow

graphics you like for use on your own web site. Not only is this illegal, it is also unnecessary, as there are many unrestricted and royalty free pictures available on the Web. Just be careful, if you have bought a collection of photos that are royalty free, to check the licensing

information carefully as there may be charges for certain types of commercial use. Traditionally, most copyright images are licensed on a 'one time, one project' basis and can attract good royalties.

Because of the potential value of images, and the ease with which they can be copied illegally, designers and photographers are looking to protect the copyright in their images using digital watermarks. The watermark can hold all sorts of information, such as who owns the copyright, the audience its intended for, and whether it is royalty free or restricted in its use.

The Digimarc ImageBridge watermarking solution (www.digimarc.com) also tracks the use of images across the Web. The watermarks are embedded through plug-ins that work with several image-editing programs, including Photoshop and Paint Shop Pro. They can also read the watermark. Additionally, there is an ImageBridge reader, which enables you to read a watermark through the Internet Explorer browser in Windows.
➡ *CorbisImages, GettyOne Images, Photodisc, Photoshop (Adobe), Stock Photo Suppliers*

FAR LEFT: Pixels are used to convert screen graphics; they are positioned together to form an image, rather like mosaic tiles combine to form a picture.

CORBISIMAGES *(www.corbis.com)*

 While CorbisImages' online gallery has more than two million images, this is still not the full picture: the total Corbis collection numbers some 65 million images. Using photojournalists around the world, their news section has the latest pictures of everything from the Olympics to the Grammy Awards, taking in the odd conflict, election or natural catastrophe.

But the main interest in the site for webmasters comes from their traditionally licensed stock images and their collections of royalty free pictures. Traditionally licensed images – where a fee-per-use is paid that is dependant on the size the picture is used, where it is used and for what purpose – can be bought and downloaded online. The searchable online catalogue covers celebrities, sports icons, famous photographers, fine art and more. As with many photo libraries, fees differ if the publication is for editorial rather than commercial use.

The collections of royalty free images cover several themes, from wicked women to medical health and schooldays. Some images are also available online. For a one-time flat fee you can use the images on as many projects as you want and rights are pre-cleared so they are ready to use.

➡ *GettyOne Images, Photodisc, Stock Photo Suppliers*

CORELDRAW

Graphic design suite. The Corel Corporation's graphic design package is now more than a decade old, and has kept with the times with the addition of web-specific features as well as the latest image-editing tools.

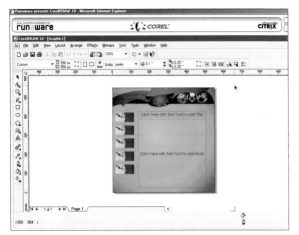

The CorelDraw vector imaging product now comes as part of the CorelDraw Graphics Suite, along with image editor Photo-Paint and animation tool RAVE.

Foremost among CorelDraw's web-specific tools is its image optimizer, which helps reduce the size of graphics while maintaining image quality. The optimizer can display four images side by side so you can see previews of the edited image in various formats and at different compression levels. You can also preset export controls for different graphic types.

As well as supporting GIF and JPEG formats, CorelDraw offers extended control over compressing and exporting to the PNG format, and RAVE will export sequences to Flash, animated GIF, AVI and QuickTime formats. RAVE and CorelDraw can produce and export rollover buttons, the former with sound clips attached.

CorelDraw increases control over the export of graphics to web pages through its Publish As HTML feature, and will alert you to potential problems before the site is uploaded. The suit can also produce web-optimized streaming PDF files, which display at the same time as they download, for the user's convenience.

➡ *GIF, Graphic Design Package, Image Enhancement Techniques, JPEG, PNG*

COUNTER

Page request counter. If you are curious to know how many people are visiting your pages, you can use a counter to keep track of the number of hits you have. A common feature on the Web, counters graphically illustrate how many requests there have been for a page, either since it was installed or the counter reset.

The counters can either be just numeric text or the digits in the counter can be artwork. For a collection of free counter graphics go to the Museum of Counter Art (www.counterart.com). A different graphic is needed for each digit but they will not work as counters unless they are included in a CGI script or you subscribe to a Counter service.

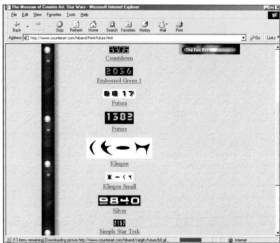

Counter scripts are available online (see Matt's Script Archive at www.worldwidemart.com). The way they operate is to open a text file, read the number in it, add one, update the text file with the new number and then display it. Alternatively, you can use a counter hosting service, so the work is done for you. You need to include the counter on the page with an HTML link, but the script is run by the server of the counter service (e.g. www.easycounter.com).

➡ *Free Web Extras, Easycounter.com*

LEFT: Sunday, Banks of the Marne by Henri Cartier-Bresson, one of the many famous photographers featured in Corbis's extensive online gallery.

CREATING A BUSINESS WEB SITE

An internet presence is now a crucial part of corporate strategy. Web sites can be used for advertising or promotion, as a sales medium, or as a conduit for contact between the firm and its customers or partners. A company's line of business will largely determine the content and structure of its web site. Retail and wholesale sales lend themselves perfectly to e-commerce, while more abstract business-to-business service providers might prefer to advertise their wares online as a gateway to conventional dealings. When planning your business site, think carefully not only about the design, but also the content – write this in a word-processing package first and get someone to proofread it before you put any of the information on your site.

1. Every company site should include an overview of the firm. An About Us section can provide a description of the core activities of the company, a brief history and details of where it is based or where its headquarters and any satellite offices are. Senior personnel should be profiled, and an organization chart added to show the hierarchical structure of staff and departments. Mission statements can also be quoted and explained. In the case of B2B concerns, case studies could show prospective clients how they could benefit from doing business with the firm.

2. Include contact details. While you can simply publish the email address of every member of staff, visitors might choose a recipient for their message at random and it

might not be dealt with at all, losing valuable business and damaging a firm's reputation. Instead, incorporate an online form and direct its contents towards a central distributor – an office secretary, for instance – who can forward the query to the most suitable party and follow up to ensure that prompt action is taken.

3. If some of the information on the site is sensitive, consider setting up an extranet service, where only registered external visitors can access certain pages using a password.

4. Add a site map which lists every page under each section heading, so that users can access a page quickly and easily.

5. Much of the design of business sites will be determined by the company's own house style. The colour scheme, for instance, may be based on the existing masthead, and the logo may be simple enough to use online. However, if a logo is too involved or a colour scheme is old-fashioned, a venture on to the Internet is the perfect opportunity for a revamp of a company's brand and image. Avoid showing the new logo off with a splash screen though – you'll risk driving customers away.

6. If a site is to be updated regularly with stories and press releases, consider a content-management system. These allow staff to write reports through an intranet front-end, and send them for instant approval to a designated editor or senior manager. Such software can take pressure off those responsible for building and maintaining the site itself.

7. Use high-end web editors like Macromedia Dreamweaver or Adobe GoLive. Both ease collaboration on sites, and simplify site-management across a number of machines. Complement the web editor with a web-specific graphics package like Photoshop or Fireworks.

8. If you are setting up an e-commerce section, don't cram all your products on to a single page. Instead, position them three or four to a page or use e-commerce software with a search facility. Many 'ready-to-go'

e-commerce packages let you create an online store quickly and easily, including Actinic Catalog, Starwebz WebShop (both CD-based offerings) and ShopSite Manager, which is a online service supplied through certain ISPs (check that your ISP supports ShopSite first). Some ISPs offer their own bespoke solutions, which you can try out online.

9. E-commerce service providers and ISPs sometimes provide credit card authorization tools so that users can buy online easily and safely; the companies that offer this service usually take a cut of each transaction, but it is worth it for a secure validation system.

10. If your business is conducted overseas, print prices in euros and dollars, or find software with a built-in currency converter. Consider translations for international customers, even if they consist of only an introductory paragraph.

11. Do not cut corners when choosing a firm to host your site. Free web space is an unprofessional no-no, and regular consumer accounts are unlikely to offer the stability required for a successful site. Find a reliable corporate account and agree to a service level agreement that guarantees maximum uptime. Server problems could damage customer confidence and cost you sales.

12. Corporate hosting accounts sometimes offer domain-name registration for free. While .ltd.uk and .com.uk domains are available, go for .co.uk and .com as these are universally recognized. If your company name is already taken – a strong possibility these days – modify it slightly by hyphenating words. Don't waste the domain name, ask the host or your IT department to set up email accounts for all members of staff incorporating the URL; this is far more professional than separate webmail or standard ISP accounts, which are still surprisingly common on company sites.

➡ *Branding and Identity, Consistency, Logo Design*

FAR LEFT: Your business may not be quite as successful as Sainsbury's, but by creating your own web site you can also set up an online store.

CREATING A PERSONAL WEB SITE

The Web isn't all about big business. The majority of the sites on the Internet were created in bedrooms and studies rather than boardrooms and studios, by webmasters who only want to share their hobbies or their thoughts with like-minded web surfers. With inexpensive software and a plethora of online services, creating family pages or a fan site is quick and easy, and can lead to bigger things: a few well-run fan sites have gone on to become the official web presence of some musical artists and sporting associations.

1. Determine the theme of the site and the target readership. If your site is for keeping in touch with far-flung family members, make sure they have web access first; there is little point in starting work on a site if you are going to be its only reader.

2. If it is a hobbyist or fan site, search for similar existing sites and work out how your site is going to be different and better. If your chosen subject already has an official site, think about how you can offer an informal alternative.

3. Plan the structure of your site, dividing the content into directories and creating a site map or storyboard illustrating each page. Stick to this structure as you build the site.

4. Choose between designing your own site or using an online site builder. Sites like MoonFruit (www.moonfruit.com) let you add your content

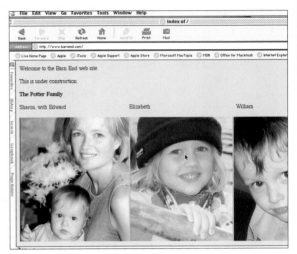

and colour scheme into a standard template. However, their inflexible formats offer few opportunities to stamp your own style on a site.

5. If you are designing the site, choose a web editor. There are several combined web editors/image-editing tools available for under £50, and Microsoft's FrontPage is a good investment if you see your site as a long-term hobby, and comes with a collection of professional-looking templates.

6. Learn a little HTML before starting on the site's design. An editor might not be producing the desired effect and by understanding some of the code, you might be able to correct it by hand. It also proves useful when viewing (and 'borrowing') the source of a well-designed page to use as the basis of your design. There are many HTML tutorials and primers on the Web.

7. Consider your image sources. Most clipart is of poor quality. Create your own graphics in an inexpensive graphics package like Paint Shop Pro. Use photos taken with a digital camera or scanned; basic image-editing tools are often bundled with digitizing hardware.

8. Add value to the site with free tools like chat forums and online polls. Such features can encourage visitors to return and help build an online community. Guestbooks and hit counters can be the source of invaluable feedback.

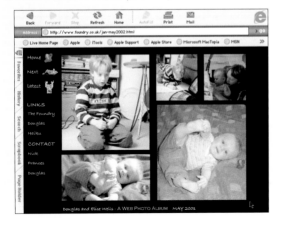

9. When the content is ready, choose a host for your pages. This could be your current Internet Service Provider (ISP), as dial-up contracts usually include around 10 Mb of free web space. Check the terms and conditions – there is probably a limit on the amount of data that can be sent from the site each month, beyond which the ISP may charge or press for an upgrade to a business account.

10. Online hosts such as Yahoo!, GeoCities, Tripod.co.uk and FortuneCity will host your site for free as part of their online communities. The catch is that your pages are obliged to carry intrusive advertising boxes which float over your content until the reader dismisses them.

11. Rather than using the unwieldy URL supplied by your ISP (usually in the format www.yourname.homepages.hostname.co.uk or sometimes featuring number codes), consider buying a domain name. URLs ending in .co.uk cost as little as £5 a year and are far easier to remember.

12. Choose an FTP utility. The better ones cost around £20, but there are plenty of free and shareware ones available. Your ISP will supply the settings for uploading your pages, or an online host may demand that you upload pages using a browser-based online form.

13. Once uploaded, ask related sites for a reciprocal link. Even rival sites usually agree. Find a web ring that concerns your topic and submit your URL. You will have to place a button and some code on your homepage that links to a random related site, but you should see visitor numbers rise in return. Publicizing the site in search engines and directories is also advisable.

14. Make some pocket money by selling products through partnership programmes. Online retailers like Amazon (www.amazon.co.uk) have schemes whereby you advertise their goods and earn a percentage of every sale in return.

15. Web publishing can be a legal minefield. Don't pass on gossip you have no evidence for and make sure the users of your message board don't overstep the libel mark as you could be liable. Don't use reports or images copied from other sites as the copyright holder is unlikely to accept your amateur status as an excuse not to pay royalties. Some television companies have even banned all fan sites for certain shows, citing 'quality control' as their justification. If in doubt, don't publish or your hobby could become very costly.

➠ **HTML, Storyboard, Uploading, Web Design Process**

ABOVE: Use the Internet to earn money: with online retailers such as Amazon, you can advertise their goods and earn a percentage of the subsequent sales.

CREATING A SCREENSAVER

Getting your web site URL known to a wider audience can be much easier if you entail the marketing might of your site's readers and offer free screensavers for download to visitors. Screensavers were introduced to prevent damage to monitor screens caused by phosphor burn-in – the imprint left on a cathode-ray tube by electrons constantly hitting the same spots when a machine was idle but its monitor left on. The simple animations soon spawned a booming novelty industry, and no PC was complete without flying toasters, scrolling words or bungee-jumping cows.

The basic style of promotional screensaver is much the same. Logos gliding around the screen is a classic design, while the more creative can invent interactive screensavers that teach the user something about your company. Shareware tools make creating basic screensavers straight-forward. A simple logo qualifies as a screensaver, and utilities that embed the correct files in a distributable format, like Softdd's Create 'n' Distribute Screensavers, are easy to find online. Good screensaver software lets you create self-extracting EXE files, which users can download and which will be installed into the Windows desktop automatically. All, even shareware ones, do this, although

you may have to pay to have some full functionality.

One of the simplest to use is Custom Screen Saver Wizard, from www.customsavers.com, which costs around £16. To create a screensaver, you simply put all your image files in one folder and the wizard imports them all. You can add some text over the image, set a display time and choose from a wide selection of images effects like raindrops, float and flying objects. You can export to ZIP and self-extracting .exe files.

An unregistered trial lasts 15 days and the CustomSavers URL will appear on any screensaver you create until registration. The program also comes in a Commercial Edition that allows company names, logos and information to be embedded in document. A Professional edition lets you sell the screensavers you create.

Screen Saver Studio has a more visual interface than the wizard-controlled Custom Screen Saver. Available from www.screensaverstudio.com, the program lets you import over 40 graphics formats and combine them with text and music, in templates that include a slideshow and a 3D spinning cube. Inter-frame transition effects like checkerboard, fade and wipe can be added easily.

Digital Workshop's Fandango provides a library of effects that you can apply to your logo such as bounce, where the image bounces within the confines of the screen, and scatter, where images are placed on

Make Screen Savers and Wallpapers.

MAKE YOUR OWN
Screen Saver

Products
- Custom screen saver Wizard
- MakeYourOwn screen saver
- Flash screen savers
- Images for Screen Savers
- Hawaii screen saver
- 3D Photo Mouse Pads

Download
Purchase
ScreenSaver Links
Help Center

Custom screen saver wizard:
- Show off your favorite photos. Send your pictures to friends and family as screen savers.
- Promote your business or your web site by giving away free screensavers. Much more cost-effective than banner advertising.
- Sell your own screen savers -- for Profit or for Fundraising. more...

MakeYourOwn screen saver:
- Display your favorite images and play favorite sound files on your PC as screen savers. more...

Webmasters: Get FREE software and earn commission by selling our popular screen saver top of one another until the screen is full. Audio clips and AVI movies can also be incorporated into Fandango screensavers.

These basic products let you select a series of graphics – your company logo, for instance – and move it round the screen in a pre-determined path to an optional audio score. That may be acceptable, but if you want to create truly custom screensavers, Macromedia Flash is the best solution.

Because Flash graphics are scalable, a Flash-based screensaver could be made available on your web site for installation on all windows systems. Third Eye Solutions' FlashJester and The Active Screen Saver DevKit (available from www.automatedofficesystems.com) both provide the means to embed a Flash animation into a screensaver and save it in a distributable format.

The rendering code used by Active Screen Saver DevKit was actually created by Macromedia and is provided to developer Automated Office Systems as an ActiveX control. DevKit also supports HTML, DHTML, JavaScript, VBScript and Java, so you could even produce interactive screensavers. You can also tell the utility to open your web page when the screensaver kicks in. However such versatility doesn't come cheap and the Windows-only DevKit carries a £140 price tag.

If you support cross-platform users with your site design, you should do the same with these promotional devices – it makes no sense to limit your advertising potential, after all. ScreenTime Media (www.screentime.com) supplies a range of products for both PCs and Macs which convert common graphics formats into screensavers.

ScreenTime Flash lets you create Flash-based screensavers using a WYSIWYG interface, even letting you enter an expiration date when your readers can come and download an up-to-date replacement. ScreenTime also produces utilities to convert PowerPoint presentations to screensavers, and its Photo & Video tool lets you embed QuickTime and AVI movies, and several leading graphics formats, into distributable screensavers.

The company's CineMac tools also convert QuickTime and Macromedia Director projects to screensavers, but it's the ScreenTime for Generator that really stands out from the pack, by letting the user build the screensaver for themselves. You create the elements that make up the screensaver – animations, video clips,

music – and create a web interface using Macromedia Generator, enabling Windows users to assemble their own custom screensaver. Official sites for Nike and The Matrix have used this technology to offer truly custom-built screensavers.

If you offer eye-catching screensavers, your visitors will return out of loyalty and also for updated screensavers, and if others visit your site as a result, this simple marketing initiative will have paid off.

➧ *Animation, Flash (Macromedia), Promoting a Web Site*

FAR LEFT: Screensavers began as simple animations but were soon jazzed up; bungee-jumping cows were particularly popular at one point!

CREATING AN ONLINE INVITATION

Web-based invitations. These not only allow you to set up the invitation online but you can also gather the responses and show the feedback on site. It does not only have to be for fun – the same system can be used for inviting clients to events, or setting up meetings.

The invitation itself can be as plain or as fancy as you like. Within the body tag, you can insert a background image (using the background attribute) or change the background colour (using the bgcolor attribute). Write out the text of the invitation, with date, time and any special information needed. Use a heading tag to style the main tile, <font face> to specify the typeface, and the size attribute to specify the size of text. Add any images or animations you may have (champagne corks popping etc.) with the <img> tag. Add some alternate text through the alt tag for anyone who might have turned off images in the browser.

You will also want some feedback from those who you have invited – even if it is just to know they're coming. The replies can be kept separate so only you can access them, or they can be added to the page, so that the other invitees can see who's coming and what they're saying.

To set up this interaction you need to create a form using the <form>…</form> tags. The information from this form has to be processed. This is almost always done by a program, or script, running on the web server. So, within the opening <form> tag you need to specify the action attribute (which is the address of the program that will process the form) and the method attribute which specifies how the information will be sent. Typically, this will be by the 'post' method, rather than the 'get' method.

Next, you need to create the input fields on the form itself. This could be a variety of types. For example, if you want to offer several choices from which the invitees can only choose one (such as 'Yes I am coming' or 'No, I am not coming') you would use a radio button. If you want them to specify how many friends they want to bring with them, you could have a drop-down list of numbers from which they can select.

Obviously you need to know who's replying, so you will want a text input field where they can put their name or other details you might want (such as a mobile phone number or what fancy dress costume they're planning to wear). To help build up some of the pre-party banter the <textarea> tag creates a text box for free-flowing comment. You can set the visible size of it using the rows and cols attributes. For example, <textarea name="comments" rows="6" cols="30">...</textarea> would create a box that would take six lines of text with 30 characters in a line. If there's more text, scroll bars appear so that it can be read. If you want to prompt people on any details to include, add your own text between the opening and closing <textarea> tags and it will appear by default.

To finish off, the form needs a submit (or send) button. This is created by using the <input> tag and adding 'submit' as the attribute. Clicking this will send the form details for processing by the program at the URL you specified in the action attribute.

Having completed the invitation and form, the complications come in issuing the invitations and processing the data. For simple forms its possible to use JavaScript or some other client-side scripting to analyse the form and return the values. But for this type of work

LEFT: An online invitation can be used to invite clients or celebrities to events or openings. Delivery may be guaranteed but acceptance is not!

it will probably need a server-side application, typically CGI or ASP. For those with no experience of programming, there are a number of online sites where you can download scripts, which can be easily modified by following the instructions given.

Having set up the invitation you need to make your friends aware of it. To do so, the script needs to send an automatic email to the party guests with a link to the URL where they can view the invite. Once they have seen the invite and responded, that information can either be collated and sent as an email message to you or set out on a web page. Alternatively, in the same way as a guestbook, the comments can be shown on the invitation page for the other guests to see.

All of this may involve some complicated programming. Your server has to support CGI scripts. An alternative is to use some of the online services that will run the whole process for you, such as www.evite.com, the more commercially oriented www.eventlauncher.com, or the more specialized www.meetingwizard.com. Most online services supply templates for the invitations, but some also allow you to send your own custom-designed invites.

➡ **Form Handler, HTML, Image Use, Interactivity, Page Layout**

CREATING AN ONLINE PHOTO ALBUM

Web photo gallery. Whether it's for a product catalogue, the list of the 10 most wanted criminals, or scenes from your friend's wedding, there are plenty of reasons to put a photo album on the Web. Naturally, to speed download time the pictures aren't full-size – you need to create thumbnail images of the photos, which are then linked to the larger photos. It is only when viewers click on the thumbnail that they are taken to the page, or pop-up, where the bigger image is downloaded.

Creating all those thumbnails and checking the links are set correctly can be hard work. But, fortunately, there are several tools to speed up the process. This section bases its information on Macromedia's Dreamweaver combined with their image editor Fireworks, but online picture galleries can be easily created with other programs, such as Adobe's Photoshop Elements.

First, choose the photos you want and put them together in a single folder. Most image types are recognized. Within Dreamweaver go to the Command menu and select Create Web Photo Album and the relevant dialog box opens.

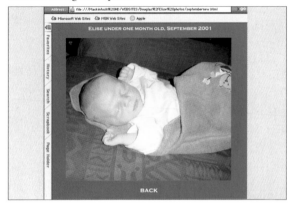

The first field is for the Photo Album title. This appears at the top of the Album page and also on each of the linked pages with the full-size images. The Subheading: and Other info: boxes allow you to enter more details about the album, but the text only goes on the gallery page. The HTML formatting for this is fairly basic, so once the album is created you'll need to go back and set the pages to your site style.

Next, you need to tell Dreamweaver where to locate the pictures, which is easiest to do by using the browse button and locating the folder concerned. As well as the source folder, you will need a destination folder where the gallery photos go.

The next settings control the size and format of your pictures. First, you have to decide how big to make the thumbnail images. Bear in mind that the larger they are, the bigger the gallery page, the slower it downloads and the fewer photos you can fit to the page. If you have several gallery pages (such as for a product catalogue or portfolio) it's best to keep the thumbnail size consistent. While there's the temptation to make the thumbnails as small as possible, an image 36 x 36 pixels is virtually useless. Generally, a thumbnail somewhere between 72 x 72 pixels to 144 x 144 pixels is about right.

Keep the Show Filenames box ticked. While adding the filenames is not particularly helpful, it does create a text field which you can go in and change to a caption later. The next choice is the number of columns the gallery will have. This needs to be worked out in relation to the size of the thumbnails and the width of your web page (commonly 600 pixels).

The quality of the thumbnail format that you select next is really determined by the type of images you have. For simple illustrations, the option which gives the best quality for the smallest file size is the GIF WebSnap 128. However, if the thumbnails are being created from photos, the JPEG Better Quality option may be more appropriate. Note that you can have the thumbnails in a different format to that for the enlarged photos. Note also that the original images won't be changed. When Fireworks creates the thumbnails it resizes and resamples the original artwork or photos.

The last option to decide is whether to enable navigation for each full-size photo page. This gives each

page browser-style options for Back, Home and Next. If this is not selected, the only way for the user to return to the Gallery is via the Back button on the browser.

Clicking OK launches Fireworks, which creates the thumbnails and full-size images to the settings you chose. Dreamweaver then writes the HTML for the pages. If you look at the code it links to two folders, one called Images and the other named Thumbnails. Both these and the index page need to be copied to your web site to display the album.

The Photo Album tool creates fairly basic HTML and does not allow any choice of font or colour scheme. However, it is easy enough to go into the HTML and link up to your normal style sheet or adapt the page as you wish. Obviously, with the image pages it is a laborious task to do this one by one. Fortunately, using the Find and Replace function it is possible to alter several pages at once. Select Edit > Find and Replace. In the dialog box that opens select Folder from the Find In:

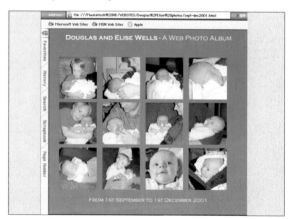

box and browse to the folder containing the Web album pages. In the Search For: box select Source Code and enter the code string you want to change, such as the background colour of the page. Put in the new code and click Replace All to apply to all the pages in the folder in one go.

➡ *HTML, Image Compression, Image Resolution, Retouching Images, Scanning, Thumbnails*

LEFT: Show off the holiday snaps you're particularly proud of using an online photo album.

CREATING A WEB PAGE

The document markup language HTML is used to build web pages. It tells the browser how to display what is on the page. It also contains the links that connect one document to another. All HTML documents are collections of tags, enclosed within less than (<) and greater than (>) brackets. Most are also container tags, that is they have an opening tag (such as <i>) and a closing tag, like </i>. The tags tell the browser how to display anything that is contained within the tags. So, <i>this text is shown in italic</i>. While HTML will still display some content that doesn't have closing tags, XHTML (eXtensible Hypertext Markup Language – the latest generation of HTML) is less forgiving and end tags will be needed.

Tags can be modified by attributes, stated in the opening tag which allow you to specify properties such as font, size, colour etc. So, <font color="#FF0000"> puts the text in red. In HTML, if an attribute has a value, that is a single word or number, it does not need to go between quote marks, but XHTML does require all attributes to go in quotes.

Similarly, HTML itself is not sensitive to case – so <FONT> is the same as <Font>. However, XHTML is case sensitive and all tags need to be in lowercase. In preparation for that it's as well to start coding tags in lowercase anyway.

Each HTML document has two main parts, the <head>, which contains general information about the file and scripts that need to be run and the <body>, which is the content that will appear in the browser window. Normally, this HTML outline for the page will be automatically set up by your web-authoring program. Typically, the page will start with a document type definition which lets the browser know which HTML standard you are following. Within the head you should also include the <title> which has the text that will appear in the browser's title bar (e.g. <title>Web Design Greats</title>).

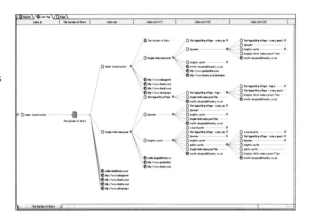

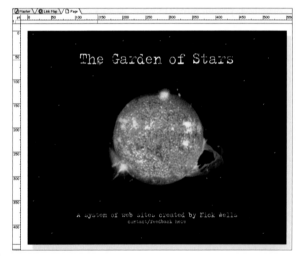

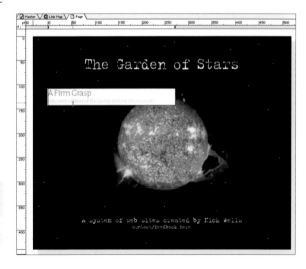

ABOVE: A site map is a very useful way of keeping track of your design, showing links within the site and to other websites.
MIDDLE AND RIGHT: A graphic approach to web design, by an application such as Freeway, can allow you to create links and see the how the site will look without an intimate knowledge of html.

By default, most browsers leave several pixels of space around the web page. If you want your page flush to the top and left of the browser window you need to set the page margins. In Internet Explorer, set topmargin and leftmargin attributes to zero. For Netscape, use the same setting in marginheight and marginwidth.

Add a splash of colour to the background, by using the bgcolor attribute in the <body> tag. If you want to get jazzy add a background image that tiles, that is repeats, across the viewable area. To do this, add background as the attribute to the <body> tag and also enter the file location for the image. Beware that the background doesn't make it too difficult to read the text on the page.

Content may not be king on all web sites, but it does need treating royally. Ensure that any content is as sharp and short as possible and free of grammatical or spelling mistakes. Design-wise, you can do a lot to help get the message across. For spacing, the paragraph tag <p>...</p> adds additional white space when it breaks the line. If you don't want the extra space use the line-break tag <br> which is also one of the few standalone tags that does not have an end tag. You can add emphasis to text with the italic or bold tags.

For greater visual emphasis, add headings to the page. There are six available, <h1> being the biggest and <h6> the smallest (too small for most viewers). With most browsers <h4> is equivalent to the size of the body text. The typeface, size and colour can all be set through the <font> tag, but this is gradually being phased out in favour of using style sheets. However, it is still needed to work with older browsers.

For visual interest add images to the web page using the standalone <img> tag followed by the SRC attribute with the location of the graphics file. By using the height and width attributes to specify the actual pixel size of the image, you effectively put a placeholder which preserves the layout as the page is downloaded. For those who have disabled image downloading, or who have non-graphical browsers, you should also use the alt attribute to provide a brief textual description of the image.

Using the vpsace and hspace attributes, you can add extra space between text and graphics but for more precise alignment it is best to use tables. A table is created with the opening and closing <table> tags followed by one or

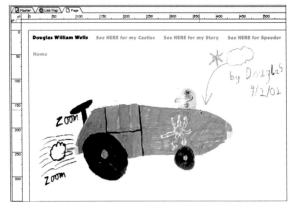

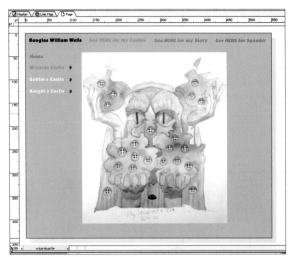

more table rows <tr>. Within each row there are data cells that use the <td> tag. By putting text or images within the data cells you can help structure the page more clearly and control the layout more precisely.

To really connect to the Web, you can create hyperlinks from either your graphics or text. Select the object you want to link and use the anchor tag <a> with the HREF attribute followed by the address (URL) of the page you are linking to. This can either be absolute for an external link (one outside your site) including the protocol and domain name (e.g. http://www.expedia.com) or relative for files on the same server.

➡ *HTML, Image Usage, Site Layout*

ABOVE: Simple navigation for pages within a web site and a direct approach to graphic design can be very effective for children's sites.

abcdefghijklMNOPQ
rstuvWXYZ
*abcdefgh***ijkLMN**
opqrstu
VWXYZ

CROPPING IMAGES

An easy but sometimes overlooked way to keep file size down is to crop the image. File size matters: with most users still connecting to the Web through a dial-up modem, bandwidth-hogging graphics are a real turn-off. One of the easiest ways to keep file size low is often the most overlooked. Simply make the graphic smaller.

A great deal of space can be saved by cropping out any extra white space, particularly with scanned images. Cutting out the background also helps to focus attention on the main element of the graphic. Cropping a bitmap image works in much the same way in most photo editors. Select the crop tool and click and drag to outline the area you want to keep. If you don't get the area right first time, don't worry, simply adjust the crop handles on the box until it encloses exactly the bit you want. When you are happy that the cropping area is in the right place, simply double click inside its borders.

If you go too far and your postcard ends up postage-stamp size, most photo editing programs will let you

undo the last step and usually several steps before that. Even so, it's worth working on a copy of the original image so that nothing is lost forever.

➠ *Graphic Design Package*

CROSS-BROWSER COMPATIBILITY

Despite the best efforts of W3C to set standards that all software manufacturers should adhere to, not all browsers display a web page in the same way.

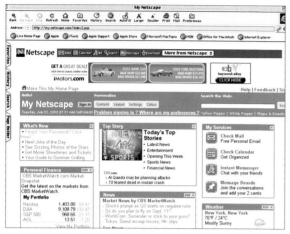

To maximize your audience, ensure that pages are compatible with the most popular browsers.

There are over 200 browsers available for PC, Mac, palmtop and even WebTV, but 95 per cent of web surfers will be using either Microsoft Internet Explorer (IE) or Netscape Navigator. Not that this duopoly makes the task any easier – versions dating back four or five years could still be in use, and there are platform issues to consider,

with the same browsers displaying the same code in very different ways on Macs and PCs.

Fortunately, after much incompatibility, Netscape 6.0 and IE 6.0 are almost identical in the way they work with HTML, although there are discrepancies in CSS, DHTML, XML and ActiveX support. Font sizes, the dimensions of form elements and spacing also vary

slightly between editions. But it is in the use of older browsers where problems occur, as your page reaches desktops where frames, CSS and JavaScript may not be supported at all.

For realistic cross-browser support, try and comply with versions 4.0 of Navigator and IE and check the page in as many browsers as possible as often as possible. This poses problems as well, though, since IE does not react well to sharing hard-disk space with older versions. Install version 4.0 alongside v5.5 and the chances are that neither version will work properly. The only solution is to install the older version on to a clean machine, or ask colleagues (not forgetting the Mac users) to check the site's appearance for you. Netscape is a little more understanding, and you can install multiple versions of Navigator provided they are in different directories.

Adding extra code to cover all bases is one solution. If you usually apply font attributes using CSS, for instance, add standard HTML instructions too. Older browsers will bypass the CSS tag and apply the HTML instead.

Use older versions of JavaScript if possible (v1.2 is widely supported by older browsers), and always include NOFRAMES and NOSCRIPT tags and offer alternatives if possible rather than just a 'Hard luck, your browser's too old!' message.

Finally, test as often as possible and clean up the code if necessary. Dreamweaver's Target Browser Check will look over your page and report any compatibility problems. Really though, there is no substitute for testing your site in the browsers themselves.

➡ *Microsoft Internet Explorer, Netscape Navigator and Communicator, Technical Limitations*

TOP LEFT: Eric Gill designed the Gill Sans typeface in 1927. It is still widely used today.

CSS

Cascading Style Sheets. These give web site developers more control over the appearance of web pages than regular HTML offers. The CSS1 and CSS2 specifications, created by the W3C to encourage web-wide uniformity, give complete control over the layout and style of every element on a web page, from text and paragraphs to tables and page margins. As the colour and layout attributes of entire sites can be set from a single remote CSS file, designers can make radical changes to the design of whole sites without having to edit hundreds or thousands of individual HTML pages.

Style sheets are even more useful in a corporate environment. With several designers working on pages, being able to define characters through a style sheet is much easier than having to refer to fonts and colour codes on every line where the slightest error could put a page out of kilter with the rest of a site. Likewise, if a head designer wants to make one change (to the size or colour of a site's main body font, for example) all they have to do is change the content of the CSS file.

Simply specifying a style name for each paragraph rather than describing the typeface, size and colour to use at length – a process called 'hard coding' – also reduces the size of HTML files considerably and speeds up page download times.

Using a graphics editing package, designers will find creating and applying style sheets as easy – and remarkably similar– to utilizing style sheets in desktop publishing packages. In fact, elements such as type size and margin dimensions can be specified in pixels, points and millimetres rather than in the clumsy relative sizes used in HTML. You can also set leading and work

spacing, variables that are impossible to change using HTML. CSS1 also sets up items like drop caps automatically, which in HTML you can only by creating additional graphics.

CSS2 brings further precision with its spacing and positioning commands. Designers can position an element to appear anywhere on the screen and set standard spacing rules for paragraphs and images. Because measurements are expressed in day-to-day values, the resulting type size will eventually be constant across browsers and operating systems. For the moment, though, the consistency is not quite there especially with regards to positional settings, and you should check any page designs in as many environments as possible before publishing.
➠ *Font, HTML, Type*

CURVATURE RANGE AND BÉZIER CURVES

Use of mathematically defined curves. The key to eye-catching design – be it static or animated – is non-linearity. Straight lines will hold little interest for the reader, while curves are easy on the eye and can express a wide range of emotions. A smooth, gentle curve conveys elegance, while longer waves can suggest a certain sluggishness. Sharp, irregular waves express awkwardness, while low, almost linear curves give the impression of speed.

Curvature range is the difference between the most linear and the most

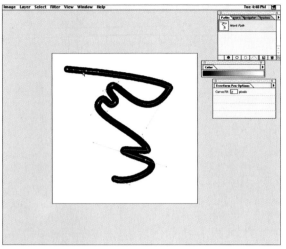

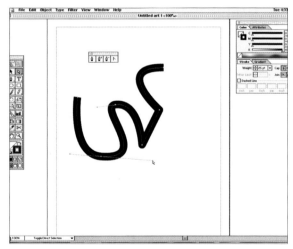

using at least four points. Two endpoints at each end of the line are connected to control points which do not lie on the curve itself but define its shape. Moving any of the four points alters the size and curvature of the Bézier, to the point that loops and sharp points can be incorporated into the curve. Up to two bends can be built into a Bézier curve, and you can even create straight lines (although that would defeat the object of creating the curve in the first place).

Graphic design programs like Photoshop, Fireworks or Illustrator make Bézier tools easy to create, usually using some variation on a pen tool. You can add additional points to the curve, which usually produces a double-sided control handle at the centre of which is the point. This handle can be turned to control the curvature of the splines adjacent to the new point. An infinite number of intermediate points can be added, but it is wise to keep the number of points low or the spline will appear as little more than a series of straight-line segments connected at jagged points.

➡ *Geometric Shapes in Design, Non-Linear Design*

FAR LEFT: Try to avoid a linear design for your web page – as Marilyn Monroe proved, curves are a lot easier on the eye, and hold attention for longer than straight lines!

curved elements of a line (technically known as a spline). The greater the curvature range, the more dramatic the spline is. Shapes with low curvature ranges, such as a straight line or – perhaps surprisingly – a circle, are less interesting and not as eye-catching as high-curvature elements like dramatic waves and large undulations. This is why ellipses and ovals are more engaging than the constant curve of circles. Increase the curvature range too much, however, and curves will become too dramatic and ultimately pointed, rendering them ugly to the viewer's eye.

Curvature range applies mathematical rules to design, and designers can thank a mathematician, Pierre Bézier, for developing the tool that today's graphics packages use to create freeform curves. Bézier curves define a curve

CUTEFTP (GLOBALSCAPE)

File transfer utility. GlobalScape's CuteFTP is one of the most popular file transfer protocol (FTP) programs for the PC, with a user base of millions of webmasters. It allows fast and straightforward transfer of files from a PC to a remote web server, as well as plenty of other features to make web site management a painless experience.

CuteFTP's basic FTP interface is a two-window affair, with the directories on your local PC on the left and the files on the server on the right. Just as in Windows Explorer, files can be dragged and dropped from one window to the other. Alternatively, files can be transferred directly from within a Windows session by right-clicking on a file and selecting a pre-set FTP site. Making a connection to an FTP server is quick and easy thanks to CuteFTP's Connection Wizard, which takes you step-by-step through the connection process.

Useful recent additions include a Smart Keep Alive feature, which prevents your FTP connection from timing out by sending stealth packets of data, and an automatic reconnect feature. Files can also be scheduled to transfer at a set time, and integration with GlobalScape's CuteHTML lets you edit HTML documents without having to download the page first. CuteFTP, and its advanced sibling CuteFTP Pro, are available from www.cuteftp.com.

➠ *FTP, Uploading a Web Site*

DESIGN BASICS

 Designers learning internet skills should remember these pointers to good web design.

1. Don't reinvent the wheel. Have a good browse around the Web, and when you find a site layout you like, view its source code to see how it is constructed. Many web-editing packages include a set of standard templates and themes, one of which should meet your needs.

2. Get your site design finalized and create templates before you start laying out pages. This will guarantee consistency and save you from having to re-edit every page just to correct a small problem. Likewise, plan your site structure using a flow chart.

3. Select a scheme of complementary colours before you begin and do not stray from these colours. Even changing colours slightly for different site sections is inadvisable, as readers might think they've been sent to an external site.

4. Choose a consistent screen resolution and colour depth for your pages. Consider working with the reasonable lowest common denominator of 800 x 600-pixel screens and 216-colour web-safe palette: a high-resolution screen and dithered colours could render your site unreadable on low-specification machines.

5. Keep file sizes small. Larger graphics and lengthy pages take longer to load and could prompt dial-up users to press the dreaded Back button. Compress image files as

LEFT: Even though elaborate images (such as Picasso's Glass and Fruit *featured here) may look impressive on your web page, users will become impatient waiting for them to download.*

much as possible and include text alternatives in each image tag.

6. Reports state that readers are reluctant to scroll down for more than $1\frac{1}{2}$ screens, so it is better to run a longer story onto a second page than to force users to scroll away from the page header and navigation bar.

7. Don't use too many images. Graphics-heavy pages take longer to download and a simple design is preferable to image overload.

8. Keep navigation devices constant. The reader should be able to return to the homepage by clicking a banner or icon in the top-left corner, and a site's main sections should be accessible from every other page. Include a contact link on each page.

9. Respect web conventions – links should stand out, and blue underline is the usual style. Make links clear, but do not use blue underline anywhere non-linking, as it proves too confusing.

10. Test your site as your readers would see it, using a dial-up connection and dropping the screen resolution and colours. Run the site across as many browsers as possible and on both Macs and Windows PCs to check its universality.

➠ *Colour Combinations, Consistency, Image Usage, User Interface*

DESIGNING A 3D INTERFACE

Although the computer screen is a two-dimensional medium, web graphics software packages make it easy to create an impression of depth to apply a pseudo-3D appearance. Using a few simple tricks, you could make your site stand out and give it a professional touch. Most of these effects can be created in image-editing programs such as Macromedia Fireworks, Adobe Photoshop's ImageReady utility and Ulead's specialist web design applications.

1. In the real, three-dimensional world, light sources cast shadows on to background objects, so adding shadows and lighting effects to a page can create the impression of three dimensions. Placing a drop shadow behind an image – whether it is a cutout, a button or a geometric shape – lifts that element off the page. If you use more that one drop shadow on the same page, keep the angle and depth of the shadow constant to suggest a regular light source; shadows slanting in different directions will look unnatural.

2. Some programs let you add inner shadows as easily as you can add drop shadows. Inner shadows usually sit inside geometric shapes and give them a sunken effect, raising the main body of the page to the foreground. Unlike drop shadows, inner shadows point towards the light source. Again, if you combine inner and drop shadows on a page, keep the angle of the light source consistent.

3. Inner shadows can be added to large white-out text headlines and banners. This creates the impression that the headline or logo has been cut out of the foreground, and works best on black or dark-coloured backgrounds.

4. Motion blur is a form of exaggerated shadow to suggest movement as well as depth. Used sparingly, it can add additional depth to a page. It can be combined with animated graphics in order to suggest that an item is moving towards the reader. This can be created simply by enlarging and shrinking the main character in an animation as it moves, to give the impression of it approaching.

5. Embossing tools use subtle shading effects to make elements such as buttons appear to sink into or raise out of their surroundings. You can apply an inset or a raised emboss effect. This works well when lifting headline text gently out of its background. Embossing works particularly well when the embossed image and its background are the same colour. This can give the effect of embossed paper or, with a light grey tint on the background and the foreground, of a stamped metal panel.

6. Textures, combined with colour and lighting, can be used to enhance the appearance of embossed elements. Brown-tinted embossed text or line-art on a wooden texture can look like a carving, while a metal textured image can resemble a coin or engraved metal nameplate. Dedicated 3D-graphics utilities let you add a light source and light type such as spot, point or distance to enhance this effect, and tutorials at www.eyeball-design.com explain how to extend the real-world feel by adding knot holes, piping, screws and even cracks and corroded areas.

7. Specialist 3D-graphics utilities include an extrude tool which automates the creation of three-dimensional images and animations. Any simple flat image such as a polygon or Bézier curve can be turned into a three-dimensional shape, and shaded, textured and lit to create a lifelike graphic.

8. Bevelling adds raised edges to buttons and other small geometric shapes. An automatic inner bevel applies a raised and textured border to the inside of the button, while the outer bevel adds an additional border to the button. The size of the border, inside or out, can be set by the user, but on smaller buttons, keep it small or there will be more bevel than button. Fireworks offers several styles so you can apply a smooth bevel, emulate convex or concave slopes, or create a frame which indents the content of the centre of the button.

9. Three-dimensional rollover buttons can be created by combining various states of a bevelled image. Fireworks supplies preset raised, highlighted, inset and inverted variations on the bevel to make creating active buttons very straightforward.

10. To create a simple 3D arrangement, create a coloured round-cornered rectangle to the size of your planned page width. Place another white round-cornered rectangle some 150 x 150 pixels in from the top left-hand corner and make it larger and deeper than your intended page size so that it bleeds off the right-hand side and the bottom of the page. Then apply an inside shadow to the top and left-hand sides of the white rectangle, and in a table-based layout (split appropriately and imported into a web design package), use the white 'background' to hold the page content and the coloured 'foreground' for the header and the menu. A slight inner bevel or lens flare on the coloured rectangle will raise the menu and header even further.

➡ *Bevel and Emboss, Eyeball Design, Geometric Shapes in Design, Graphic Design Package, User Interface*

LEFT: Using lighting effects to create shadows or a 3D effect, you can brighten up your web page.

DESIGNING FOR DIFFERENT RESOLUTIONS

In designing for the Web, it is important to bear in mind that users will be viewing your pages at various sizes. Given people's reluctance to scroll, particularly horizontally, it is important to try and fit your page within the likely screen size of most of your visitors. If this is Web TV then you only have a maximum of 540 x 384 pixels. In fact, the majority of people view web pages at 800 x 600 (that is 800 pixels on each of 600 lines) although a significant percentage with 17-inch monitors are likely to have a screen resolution of 1,024 x 768 pixels.

Even if you decide on a particular resolution, the chances are the actual viewing area within the browser is likely to be smaller than the maximum possible. For instance, most users do not set their browser to fit the screen. In addition, browsers have different combinations of menu and tool bars that users can select. These may take up to 150 pixels of vertical space. Consequently, your site should be designed for a smaller window by adding extra space at the margins. Alternatively, rather than designing tables to specific pixel sizes you could use percentages so they fit whatever the viewing area.

➡ *Screen Resolution, Technical Limitations*

DHTML

Dynamic Hypertext Markup Language. The aim of Dynamic HTML (DHTML) is to take the ordinary text-and-graphics web page and bring it to life. Using DHTML, content on the page can change and images and text can move, appear, disappear or change style as wanted. What's more, all the coding is in the client-side so there are no delays with requests going to and from the web server.

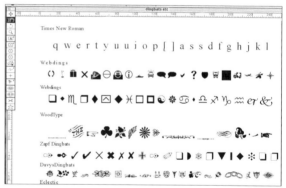

In fact, DHTML is not a single identifiable product in the way JavaScript is. Instead it is a combination of technologies, including HTML, JavaScript and CSS, that enables designers to control each element on the page. In effect, it allows you to hide or show objects and move them around, by changing the CSS positioning properties. No plug-ins are required and files are small as they are text files, which are quicker to download than graphics files, and render faster than alternatives such as Flash. The main fly in the ointment is the variable support for DHTML among the different types of browser. Although there are workarounds, it is not yet totally cross-browser compatible.

➠ *Animation, HTML, iFrame, JavaScript, Site Navigation*

DINGBAT

Decorative typeface. Sign off with a heart-shaped drawing, add a finger pointing to a text input box or put a tick by a correctly completed form – these are all

ABOVE: When designing your web page, bear in mind that users will be viewing your pages on different sized screens.

dingbats; a simple decorative typeface made up of graphic images.

The assortment of icons and symbols are more commonly called Zapf Dingbats after their creator Herman Zapf. Dingbat itself has become a generic name for any font where the different characters are made up from small decorative graphics. The arrows and pointers can be used as part of navigation elements while some of the icons and symbols are good as stand-alone characters, to mark either the beginning or end of a section of text. They can also be used to add some fun and style to bulleted lists, although the effect wears off with overuse. If they are used with lists do not use the <UL>...</UL> tag as this will automatically add the default black dot bullets for each list item.

Dingbats can be used as clipart or larger illustrations (such as the base image). The font can be rasterized in Photoshop, by right-clicking on 'layer', and coloured using the brush options.

➠ *1001 freefonts.com, Font, Fontfreak.com*

DISTORTION TECHNIQUES

The filters featured in graphic-design applications can be sorted into two groups: non-texturizing effects, which alter the colour of pixels but do not technically 'distort' the image; and texturizing effects, which physically distort groups of pixels to create unusual effects.

The most basic non-texture effect is to alter the brightness of an image in order to promote or demote it in relation to other elements in the composition.

Blending it with a background colour is one option: darken an image on a black background or lighten it on white and you can place almost any image or text element over it, including a fully saturated version of the same image.

If you wanted to place an image in the background of a montage, but it was proving too bright to allow coloured text to stand out over it, you could reduce its prominence by desaturating it and converting it to greyscale.

Similarly, your graphics package will let you render the image in shades of a colour featured in a site's overall scheme or that complements the colour of the foreground element.

Such effects can be mixed and applied to different parts of an image using masks. Use sparingly though – desaturating one part of an image and increasing the saturation on another can lead to garish colour clashes.

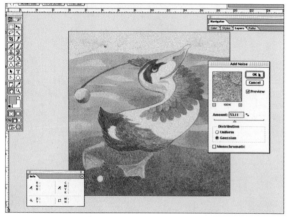

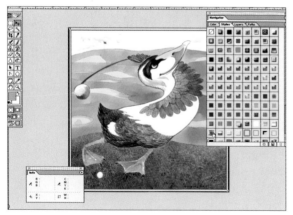

Most effects are in the texturizing camp. These tools edit selected areas of an image by distorting the order of the pixels. There is an endless stream of such filters, and while some are merely eye candy, a few can be useful when created montages and illustrations.

Like desaturiztion, the blur filter merges an image with the background by softening its texture, making the eye think that it is out of focus and therefore further away. The motion blur and wind filters add movement to static objects by adding a trail of smeared pixels to a blur, but their use should imply a natural movement. Motion blur can be applied as a shadow which also lifts an element above the surface of the screen.

The diffuse, mosaic, noise and sharpen filters are the opposite of blur, as when used in moderation, they create crisp, sharp images. Use them to sharpen an object at the front of your composition.

Finally, you will also find naturalistic texture filters like slate, metal or wood. These can create interesting effects, but only when applied globally to a completed image rather than selectively.

➠ *Artful Distortion, Graphic Design Package, Image Manipulation*

DITHERING

The number of colours a monitor can display depends on its bit depth. A 24-bit monitor can show millions of colours while an 8-bit colour monitor can only display 256. Although a 24-bit colour monitor is not going to have any problems displaying an image with thousands of colours, the 8-bit monitor does. The browser's workaround is to dither the extra colours, i.e. it blends two of the colours it does have in its palette to approximate the additional ones it needs. The result can make the images look rather speckled and there is the added complication that browsers on different systems have different palettes, or CLUTs (colour look-up tables) to which they refer to mix their colours.

One way to solve this problem – at least for the flat colour GIF files that are mainly affected by it – is to only use colours in the web-safe palette. This is a selection of 216 colours that are in all the main system and browser palettes. Consequently, the colours will appear the same, or as near as they are ever likely to, whichever computer they are viewed on.

➠ *Colour, Image Compression*

ABOVE LEFT: By using naturalistic textures, in Photoshop for example, you can create impressive results.

DOMAIN NAME

Part of the URL or address that identifies a particular web site. For instance, microsoft.com is the unique name that identifies the web pages for

The translation of a site's domain name into the IP address needed to locate it is done by DNS servers. If one server does

software company Microsoft. The .com suffix reflects the type of organization the site belongs to, such as .com for commercial organizations, .gov for government and .org for non-profit bodies. This part is called the top-level domain. New ones have recently been introduced, including .info for information services and .biz for business. Microsoft is the unique name that identifies the company or organization.

In fact, domain names are really a convenience for web users as we find it easier to remember names, rather than numbers. To locate a site on the Internet the domain name needs to be translated into its IP address. This is a block of four numbers separated by periods.

not know the number of a particular domain name it queries another, and so on down the network until there is a response.

➡ *Web Hosting*

DREAMWEAVER (MACROMEDIA)

Web editor and design package. Macromedia's Web editor Dreamweaver lies at the heart of a website production system that includes the dominant multimedia standards Flash and Shockwave. Dreamweaver is a favourite with professional web designers, but can cater for users of all degrees of experience.

The program offers several ways to create a web page. Designers can sketch a design for a site in a graphics package and then trace table elements, text areas and images over it. This way, they can output to a regular page, or to the little-used layers-based format, which ensures pixel-perfect design in the latest browsers.

Alternatively, you can create your pages in Dreamweaver's WYSIWYG display window, entering text and adding other elements from images to animations and applets. A tabbed Window also gives access to the HTML source, should you want to check why an effect isn't working as it should. The high-end text editors BBEdit for Mac and HomeSite for Windows are bundled with the program and will check your HTML for errors and compatibility with all the latest and old versions of browsers.

Control of Dreamweaver is via floating tabbed toolboxes, Properties being chief among these. It displays all the variables for a selected element, so if you click on a section of text, it will show you the font, size, colour for that element.

Site-wide consistency can be achieved using Dreamweaver's HTML styles. Styles let you save a set of attributes which can be assigned to characters or a paragraph with a single click. Dreamweaver then applies all the correct HTML codes to the text for you. A more efficient option is to use cascading style sheets (CSS), for which Dreamweaver has full support. The program also supports Java and ActiveX items, and Flash animations and graphics are linked dynamically to Flash and Fireworks respectively.

Dreamweaver boasts impressive site control features. You can view your entire site as a conventional Windows/Mac directory or as a tree structure. FTP links can be established to a remote server and updated pages uploaded automatically. If a group of colleagues will be editing the content of your site's pages, they can add comments to any elements they have worked on for future reference.

Another bonus for group working is that Dreamweaver's template system can be used to specify which areas of a page can be edited and which are locked. This should prevent pages from accidental mis-editing. The program's template system is a great boon, as any amendment to the base template will be replicated in any of the pages or other templates created from the original. This is useful when you have an afterthought to a design that requires global replacement.

➡ **HTML, HTML Editor**

CENTRE: Dreamweaver's template system allows you to make global changes to your design.

DYNAMIC NAVIGATION

Interactive and expanding navigation tools. Dynamic navigation, where menu items break out of the static to offer more options or simply to emphasize interactivity, livens up a web site, engages the reader and offers a convenient way to make the most of limited screen space.

The simplest form of dynamic navigation device is a rollover: a change of colour or image when a mouse hovers over a button draws the reader's attention to a link. Distance rollovers are even more useful, as the changing remote graphic can give text descriptions of the contents of the destination page.

Dynamic drop-down menus can be great space-saving devices. If your site is divided into 30 sections, it is impossible to run a horizontal menu across the screen, and impractical to run a lengthy menu down the side of the page. Instead, you can group the sections under a few main menu headings, which when hovered over or clicked on call up a menu containing the subsections, just like application menus.

The easiest way to do this is to use a standard form drop-down list which uses JavaScript's windowOpen control to open a destination URL as soon as the menu is released or when the user clicks a 'Go' button. These can be created easily using tools built into the best web editors, or by customizing code which is freely available from JavaScript libraries (such as http://javascript. internet.com/navigation).

Web design packages can create variations on these menus by adding colour and images. Make sure it's clear to the reader that this is still a menu though. Displaying the 'Select a Section' option by default (and routing it back to the same page) is a good idea. Flash menus are equally impressive and easy to create, but Flash-less visitors will have no way of navigating your site.

DHTML can be used to add fly-out hierarchical submenus to menu items, like the directories on Windows Start Menu or the Mac's Apple Menu. You can also hide menus under tabs which the reader can drag in as required. Scripts to create these kinds of menus can be found at DHTML repositories like DynamicDrive (www.dynamicdrive.com) or Web Reference's HierMenus Central (www.webreference.com/dhtml).

Java applets are available to control vertical hierarchical menus. Click on a menu item on the left of a page and a list of subtopics will appear under that item, with the other main topics moving down to accommodate it.

➡ *DHTML, Java, JavaScript, Rollovers, Site Navigation*

DYNAMIC WEB PAGES

Interactive web pages. Originally, web pages were static – the content did not change from the time the page was initially created. But now a variety of technologies have brought movement and change to the Web. Animation, whether a simple animated gif or a flash movie, can create dynamic effects on the page. Similarly Dynamic HTML (DHTML), which is a composite of cascading style sheets (CSS), CSS positioning and JavaScript, will change what is displayed in the browser window. The movement comes either as a result of some interaction by the user or from following some script. So, for example, menus can slide out automatically, animated objects float round the window, etc.

The most dynamic sites are where content is generated by server-side programming – at the time the user asks for

the page. Usually the information is stored in a database. When the page is requested the content is merged into page templates and delivered to the user. Dynamic web pages like this will normally be marked .asp (for Active Server Pages) or .jsp (for JavaServer pages). A typical example is a search engine page where each query results in a new page being created with the results of the search.

➡ *Animation, DHTML, Marquee*

EASYCOUNTER.COM *(www.easycounter.com)*

Web page counter; a counter hosting service that takes the hard work out of tracking visitors to your web pages. Depending on your site's popularity, it can be encouraging or disappointing to see how many visitors have come to your web site. It is something that most web-site owners will want to know, though. Although some professional web-hosting services offer user-tracking statistics, for smaller sites this job can be done by a web page counter.

Sites like Easycounter.com offer a free counter hosting service. There is a small bit of HTML which needs to be included in your code to place the counter on the page, but the script that operates the counter runs on the Easycounter server. You can place a separate counter on several pages and view all the counts simultaneously. Counter results can also be emailed to you on a regular basis. Not only will the counter keep tabs of how many have visited your page, it can also track the number of hits since the counter was reset (as it may have been after a major design update).

To keep the service free, it is supported by advertising. That means your counter will have an advert with it, but there are several designs so it does not need to be too obtrusive.

➡ *Counter, Free Web Extras*

LEFT: Animation has advanced immensely; if used to its optimum it can create dynamic effects on your web pages.

EPS

Graphics file format. EPS is a vector format that can also contain bitmap graphics. It is good for printing to postscript printers, but it is not as useful for web design. EPS stands for Encapsulated PostScript. An EPS is a vector graphics file format, i.e., the elements are described by mathematical formulas rather than by mapping the image to pixels. As a result, files are generally smaller. Images can also be

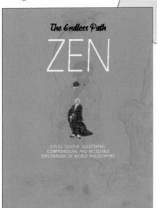

scaled up or down without the quality being affected.

EPSs are unique in that they can contain both vector and bitmap graphics. They will have a low resolution bitmap image, usually a TIFF, as the header graphic. EPSs have to be placed or imported into a program to view. Typically, this will be a desktop publishing program, such as QuarkXPress; a word processor, such as Word; or an illustration program, such as FreeHand. When you view the file in these programs it is usually the low resolution header graphic that you see.

The EPS really comes into its own when it is printed – which can only be done on a postscript printer. If it is printed on a non-postscript printer, only the bitmapped header graphic appears. As it is low resolution – usually 72 dpi – it will appear very blocky.
➡ *File Type*

ENABLE FILE DOWNLOADING FROM A WEB SITE

File transfer from the Net. To enable a file to be downloaded from your site, simply put it in the main directory on your server and create a link to it in the HTML. For instance, to download a whitepaper written in Word you would simply have <a href="whitepaper.doc">Download whitepaper here</a>.

It may be that your browser has a helper application or plug-in which enables the browser to automatically display or play the file. This is possible with some sound and video files, PDF files and Flash or Shockwave files. If it is not possible to play the file directly, a dialog box pops up giving the user the option to save the file to their hard drive.

To reduce download time, compress the files using a program such as WinZip. If your server is still struggling to download the file in a reasonable time use an FTP server instead. Files download quicker from an FTP site than they do from a Web server. You need to make sure your FTP server allows anonymous read access to files and include the relevant link in your HTML. It will be something like <a href="ftp://ftp.yourdomain.com/downloadfile.zip"> Download file </a>.
➡ *HTML, PDF, WinZip*

EYE FLOW

Guiding users through pages. Web pages can be so busy that a first-time visitor may find it hard to work out where to start. By laying out pages according to certain rules, you can guide readers around the screen and offer a comfortable and engaging browsing experience.

The reader's eye naturally flows from left to right and from top to bottom. The smoother that process is, the more information will be received and processed. When a page is opened, the reader's eye will fall on the top

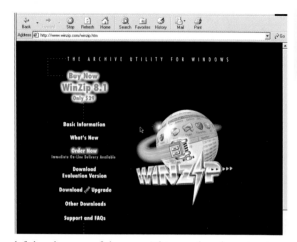

FAR LEFT: *Regardless of what you need, whether it is ancient text or the latest information on the Internet, bear in mind that the reader's eye naturally flows from left to right.*

left-hand corner of the page. This may be where the site banner or menu is placed, and is probably not an ideal starting point. To emphasize where you want your reader to begin, contrast it significantly from the other elements at the top of the page – use a contrasting colour or bold font so that it stands out, or a large, bright logo which pulls the eye in. Crosses work particularly well in this respect.

Make sure all your pages are top-heavy. Once the reader is hooked in, guide them gently down the page by reducing the emphasis, breaking up paragraphs with light crossheads. The least important page elements can go where the eye is least likely to notice, in the far right-hand side. Play them down using smaller text and subtle graphics.

➠ *Alignment, Non-Linear Design, Spacing*

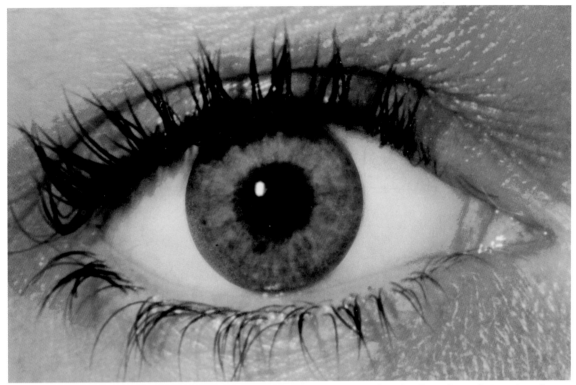

EYEBALL DESIGN (www.eyeball-design.com)

Online design tutorials; a site for special-effects wizards who want to chat online to fellow enthusiasts. Once past the slightly confusing splash page – the revolving balls are actually shortcuts to the site but don't always respond to the user's click – there is a wealth of material covering special effects (FX) in Photoshop. The heavily designed site may appear a bit sombre in parts, but it does stimulate a lot of activity. The site runs regular weekend design challenges and also spreads information in novel ways. Several tutorials are live – using IRC (internet relay chat) – and the site comes with a handy time-converter link so you can work out when you need to be up to catch the programme. It also supports SVG (scalable vector graphics), the new image format agreed by the W3C. The XML-based standard can add animation and interactivity to the page but is hampered by the fact it needs a special viewer.

Eyeball-design's chat links are also used to create a talking shop where Photoshop enthusiasts can communicate with each other. Alongside is an interface depot, not for one-to-one meetings but a file exchange scheme for any interface patterns, textures or Photoshop files that you have created and are happy to share.

➡ *Designing a 3D Interface, Geometric Shapes in Design, Non-Linear Design*

FEEDBACK FORM

Method of gaining feedback from users. It's good to have some form of communication with your web-site users. The easiest way is the mailto: link which enables them to send a message, but sometimes more structured information is needed. Forms are an ideal way to send feedback or request information.

The form is set up with the <form>…</form> tags. Within the opening tag itself you need to specify the action attribute (the address of the program that will process the form) and the method attribute (which specifies how the information will be sent). For small forms use the 'get' method; for more complicated forms, particularly where security is important, use the 'post' method.

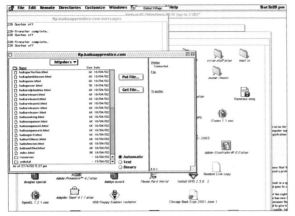

While the forms themselves are relatively unproblematic, the data will need processing. For a simple form it may be possible to use JavaScript or some other client-side scripting to analyze the form and return the values. Otherwise the users' responses need to be sent to an email address or to a server-side application, typically CGI or ASP, that can handle them. For those who do not want the hassle of programming, there are a number of online sites where you can download easily configurable scripts.

➠ *HTML, Form Field, Form Handler, CGI, Response-O-Matic*

For a feedback form you will probably want a text input field where visitors put specific information, such as their name, as well as a text box where they add general comments. For single-line text use the <input> tag with the attribute type="text". You can control the length of the visible field by using the size attribute. To limit the number of characters users can enter, add the maxlength attribute.

The <textarea> tag creates a text box for free-flowing comment. The visible size is set with the rows and cols attributes. For example, <textarea name="feedback" rows="4" cols="25">...</textarea> would create a box that would take four lines of text with 25 characters in a line. Any more than that and the box would scroll. If you want to prompt people on details to include, add some text between the opening and closing <textarea> tags.

To round off the form, add a submit button, created by using the <input> tag and putting "submit" as the attribute. Clicking this will send the form information to the URL previously set in the action attribute.

FILE

A collection of information. Information on the Web is stored in a variety of file types, marked by an extension. A file is a collection of information that has been given a name, or filename. There are many different kinds of files but on the Web the most common are data files, text files, graphics files, audio files and video files.

A basic web page is stored as a text file, although it is given the file extension of .htm or .html. Hand-coders using Notepad need to be especially careful as this program saves documents as .txt by default. If it is not saved as .htm or .html it will not be recognized by the browser.

Generally, servers are sensitive to file extensions and the correct one must be used or the link to the file will not work. For instance, picture files must also have the correct suffix, such as .jpg or .jpeg for JPEGs, .gif for GIFs, and .png for PNG files. It is also important to follow the naming convention supported by your web server, otherwise no file will be found.

Once your site is complete, the HTML documents, graphics and other media files need to be uploaded to the server. This is done using FTP (File Transfer Protocol), which is the standard way for moving files between computers over a network.

➠ *File Type*

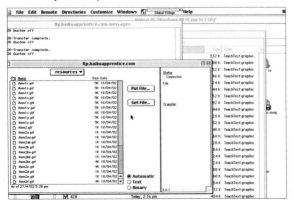

TOP LEFT: Eyeball design provides special effects enthusiasts with chat links, tips and tutorials.

FILE ORGANIZATION

Before you start building the pages that will make up your web site, decide how you want to store their constituent .htm, .gif and .jpg files on the server. If a web site consists of less than 20 pages, you can safely put them all in the one top-level directory. To preserve order on larger sites, files can be divided into directories based on the site's menu structure. If your site is particularly complex, you can create further subdirectories. Each directory should have an index page (index.htm or equivalent).

Create a separate directory for images at the top level to ease management. Other resources, like Flash animations or movie files, should also be assigned a separate directory.

When referring to files, use relative rather than absolute links. A relative link refers to a second file according to its relationship with the first, for instance images/banner.gif rather than the absolute http://www.servername.com/images/banner.gif. This makes it easy to move the site wholesale to another server or to a CD.

The best web editors can track changes to a file's name and location, and update all the references to that file across the site. Update the site cache regularly to keep this useful feature running smoothly.

➡ *Asset Management, Naming Convention, Web Site Structure*

FILE SIZE

File size is critical on the Web to minimize download time, so a variety of compression techniques are used to make files smaller. The size of a file is measured by the number of bytes it takes up, where a single byte represents one letter or character. Typically, file sizes will be shown in either kilobytes (KB), which is 1,024 bytes, or megabytes (MB) which is just over a million bytes (1,048,576 bytes).

On the Web everything that is viewed in the browser – the HTML document, graphics files, etc. – has to be downloaded, usually over a dial-up connection. In real terms, even with a good 56 Kbps connection, that is unlikely to mean transfers of more than 2–5 KB per second. Consequently, web designers are advised to keep their pages to 30 KB or less.

To minimize file size and reduce download time most graphics files are optimized for the Web in a compressed format. Compression works by removing repetitive information and spaces. GIF files use a 'lossless' system which does not affect the quality of the image, unlike

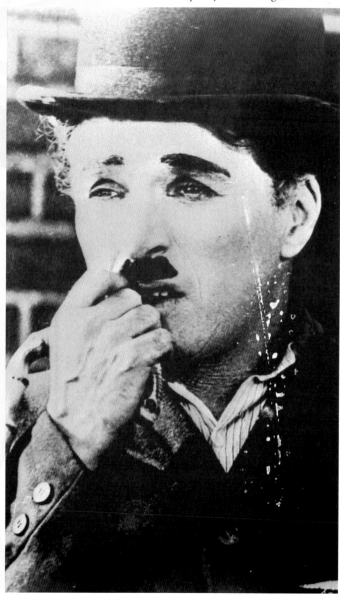

JPEGs which use 'lossy' compression, where the file is reduced in size by removing data from the image. HTML can also be optimized by removing excessive characters such as spacing and comments.

Many of the programs and files stored on the Internet are also compressed and have to be restored to their original format before being used by utilities such as WinZip (for Windows) or StuffIt Expander (for the Mac).

➠ *Page Download Time, Byte, Image Compression*

FILE TYPE

The format of a file. Different file types have different file formats, or ways of organizing the information they store. These are shown by the file extension – the three or four letters that come after the period at the end of a filename. Web servers add a header to each document they send to the browser, which indicates what type of file it is. This lets the browser know how to

LEFT: When organizing your files, create a separate directory for Flash animations or movie files.

handle the file – i.e. whether to open it in a window or launch the appropriate plug-in or helper application.

There are many file types on the Web; among the common ones are:

.htm or .html	A web page that can be viewed by a browser or other HTML-compatible program.
jpg, .gif, .png	Image file formats used on the Web.
MP3	Because of its near CD-quality MP3 is commonly used for distribution of music on the Web.
.rm	Streaming video.
.avi, .mov, .mpeg	Digital video formats.
.pdf	Portable document format that needs the Adobe Acrobat reader to be viewed.
.zip	Compressed file that needs to be unzipped (decompressed) before viewing.

➠ *File, BMP, EPS, GIF, JPEG, TIFF*

FILTER

Photographic special effect. In photo-editing programs a filter is an effect that can be added to an image. Some of them are like traditional photographic filters, but many add special effects to the image, such as tiles which break the digitized photo into a series of tiled images. Filters are applied to bitmap images. In drawing programs, such as Illustrator, they can produce the same range of effects on vector graphics.

Effects can be subtle – such as the blur or sharpen filters which can gently retouch a photo – or wild like the

Emboss or Wind filters. For that hand-painted touch try the brush strokes or sketch, while you can add a bit of light to the subject with a lighting-effects filter.

While most photo editors come with a number of standard filters, there are also third-party packages which can be imported into the program and run from the menu bar alongside the other filters.

Filters can usually be applied either to a whole layer or just a section of it; however, applying the effect to just a section can leave a hard edge between the filtered and non-filtered areas. To compensate for this, it is best to feather the selected area before applying the filter. In some programs you can also lessen a filter's overall effect by applying the fade command.

It is also possible to boost a filter's effect. To do so, increase the brightness and contrast values on the layer you have selected, before applying the filter. If you want to make the effect look less artificial then it's a case of more is better. Apply more than one filter and the effect looks less computer-generated.

Effects are generally grouped into sections. For example, in Photoshop, Artistic filters such as Plastic Wrap, Neon Glow or Coloured Pencil give a more natural, homespun look to images. Blur filters, of which there are several types such as Gaussian blur or Motion blur, smooth transitions by averaging the pixels next to hard edges. Brush strokes give that painting effect, while distort filters live up to their name. For example, the Twirl gives your image a twister-style effect. Noise filters add or take away speckles of colour, while render filters add that cool 3D shape or cloud pattern to add depth to a view. Become an impressionist with stylize filters, such as Emboss or Tiles, or add a grain or glass effect with a texture filter.

➡ *Image Enhancement Techniques, Graphic Design Package*

FIREWORKS (MACROMEDIA)

Web-enabled graphics design package. The graphics weapon in Macromedia's web arsenal is Fireworks, an easy-to-use program which lets web newcomers and professional designers create optimized, high-quality graphics with ease.

It is important to stress that Fireworks is not a high-resolution graphics program of the same calibre as Photoshop, and it is not suited to preparing images for print. Its primary role is for creating simple vector graphics such as buttons, dynamic elements like rollovers and animated GIFs, and optimizing images for publication on the Web. With this in mind, Macromedia has kept the interface – and the feature set – straightforward but powerful.

Adding a drop shadow or embossed effect to an image is simply a matter of entering the settings into a tabbed dialog box, while making a button change its state when rolled over or clicked on is all done automatically, as Fireworks calculates the bevels and shadows accordingly.

Image maps are just as easy to create by adding 'hotspots' to the active areas of a graphic.

When exporting graphics, Fireworks offers a four-up display, letting you preview your image with different degrees of compression and a range of colour palettes before choosing the one which strikes the right balance between appearance and file size.

It is possible to create a whole page design in Fireworks before importing the graphics into the program's Dreamweaver sibling. When you export such large images, Fireworks will slice them up into smaller parts and even single-pixel spaces for faster loading, and create an HTML document to rebuild the image in Dreamweaver.

Fireworks' interface shares a common look and feel with Macromedia's Flash and Dreamweaver software, and boasts ties with both sibling products. As well as a common interface, Flash will import graphics and animations from Fireworks, while all rollover graphics or sliced images and their accompanying HTML can be imported into Dreamweaver.

➡ *Dreamweaver (Macromedia), Flash (Macromedia), Graphic Design Package*

FIXED-WIDTH PAGE DESIGN

 When you design a web page, you have no way of predicting the size of screen and the browser that a reader will be using when they enter your URL. On a large screen, short columns of text can stretch across the page to the point of illegibility, while small graphics can disappear across the wide expanse. On smaller screens, large graphics dominate to the detriment of the words, menus and other page elements.

You can reduce the risk of this happening by designing pages to a set width. If you use a resolution above 640 x 480, you might have noticed that the page content of many professional sites stops about three-quarters of the way across the screen. This is because the site editors have catered for the lowest common denominator and placed the content of the page within a 600-pixel wide table. On a screen displaying a resolution of 640 x 480 pixels, the page would fit snugly within the confines of the monitor and, with fixed font sizes through the use of cascading style sheets (CSS), the text and graphics sit exactly where the designer intended.

If you choose a fixed-width design, you first have to choose a width to design to. According to TheCounter.com (www.thecounter.com), almost nine out of 10 internet users currently use resolutions of 800 x 600 or more, with only four per cent operating a 640 x 480 screen. With almost 500 million web users worldwide, four per cent is still a significant figure, but if you want to get more content on to your page, the 800 x 600 option strikes a good populist balance.

The fixed width is specified by adding a <TABLE WIDTH="XXX"> command after the <BODY> tag on the page. 'XXX', however, will not represent your chosen screen resolution, as you have to allow for the borders of a web browser's window and its right-hand scrollbar. As a result, the working area of a 800-pixel wide screen is only 760 pixels, and a 640-pixel wide screen is reduced to just 600.

Because the fixed-width page will end abruptly on larger screens, make sure the design defines the page borders clearly. This can be done by adding a coloured panel on the right-hand side of the fixed-width table, or by heading and footing the page with a colourful full-width logo. This way the swathe of empty space, which could appear on larger screens, will not look so out of place.

➡ *CSS (cascading style sheets), Cross-Browser Compatibility*

FLASH (MACROMEDIA)

Scalable vector-based animation tool. Macromedia's Flash has become the industry standard for low-bandwidth interactive animations, presentations and even applications over the Web. The Flash program, currently at version 5, lets designers create content for distribution to the 414 million systems that currently run the Flash Player.

As part of Macromedia's powerful arsenal of internet tools, Flash integrates tightly with its siblings, particularly the Dreamweaver web editor and FreeHand vector graphics package. Elements can be imported seamlessly from one package to another and back again for re-editing, and interactive buttons, text elements and drop-down menu styles can be created in Flash and configured to suit a specific page or site in Dreamweaver. Because Flash objects (or symbols) are scalable, they can be imported into Dreamweaver and enlarged or reduced with no loss of quality.

Macromedia offers an online extensions library called Smart Clips, which gives free access to ready-made Flash elements for users to download and incorporate into their Flash animations.

The basic Flash interface consists of the Timeline, the main 'Stage' window and a series of tabbed toolbars and palettes. The stage shows how the Flash window would look at a given time in the animation, and scrolling along the Timeline allows you to move elements and set objects accordingly. Simple animations are straightforward, thanks to Flash's Tweening tools. Short for 'inbetweening', these let the user set starting and finishing points for an object and calculates the movement, morphing pattern or colour changes in between. Audio clips, bitmap images and digital movies can also be built into sequences.

As well as diverting animations, Flash can be used to create powerful interactive web applications using Macromedia's ActionScript, which has the same structure and syntax as JavaScript but which can be authored graphically in Flash. The software also offers connectivity to databases and middleware applications via standard XML protocols.

➡ *Animation, Animation Using Flash, Flash Player (Macromedia)*

FAR LEFT: Integrated with other Macromedia applications, Flash can be used to create animations, presentations and even applications.

FLASH PLAYER (MACROMEDIA)

Plug-in for playing Flash animations. Flash has become the industry standard for low-bandwidth, interactive scalable animations, and browser developers and proprietary ISPs like AOL have acknowledged this by adding Macromedia's Flash Player to their latest releases. Standalone streaming video players like RealPlayer and QuickTime can also play Flash content.

Flash Player is essentially a plug-in that integrates seamlessly with a browser to play any Flash content included in a web page. Content created using the current version of Flash can be viewed on more than 88 per cent of the world's PCs, and as of December 2001, over 414 million users had a Flash Player loaded on their systems.

The Flash Player is backwards-compatible, so content created using Flash version 2 could be played on the latest Flash Player. However, to play the latest Flash content, the latest player is required. Fortunately for users and content providers, if the correct version is not detected, the latest edition (weighing in at around 200 KB) will be downloaded free of charge. Alternatively, users can download the Player themselves from www.macromedia.com.

Macromedia makes tweaks, enhancements and bug fixes to the Player every few months, so if you are a developer, sign up to receive regular news and updates from the software company.

➡ *Flash (Macromedia), Multimedia*

FONT

Text formatting. Fonts have become synonymous with the idea of typefaces, but in fact they encompass other features, such as size, weight and spacing. In HTML you can specify font properties, such as size, colour or typeface, using the <font> tag. However, this is being phased out in favour of using cascading style sheets (CSS) which offer greater control of additional features such as leading and word-spacing. Even if you do specify different styles it does not give you total control over how users will see your pages. Visitors can, in fact, override the typographical elements you set, such as the typeface or font size. You can specify a font which will override the browser default, but this will only show up if the user has that particular font on their machine. What's more, different platforms treat font size differently. On the Macintosh a 12-pt font appears as roughly that, while Microsoft, in order to make the font easier to read on screen, makes it much larger. In addition, each platform has its own range of standard fonts. So, if you specify fonts in HTML, or cascading style sheets, it is more like making a recommendation than taking firm control of what's viewed.

➡ *Formatting Text Using HTML, Typography, Type, System Font*

FONTSEEK.COM *(www.fontseek.com)*

Specialist search engine. Stuck for a font? Fontseek is a search engine that can access more than 55,000 fonts in its database, commercial and freeware. Despite the fact that there are only a handful of fonts that most browsers are able to recognize – or that we can safely

assume users have on their machine – there are many thousands more available online. From decorative faces to symbols, if there is a font you want to find the chances are you can locate it through FontSeek. This search engine has the distinction of including commercial fonts

FLASH PLAYER - FONTSEEK.COM

BELOW: Fontseek.com comes in a variety of European languages and tests whether your fonts and operating system support the Euro sign.

as well as online freeware. It also has a useful page linking through to the main commercial font foundries, such as the expressively named Linotype – Hell, Agfa Monotype and Berthold. It also lists and ranks the main sites on the Web where you can download fonts. Once you have them, it has links to tools (some freeware, some shareware) for managing, converting or previewing fonts. Most usefully in these days of European expansion it offers a freeware program called EuroCheck, which will test whether your fonts and operating system support the Euro sign. It also comes in a variety of European languages.

➡ *Free Web Extras*

FORM FIELD

 Information entry point. Form fields are the areas on a form where users enter requested information. The most common method will be through a text field, where visitors are prompted to enter details, such as a name or address. Where longer comments are needed a text-box field can be added. Selection-type form fields, such as check boxes, radio buttons and drop-down menus are also used to gather information.

There may be occasions when you want to disable certain form fields, such as following an earlier selection the user has made. Normally the browser will grey out these fields so they cannot be accessed. For the selection-type form fields the disabled attribute will prevent users from choosing them. For text input fields and text boxes, the 'readonly' attribute stops readers from entering any information. However, users can still read the content so this can be a handy way of presenting licensing agreements or legal disclaimers that you would not want the visitor to change.

Entire fields can be kept from the user's view by setting the <input> type to 'hidden'. These are generally used to help with form processing, where different actions occur depending on the form involved. For instance, if a form is for a new membership it might have a hidden field marked 'new'. This would be processed differently to a form where membership details are simply being updated, which would have the hidden field set to 'update'.

➡ *Feedback Form, Response-O-Matic*

FORM HANDLER

 Processing and interpreting data from HTML forms. The best-looking forms are worthless unless you have some way of accessing and manipulating the information that readers send in. Form handlers are separate scripts that take this information and process it.

The simplest form handler is built into HTML. The mailto: form simply takes the information a user enters and sends it to a specified email address. While this is easy to set up, it does have its drawbacks. Many users do not have the interlinked browser and email software that mailto: requires, and the information webmasters receive via mailto: is unprocessed and little more than a string of answers with no questions to guide their analysis. To overcome this problem, Common Gateway Interface (CGI) scripts that handle simple forms are freely available on the Web, and often come as part of a package from an Internet Service Provider (ISP). They can be written in any language – Perl, C, VisualBasic or Java – and all the designer has to do is to reference the CGI script's URL in the opening line of the form and follow the instructions given to specify an email address for delivery of the responses. CGI scripts commonly available online process incoming survey data into charts and graphs, and compile message boards and chat forums.

➡ *CGI, Form Field, Maintaining Site Interest*

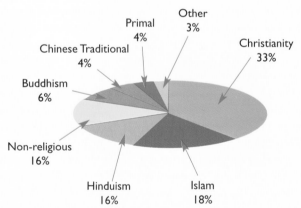

PROPORTIONS OF THE WORLD'S MAJOR RELIGIONS

FORMATTING TEXT USING HTML

 For the most basic formatting you can break up your copy and add white space. The paragraph tag <p>…</p> adds additional space when it breaks the line. To change the flow of text without adding the extra space use the line-break tag <br>.

The typeface, colour and size can be controlled with the <font> tag to create a style for the content. The size is not an absolute pixel value, but is relative to the default font size. The size values are from 7 (the largest) to 1 (the smallest). Each step in size is about 20 per cent different. So, if the <font size="4">…</font> it is roughly 20 per cent larger than the default text size which is usually size 3. It is also possible to set values relative to the default size 3 by using a plus or minus sign. However, as the browser won't show anything bigger than size 7, the maximum relative value is +4 (that is the default 3 + 4).

You can change the default font size by using the <basefont> tag. If you place this in the head of the document it will affect all the text. If you place it in the body of the copy only text after it will be altered.

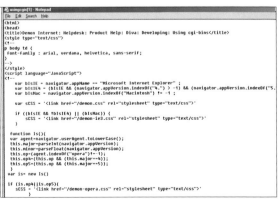

Similarly, through the font tag you can specify the typeface, or range of typefaces (<font face="fontname">…</font>, or the colour <font color="colorname or hexadecimal number>…</font>. However, the font tag is being phased out in favour of using CSS. Although not fully supported by older browsers they have the advantage that a single change in style can be applied across the site, whereas with the font tag it needs to be changed in each place it is used.

Inline styles are put in the flow of the text to add emphasis, without affecting spacing in the way block element tags such as paragraph breaks do. Inline styles can italicize text <i>…</i>; embolden it … or add an underline <u>…</u>.

For greater visual emphasis, text headings can be given different sizes. There are six available <h1> being the biggest and <h6> the smallest. As <h4> is equivalent to the size of the body text the main ones used are <h2> and <h3>.

➡ *Font, HTML, System Font*

FAR LEFT: CGI scripts available online are useful for converting data into charts and graphs, such as this pie chart of world religions.

FRAME

The FRAME tag allows a browser window to be divided into a number of frames – independent but interlinked pages. Frames are often used where one frame holds a permanent navigation bar that remains static while the content in another, larger frame changes. This gives the reader the comfort of a constant navigation device, while giving the webmaster an easy way to add an item to the menu without having to recall all the published pages. Another common use for frames is as a placeholder for a static site title and logo, sitting horizontally at the top of the page.

Pages are divided into frames using the FRAMESET tag. This tag sits in the parent index.htm. If you use web-editing software, there should be a facility for creating a frameset before working on the content of each frame individually, but in either case, every frame will have to be assigned a name. This is so that you can load fresh content into another frame using the TARGET="framename" attribute of the A HREF hyperlink tag.

When defining your frames, you will have to specify a source for the initial content. This is done using the SRC attribute of the FRAMES tag: <FRAME NAME="main" SRC="content.htm"> would load the file content.htm into the frame called 'main'.

The FRAME tag also lets you determine whether a reader should be allowed to alter the dimensions of your frame layout (adding NORESIZE to the FRAME tag locks its borders) and whether scrollbars should be included (the SCROLLING= variable can be set to NO, YES or AUTO).

If you want to load a page outside the frames setup – for instance if you are sending a reader to an external site – targeting '_TOP' will update the entire browser window.

Inline frames act as windows within a page, and can be added using the IFRAME tag which supports the same attributes as FRAME. However, iframes are only supported by Internet Explorer.

If you use frames, keep the number of frames in a page to a maximum of four, and bear in mind that search engines may direct users to a specific 'orphaned' frame rather than the parent index page of your site. As a workaround, add a link from the bottom of each frame

back to the index page. However, users will still not be able to bookmark individual frames within your site, only its index.

➡ *Frameset, Iframe, Navigation*

FRAMESET

The FRAMESET tag defines the layout of a frame-based web page, and sits in the index.htm file (or equivalent) of your site. Unlike a regular html page, a Frameset page has no body, and holds only the Frameset tag – all the colour and design data is included in the connecting frames pages. It can, however, have meta tags applied to it, and you should use the META CONTENT tag to tell search engines what your site is all about.

Frames are defined by columns and rows. Sketch out the design of your frameset and determine whether your page is split into horizontal rows or vertical columns.

If you have a navigation column on the left and a main content area on the right, for instance, it is a column-based page, but if these two columns sit beneath a static page header, it is a row-based layout. The first FRAMESET tag sets up the rows and columns that make subsequent FRAMESET tags nested within the first.

To create a frameset with a header and two columns beneath it, you could use this code:

```
<frameset rows="64,*">
<frame name="banner" src="banner.htm">
<frameset cols="150,*">
<frame name="contents" src="content.htm">
<frame name="main" src="main.htm">
</frameset>
</frameset>
```

The numbers in the quotes define the depth or the rows and the width of the columns in pixels. The '*' value tells the browser to create a frame with whatever depth/width remains in the window.

By default, all frames have visible borders, but these can be hidden by adding 'BORDER=0' to the FRAMESET tag, or coloured by adding the 'bordercolor="colourname"' attribute.

➡ *Frame*

FREE-CLIPART.NET (www.free-clipart.net)

Free graphics. Another treasure trove of ready-drawn art for those who don't have the time or skills to create their own. As the top strap of the site makes clear, it has two distinct advantages over some of its rivals. There is no need to register in order to download the graphics. There are also none of those annoying pop-ups, although the site has its fair share of flashing and blinking adverts.

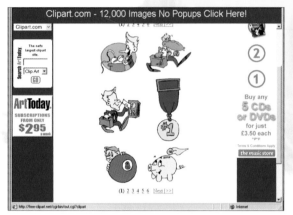

It is very clearly organized. All the art work is divided into four main areas – animated GIFs, backgrounds, clip art and icons. Within each area there is a host of sub-categories. For example, in the clip art section there are those you would expect, such as food and drink, sports, and holidays, and a few you wouldn't, like chemistry (which, amazingly, has some 112 entries) and western & rodeo.

In keeping with its very clear organization, when you select the graphic you want there are clear instructions covering how to download the image, not only for different browsers (Netscape and Internet Explorer), but also for different platforms (Macintosh and WebTV).

➡ *Animated GIF, Background Image, Clip Art, Clipart-graphics.net*

FREE WEB EXTRAS

True to the open nature of the Web, there are many free resources available online – whether it's just for technical advice or free programs, graphics, fonts, and scripts. The quality is variable and 'free' is often loosely defined: most sites are commercial and 'free' material has to be paid for somehow.

With 'free' ISPs, online web hosts (www.angelfire.com) or other online services such as Easycounter (www.easycounter.com) the free service is paid for by advertising. It also acts as an inducement to try their paid-for services in the hope you will opt to subscribe to a more fully-featured or ad-free version. This is also true of software programs such as the firewall ZoneAlarm (www.zonealarm.com) or the meta-search engine Copernic (www.copernic.com). Both offer free products which work well, but the more advanced (and useful) functions are only available in a paid-for version.

On the design front, enthusiasts make sure there are plenty of free resources and many of them can be found through www.top20free.com, while free webmaster tools, such as guestbooks, search engines, email processing etc., can be found at www.freesitetools.com.

➡ *Counter, Font, Form Handler, Guestbook*

FREE WEB GRAPHICS

Design tools online. Free is a relative term when it comes to graphics on the Web. Even images that claim to be '100 per cent FREE' may have licensing restrictions attached to them, for example, they may only be used on personal sites and not for commercial purposes. Similarly, sites such as www.aaaclipart.com offer free images, but it is only the first page of images in each category that is free. To access the others you have to buy a subscription.

Despite this, though, there are hundreds of free sites offering everything from backgrounds, icons, animations, bullets and of course clip art. For links to some of them check out www.top20free.com, which can direct you to

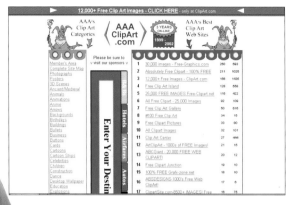

such offerings as celebrity wallpaper, www.virtuous.co.uk/fantasy/index.htm or www.lovepoemsandquotes.com for those in need of romantic quotes. Be wary of using images taken from 'fan' sites, as they may not have copyright to use the images or pass them on. Most stock photo libraries (e.g. www.corbis.com) will offer free images as a taster for their commercial offerings. If you decide you want a more decorative font to use in logos etc., there are plenty of free fonts for either the PC or Mac at sites like www.1001freefonts.com.

➠ *Clip Art, Stock Photo Suppliers*

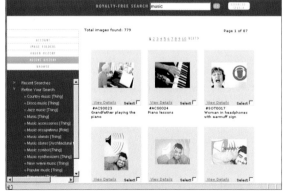

LEFT: Choose a favourite celebrity from a free web graphics site to use as your computer's wallpaper.

FREE WEB HOSTING

It is possible to get your web site hosted for free, but there are drawbacks that often mean this service is unsuitable for larger sites. As part of their package many Internet Service Providers (ISPs) will offer their customers web space. With free ISPs this will often be ad-supported like their other services. Where you pay for internet access, it will be part of the package. Some ISPs offer quite a sizeable amount of disk space (25–50 MB), which would be costly on commercial web-hosting services.

Most of the major portals also offer free web-hosting services – for example Lycos has Tripod and Angelfire; Yahoo! has Geocities; and MSN have their own personal communities. Free sites are limited in what they offer; space will be limited to about 10–20 MB and the URL normally includes the name of the hosting service.

Because many sites will be on the same server, access can be very slow at peak times. Most free web-hosting services offer a range of add-ons, such as online albums, guestbooks, page counters, etc. Their main drawback is

that the free services are paid for by the banner advertising put on your site. To access an ad-free service you normally have to subscribe to a monthly fee-based plan.

➡ *Angelfire, Domain, Geocities, Tripod, Web Hosting*

FREEHAND (MACROMEDIA)

Vector illustration package. FreeHand is Macromedia's vector graphics design application. Now at version 10, the program has made the successful transition from a print publishing tool to an all-round

graphics package that combines professional design tools with web-specific functions.

FreeHand shares a common interface with its Macromedia web design siblings, and the crossover is particularly prominent with Dreamweaver, Fireworks and Flash. Vector graphics can be imported into other members of the Macromedia family, and simple Flash animations can even be created and exported from FreeHand.

FreeHand boasts a powerful set of design tools. As well as the standard shape-drawing tools, freeform objects and curves can be created and modified using a Bézier-style pen tool. Fills include a collection of patterns and gradients, and a new true contour gradient tool lets designers add realistic contours and lighting effects to any vector object or typeface – you just select the central light source and the software creates the effect.

Eye-catching effects can be created using FreeHand's symbol-painting tools. An object can be distributed across a path using standard brush strokes, or the 'graphic hose' can be used to spray a random selection of themed graphics across a page. Imported objects and text can also be warped to create engaging effects.

FreeHand's perspective grid is a great boon. Objects and words can be attached to a one-, two- or three-point perspective grid, and FreeHand automatically warps them to meet the perspective. Objects closer to the vanishing point scale down, and altering the angle or distance of the grid automatically adjusts all the items attached to the grid.

FreeHand boasts full integration with Flash, and in fact Macromedia's Flash FreeHand Studio puts both programs in one box. Simple Flash animations can be created and tested in FreeHand, and exported to Flash or Fireworks. Alternatively, animations can be exported in layers for additional editing in Adobe's Photoshop.

The Flash Navigation panel lets you add interactivity to animated sequences created in FreeHand. A URL editor allows hyperlinks to be added to movies, and other

BELOW: Create surreal warped effects for your site, like those in Salvador Dali's paintings, using Macromedia Freehand.

extensions let you apply Flash actions to graphics and text within FreeHand before exporting to Macromedia Flash. Importing even older FreeHand files into Flash is merely a matter of dragging and dropping them into position. For additional web functionality, FreeHand also exports to the Adobe Acrobat PDF format and lets you add hyperlinks to PDF files.

➦ *Dreamweaver (Macromedia), Fireworks (Macromedia), Flash (Macromedia), Graphic Design Package, Illustration, Vector*

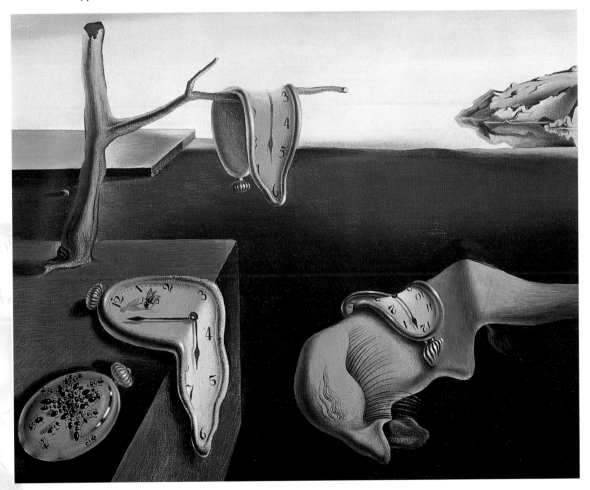

FREEWAY (SOFTPRESS)

Visual web design application. SoftPress Freeway is a rarity among web editors as it does not require any understanding of HTML and is not constrained by

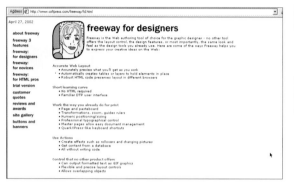

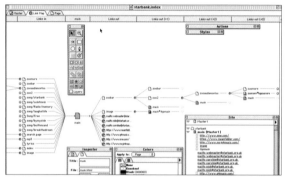

the limitations of the Web. Freeway – available for the Macintosh only for around £200 – provides an easy route from page design to the Web, as its interface is based on desktop-publishing package QuarkXPress, right down to the keyboard shortcuts. Designers can lay out pages as they would in QuarkXPress, and Freeway will export all the code and graphics for publication.

Users can view and edit the HTML code as they work, but they should not have to, as the HTML export adheres tightly to standards, with options to write HTML 3.2, HTML 3.2 with cascading style sheets and HTML 4.0.

Built-in image processing means you can import layered Photoshop files, PICTs and TIFs, position them in regular or custom frames and Freeway will export them as GIFs or JPEGs. Flash and QuickTime movies are supported, and text can be saved as graphics. Rollovers and image maps can be applied. Users can write or import third-party code like JavaScript pop-up menus or controllers for importing database content, and Freeway can create a visual map of a site's links to ease navigation.

➠ *HTML Editor, Web Standards*

FRONTPAGE (MICROSOFT)

Web-editing package. Microsoft's FrontPage offers a trouble-free way into web design for users of the software giant's many office software products. FrontPage shares a common look and feel with other Microsoft applications and makes it easy to get your first web site up and running. Designers can produce professional-looking pages straight away, thanks to a selection of around 60 templates, which run from plain pages and simple tables to various frame arrangements, feedback forms and FAQs.

FrontPage also offers a

range of themes, which are collections of colour palettes, button styles and background images.

If you choose to use a style, then producing a professional looking page is easy, as all your font and graphic issues are dealt with and you can create new buttons based on the themed sets. More themes can be downloaded from the Web.

FrontPage's graphics handling stands out when it comes to resizing pictures on the page. Images can be resized on-screen, and the program will resample a new image to that exact size. Alternatively, a page full of large images – a photography portfolio, for example, can be converted into a page of smaller, fast-loading images,

BELOW LEFT: Use Microsoft FrontPage to get your web site up and running.

clicking on which brings up the larger original in a pop-up window.

Applying advanced features such as Dynamic HTML and CSS is just as easy for first-timers. FrontPage features a drop-down list of DHTML text effects, and paragraph and character styles can be implemented from another menu for easy uniformity across the site.

FrontPage boasts excellent site management tools.

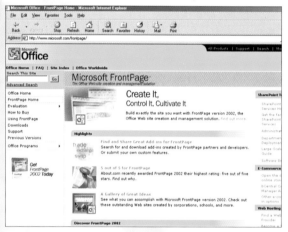

Changing the name of one file or graphic will automatically be reflected in the links to that page from other pages. Navigation tools mean that you only have to visit the Navigation control panel to link all the section indexes in your site and specify which parent pages should link to child pages.

Your web page can be viewed as a tree structure, and reports can be pulled to show missing and slow pages. The download speed for a page appears in the corner of your screen, and you can adjust the anticipated modem speed to compare load speeds at various dial-up, ISDN and network speeds.

Microsoft supplies a range of FrontPage extensions which include form handlers, online shopping carts and other CGI-style utilities. If you intend to take advantage of these tools, make sure your ISP supports FrontPage on the server side as not all do.

➡ *HTML Editor, Image Composer, Microsoft*

FTP

File Transfer Protocol; the fastest, most efficient way to transfer files, particularly over the Internet. On the Internet there is a separate protocol, the

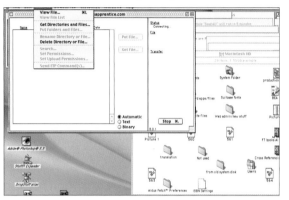
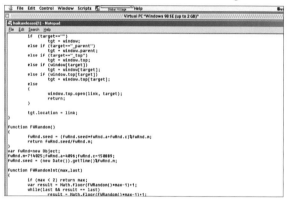

Hypertext Transfer Protocol (HTTP) used by browsers for transferring ordinary web pages and any small graphics files used. However, for the vast stocks of software, music files, and archives available on the Net, something more structured is needed. FTP covers the type or error checking in force during transmission, the compression used and how the computers will mark that they have finished sending or receiving data. Using FTP, a client program, such as CuteFTP or LaplinkFTP, connects to the server that holds the files wanted.

FTP sites usually offer a much wider selection of files than ordinary sites are able to. To store as many as possible, most files will be compressed. Downloads from FTP servers are also quicker than from a web server. As the fastest and most efficient way of moving files between computers, FTP is also used to upload completed web pages from your computer to a web server.

➡ *CuteFTP, LaplinkFTP, Server, Uploading a Web Site*

FUNCTIONALITY

Despite constant advances, by its definition as a mark-up language, HTML is mainly concerned with the appearance of web pages rather than true interactivity with the reader. Using additional tools and server-side software, it is possible to tailor a site to individual users, react dynamically to reader input and interact with database content to offer search, message boards and e-commerce tools.

The most common way of extending a browser's functionality is to use JavaScript routines. While often used to create image rollovers and visual effects, JavaScript is ideal for small personalization tasks – detecting where the user is based and adding their local time to a page, for instance. It is also suited to small calculations and form verification, such as for checking that a credit-card booking form has been completed correctly.

Most current server-side functionality will be in the form of CGI scripts usually written in Perl or C. There are thousands of CGI scripts available to buy online (as well as less stable free scripts) for building shopping carts, password protection, online auction systems, searches, guestbooks and polls. Similar applications created Active Server Pages (ASP) are beginning to proliferate. ASP pages perform the same functions as CGI scripts, but use Visual Basic-style tools.

➡ *ASP, CGI, JavaScript, Perl*

GEOCITIES

Web hosting service. Geocities is Yahoo!'s web site hosting service, which claims to be the largest homepage community on the Internet. As with most of the major web-hosting services, the basic package is free and ad-supported. Those who want their site to be ad-free and to benefit from more generous web space and additional functions (such as their own personal domain-based email) must subscribe to one of the monthly fee-based premium services.

A simple site can be built using the Yahoo! PageWizards. Alternatively, for drag-and-drop editing without any HTML coding, Geocities has its own

PageBuilder software. As with other web-hosting services, the whole process is eased by having pre-built templates that can be easily personalized. There are a number of add-ons available, from free content (stock quotes and news headlines) to guestbooks, page counters and email forms.

Because of Geocities' size, there is a ready audience for any site it holds. The Member Pages Directory boasts thousands of different categories under which your site can be posted, enabling you to link up with others operating in a similar area.

➠ *Angelfire.com, Free Web Hosting, Tripod*

GEOMETRIC SHAPES
IN DESIGN

Combining linear shapes. Just as primary colours are the basic building-blocks when using colour, so designers should master use of the basic geometric shapes before working on the overall layout of a web site. Linear shapes are uninteresting and do not draw the reader's eye in, but lines, circles, rectangles and ellipses can be combined to make an inviting, engaging homepage. There are several points to remember when using geometric shapes in design.

1. The most basic geometric shape is the straight line. HTML's own horizontal rule <HR> tag lets you break up paragraphs with lines, but its own default style lacks something in form. The standard rule is a bevelled line which, while applying a 3D effect to the page, is probably out of keeping with your site's design. Fortunately, the NOSHADE variable flattens the rule, and a COLOR= attribute lets you tie its colour in with the overall scheme of your page. Run each rule as a percentage of a cell width so that it doesn't slice the page into stark rectangles.

2. Vertical lines can apply an overly rigid grid effect to a page and should also be used sparingly. In graphical terms, however, they can be used, especially when combined with horizontal lines to form crosses, to draw the reader into the most important part of the page. Eyes

naturally follow lines, and lines can be used to coax a reader around the page from item to item. Adding an arrowhead or a bullet to the line enhances this effect.

3. Given that every PC screen is rectangular, it is no surprise that rectangles are so common in web design. Increased use of table-based design means that pages tend to be divided into shaded boxes, which neither please the eye nor encourage movement around the page.

4. Play down the impression of a page full of right angles by not shading boxes and increasing the cellpadding attribute of the table tag to create some space around the text. White space also emphasises the content.

5. Round-cornered rectangles are less austere than right-angled boxes. Use them to hold large blocks of contents, such as menus.

6. Graduated fills can help lose the impression of a rectangle by blending an object like a page header with the rest of the page.

7. Mixing rectangles of different colours and applying borders of different weight on a page can be eye-catching, provided you include plenty of white space in between, to create a non-linear effect.

8. Complete circles are rare on the web as all elements of HTML are essentially quadrilateral, and full circles are not ideal placeholders outside splash screens. Their linearity also makes them less eye-catching than ellipses.

9. Coloured half- and semi-circles in the inside corners of rectangles help to break up the linearity of the right angles. Similarly, light ellipses act as good page and table backgrounds.

10. A semi-circle added to the end of a rectangle creates a good lozenge effect for dynamic-looking menu items, while quarter-circles can smooth the corners of boxes.

➠ *Curvature Range, Non-linear Design*

GETTY IMAGES (www.creative.gettyimages.com)

Online image library. Getty Images now own a number of famous photo libraries, including the Image Bank, Stone and the Hulton Archive with its unique collection of pictures of historic figures. For designers, the centre of this library of millions of images is the 'Creative' section. It provides a master site from which you can search across the different catalogues of photos and illustrations to find the image you need.

Images are either rights-managed or royalty free. Rights-managed photographs are priced and licensed for the particular purpose for which they are going to be used. Generally, it's one fee, one use. Royalty free images may come separately or as part of a themed collection sold on CD-ROM. The price is based on the size of the photo, not how it is used. In fact, once bought it can be used many times.

As the Web is now a truly multimedia experience the photo libraries have gone beyond still images. Gettyimages.com has a section called 'Motion', which is a searchable archive of more than 30,000 hours of cinematography footage.

➡ *Copyright Images, CorbisImages, Photodisc, Stock Photo Suppliers*

ABOVE: Part of Getty Images, the online image library. Hulton Archive stocks a unique collection of historical images.

GIF (GRAPHICS INTERCHANGE FORMAT)

Graphics Interchange Format; graphics file format. The first and still one of the most popular formats for online graphics. Pronounced with a hard G, the GIF was initially created by the online service provider CompuServe. Its popularity stems from the fact that it is cross-platform, so can be viewed on any computer, and that it compresses files to save download time. It uses a 'lossless' system, whereby there is no degradation in the quality of the image. However, it may mean that the file size is larger than a similar image as a JPEG, which uses a 'lossy compression' scheme in which nonessential or repetitive data is removed from the image to make the file smaller.

As a result, GIFs are best used for images with a few, flat blocks of colour, such as logos or simple illustrations. Where there are subtle changes in colour, it is better to use JPEGs which can support 24-bit colour. GIFs are 8-bit and can only have 256 colours. The oldest version, called variously GIF87a or CompuServe GIF, has been replaced by GIF98a which provides a number of additional features, including support for interlacing, transparency and animation.

➥ *File Type, Image, JPEG, Vector*

GIF OR JPEG?

The overwhelming majority of images on the Web are in one of two formats, GIF and JPEG. The rules that determine when to use one format ahead of the other are clear cut, but many designers seem to pick their

favourite image format and use that every time. This can lead to poor image reproduction and unnecessarily long download times.

The key to using the right format is understanding how each is compressed. JPEG is a 'lossy' format, which means that the size of the original high-resolution file is reduced by discarding unnecessary pixels, those parts of the image that the eye is unlikely to miss. If several shades of blue are in close proximity, for instance, a graphics package would replace them with an 'average' blue.

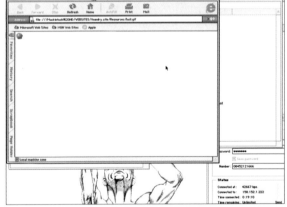

GIFs are compressed by reducing the amount of colours in the palette to a maximum of 256 colours (although using a web-safe 216-colour palette when creating GIFs is advisable). By contrast, JPEGs have an unlimited colour palette.

Bearing this in mind, it is better to use GIFs when saving simple, bold vector graphics like page backgrounds, company logos and menu items, or two- or three-colour

text blocks such as buttons and banner headlines. Simple rollover graphics are also more suited to the GIF format, and GIF is the only choice for simple animated graphics – there is no JPEG variant.

JPEG is ideal for colourful images like photographs. You can specify the compression ratio to strike a balance between quality and file size, but bear in mind that smooth graduated areas such as blue skies can break up dramatically at all but the lowest compression levels, and white backgrounds around people can compress to unwanted halos.

A third format, the portable network graphic (PNG) is beginning to appear across the Web, and as a lossless format could become a replacement for both GIFs and JPEGs. However, PNG files tend to be larger than their GIF and JPEG equivalents, and until faster internet connections become commonplace, PNG will stay in third place. It does offer higher image quality, however, and if you are designing for a fast intranet, may be worth considering.

If you are ever in doubt as to which format to use, all the leading web graphics packages let you preview exported images alongside the original so you can tweak settings and try different formats before committing.

➡ *GIF, JPEG, PNG*

ABOVE: Use the image format JPEG for photographs, but remember that smooth, graduated areas, such as the blue sky shown here, can break up dramatically at high compression levels.

GIF BUILDER FOR MAC

Animated GIF utility. GifBuilder is a free utility for creating animated GIF files on Macintosh computers. You can input PICT, GIF, TIFF or Photoshop files, a QuickTime movie or the layers of an Adobe Photoshop file, specify frame delay and optional looping settings and the utility will export an animated GIF which can be incorporated into any web page.

The Frame window lists the individual GIFs which make up the animation, along with the frame delay and whether the image has a transparent background – this makes the transition between frames quicker and can be added to individual frames using GifBuilder.

Images are exported in the GIF89a format in greyscale, 1, 2, 4 or 8-bit colour palettes, or can be fixed to the standard Mac or custom colour palette. Dithering can be switched on or off as required (and tends to produce a larger, slower-loading image), and files can be saved as interlaced. You can also set the disposal method for each individual frame. This governs frame transitions and is used to optimize each GIF as far as possible.

Free to download from http://homepage. mac.com/piguet/gif.html, GifBuilder has not been updated since January 1997, but is still popular with Mac-based webmasters.

➡ *Animated GIF, Animation, Dithering*

GIF CONSTRUCTION SET

Animation builder for PC. Alchemy Mindworks' GIF Construction Set for the PC combines all the standard tools for creating moving images, with innovative features not found in regular web-graphics packages.

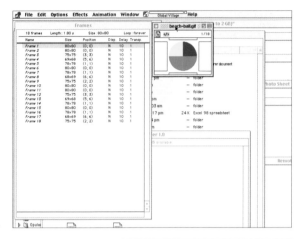

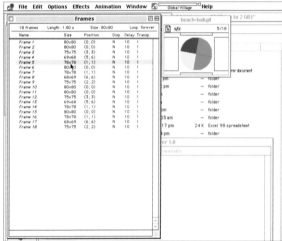

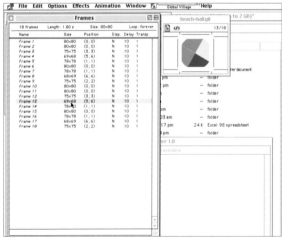

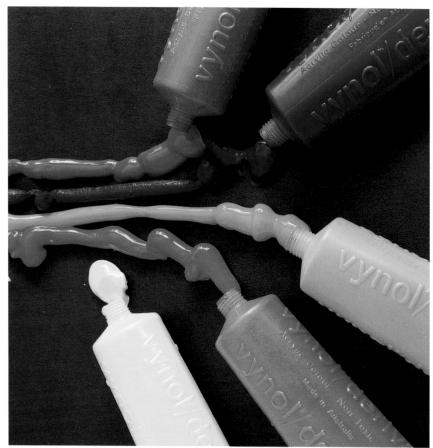

be created in seconds by typing in the desired text, and imported images rotated a user-defined number of steps. Best of all is a preset Transition effect that lets you select the transition between a series of images from a choice of 20 that includes wipe, dissolve and rollover. Once an image is complete, the Supercompressor will squeeze its file size down as much as possible before exporting to GIF, AVI or MNG formats.

➡ *Animated GIF, Animation*

GIF89A

Graphics file format. The main advantage of this newer GIF standard is its support for transparency. This allows you to make one of the colours invisible – often the bottom one – in order for the background

Available as shareware from www.mindworkshop.com /alchemy/ ($20 to register), GIF Construction Set Professional offers a step-by-step path to building clips, using its Animation Wizard. This asks a series of questions regarding frame speed, looping and palette, and builds the animation in seconds. You cannot create your own graphics using the program, but imported images can be cropped, flipped and rotated before starting on an animation. RGB colour balance, brightness and palette size can also be edited.

If you do not have a drawing program, you can still create eye-catching animations with the utility's preset routines. Scrolling LED signs and colourful banners can

colour of the web page to show through. Without it, there would be an ugly white box around many of the graphics on the Web.

GIF89a (named rather inelegantly after the year it was developed) also supports interlacing. This is where graphics flow on to the page either row by row or column by column and means that a rough version of the graphic appears before the whole image is downloaded.

Where the GIF stands apart from other online graphic formats like JPEG and PNG is in its support for basic animation. Animated GIFs work in a similar way to thumbing through a flip book. A series of images are compressed into a single GIF file using special software. The animation effect is produced by the browser looping through the images sequentially. Hence you can have the dog wagging its tail, the flashing banner ad etc.

➡ *File Type, GIF, Image, JPEG, Raster, Vector*

ABOVE: Edit the RGB colour balance, brightness and palette size of imported images using a GIF Construction set.

GOLIVE (ADOBE)

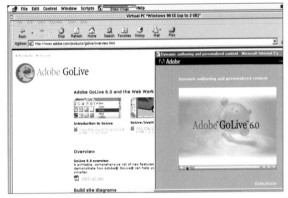

Web design and editing package. Adobe is renowned for its graphics software, and the company's web design and editing tool, GoLive, is certainly a design-led application. Beyond simple page design, the package offers networked site-management tools for workgroups and automated links to dynamic database content.

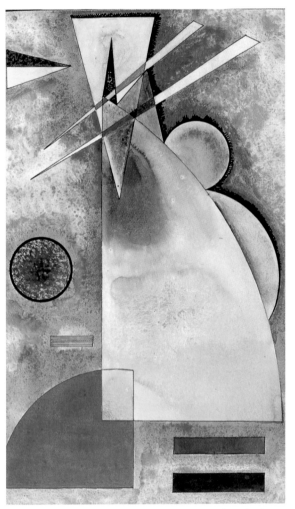

Pages can be designed graphically in GoLive's visual interface, and tabbed windows switch to the HTML source and a web preview. A split-screen view is also available, and the visual tag editor can be used to view and edit source code from within the layout editor as you work. A design grid can be laid across a page and elements placed accurately before the page is exported as a table-based design.

Images created in Photoshop and Illustrator can be dragged and dropped into position on the page, and as GoLive links dynamically to the sister products, minor adjustments to images – resizing, re-exporting and changes to the colour palette – can be made without opening a second application. Likewise Photoshop files can be imported into GoLive and divided into manageable sizes for export, and Flash animations, as well as rich media like streaming QT movies and SMIL files, can be created using visual tools.

Cascading style sheets are created and edited visually so that the user can see exactly how an element will look once a style is applied, and paragraph styles are easy to apply using the HTML Style palette. At any point, the Site Reporter tool can run a check on the code to ensure it complies with standard HTML.

GoLive's site management tools are powerful whether the software is used by one designer or a whole team. The site structure can be created as a tree hierarchy, a visual map that can be exported in PDF or Illustrator formats for presentation purposes, or used as the basis for an automatically generated text-based site map.

Adobe's Web Workgroup Server allows workgroups to share and manage GoLive files. The system manages check-in and check-out of files, tracks changes and performs site-wide link management. Security settings control access to certain team members, and locked editable regions can be defined on page templates so that editors can work on text elements without affecting the overall design of the page.

GoLive eases the process of adapting print-based content for the web automatically, and e-commerce sites and personalised pages can be created and managed through ASP, PHP and JSP database-driven content. Pages can be converted for wireless devices using a selection of plug-ins and emulators.

➡ *Illustrator (Adobe), Photoshop (Adobe), Web Design Process*

GRADIENT

Colour variation. Rather than have a solid block of colour as a background to a web page or graphic it can be more effective to have one colour fade into another. This is called a gradient, or occasionally referred to as blends.

Most graphics editors work in a similar way. They have the colour chart or thumbnails from which you can select the colours to blend, and a number of gradient designs. These designs can be rotated by changing the angle value. For a simple two-colour gradient you chose the initial colour and the end colour. You can also set the transparency of the individual colours. This is not possible in some graphics editors where there are more than two colours. Changing the transparency value affects the opacity of the whole gradient rather than the individual colours.

Be aware that while gradients look fine on monitors set to display 16-bit colour (tens of thousands of colours) or higher, they will appear a bit dotty (speckled) at 8-bit (256 colours). It is worse with certain colours, so set your own monitor to 8-bit colour to see how it will look. Also, bear in mind that gradients increase the number of colours in an image, and therefore will increase the file size.

➡ *Graphic Design Package, Image Enhancement Techniques*

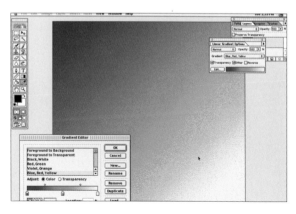

TOP LEFT: When one colour fades or blends into another it is called a gradient. In Kandinsky's work, shown here, red fades into orange.

GRAPHIC DESIGN PACKAGE

Not only are there more and more graphic packages becoming available, but they are also getting increasingly complicated to use. The range of special effects you can create is startling, even using a basic package. A mid-range product like JASC's Paint Shop Pro, for example, is useful for those using a PC who want a low-cost package. This allows you to add a series of 3D effects – such as cutouts, drop shadows, or bevels. You can age a photo to look like an old newspaper, turn it into sepia, or add a neon glow; You can change the image's shape, alter the perspective, skew the photo, twirl it, or warp it; if that's not enough you can then add texture effects to give the image the look of stone, tiles, mosaics, leather or even fur.

Whatever the source of the image and the effects added, it will need to be saved as a GIF or JPEG to be used on the Web. Most of the graphics packages will come with special image optimization tools to keep the file size as small as possible.

The tool of choice for most professional web designers is still Photoshop, which is also the industry standard in the print world. It does have web-oriented features, such as the Save to Web option which previews an image in different file formats and compression rates. For more sophisticated web effects, such as animation and rollovers, it usually comes bundled with Adobe's ImageReady software that writes any JavaScript needed.

Macromedia's Fireworks has the advantage that it has been designed from the start as a web graphics package. It is also closely integrated with Macromedia's web-authoring tool Dreamweaver, so you can edit images on the page and any changes are saved in the graphics file. It also combines tools for handling both vector (pictures using simple lines and curves that are described by mathematical formulas) and raster (pixel-based) images. This has the advantage that you don't need to switch between a drawing (vector) program and a

bitmap editing program to save the file for the Web. It does have a lot of useful features including side-by-side comparison of files to be exported, animation effects and rollover buttons.

Some designers use vector drawing programs, such as Illustrator or Freehand, to set down the basics of their image. The most recent versions of Photoshop (version 6.0 onwards) also support vector tools. These programs can also save the files directly as GIFs but file optimization is usually better if they are first opened in a Web graphics package before being saved for the Web.

➡ *CorelDraw, Fireworks (Macromedia), Freehand (Macromedia), Illustrator (Adobe), Paint Shop Pro (JASC), Photoshop (Adobe)*

GRAPHICAL LINKS

Image-based links. Images are for more than decoration. Just like text they can also be used for links, whether it's a single image, an image map or a thumbnail.

In its simplest form, the easiest way to link a graphic is to highlight it in your web-editing program and select, or write in, the URL of the file you want it linked to. Normally you can tell that there is a link, or hotspot, in a picture because the mouse pointer changes shape from an arrow to a hand.

More creatively, a single graphic can have several hotspots – or links – within it. The image is linked to different pages depending on which area of the graphic is clicked. For example, a pet shop web site might have a graphic with the different animals it sells. Clicking on one of the hotspots could take you through to a linked page with more information about that particular pet or the foodstuffs that are available.

There are both client-side and server-side image maps. Client-side is speedier for the user, as all the information needed to respond to their click is held within the Web page itself. Server-side image maps, although they are slower, are compatible with all browsers while client-side image maps don't work with some older version browsers.

A client-side image map has three elements: the graphic file itself; the USEMAP attribute within the <IMG> tag which identifies which map to use and the map file itself, shown by the <MAP> tag. Most web-authoring tools will generate the image maps for you. Within the <MAP> tag there are <AREA> tags for each hotspot in the image. Each of these area tags identifies the shape of the hotspot, the co-ordinates of the pixels and the URL that they link to.

Rather than a single imagemap, it can be more efficient for download time to create a 'faux' image map. This is just a composite image made up of individual graphics put right next to each other so that they appear to form one seamless image. The individual images are linked to different pages in the normal way for any graphic. But as individual graphics they can be optimized to produce a smaller file size in total than if they are combined together in one big image.

One other type of graphical link comes with thumbnail images, which are often linked to full-size versions of the same image. Thumbnails are handy if you have lots of images – such as for a product catalogue – as they download more quickly than the full-size version. Users only have to download the full graphic for products they are particularly interested in.

➡ *Anchor, Graphic Design Package, Link, Target*

LEFT: Graphics can be used to link to different pages, for example a pet shop web site might use a graphic of a hamster to link to a page on keeping hamsters as pets.

GREYSCALE

For a stylish retro look, it is possible to convert colour photos into greyscale images. It will automatically become an 8-bit image, as the palette contains only 256 shades of grey. It can help reduce file size, and consequently download time, if you are converting it from a file with thousands or millions of colours.

Most graphics programs give you the option to convert a file to greyscale. Alternatively, you can scan the picture in as greyscale. It can also be used to create special effects, such as adding a metallic look to a picture. More importantly, the greyscale function can be used to check on the contrast of pages on your site. A high degree of contrast between text and the background improves the all-round readability of the site.

To check how your pages rate, take a screen grab of your site and open it in a graphics editor, such as PhotoDraw. Choose the Greyscale option and convert the grab. This will show if there is sufficient contrast between the various elements on the page. Don't forget, this is particularly likely to affect colour-blind visitors who have problems distinguishing the contrast between certain colours.

➥ *Graphic Design Package, Image Mode*

GUESTBOOK

Digital comment board. One of the easiest ways to interact with your visitors is through a guestbook. Users to the site simply fill out a form and make their comments which the guestbook program adds to the existing HTML file. This way, visitors can read the comments from other users. Most guestbook programs put the newest messages on the top. There are a few which operate in reverse.

Most guestbook programs are CGI scripts, which your server must be capable of running. If it isn't, there are some sites that will host your guestbook for you. Rather than write your own script, there are several available on the Web, such as at Matt's Script Archive: www.worldwidemart.com/scripts and Extropia at: www.extropia.com.

A good guestbook script should have several different features. It should, as a matter of courtesy, send an email thanking each visitor who leaves a message. At the same time, it should send another email to the webmaster or site manager to let them know that a comment has been added. This is partly to save time constantly checking the site, but also so that the content of any new messages can be checked. After all, the guestbook is part of your site's image – you don't want obscenities or advertising plugs to get in the way of genuine messages. Some scripts will filter swear words for you.

➥ *CGI, Free Web Extras, HTMLgear*

HEX CODE

Colour values; in order to display on a web page, every colour has to be converted from its RGB value to its hexadecimal equivalent, using a hex code.

Every colour displayed on your web page is created on the monitor by different combinations of three coloured lights – red, green and blue. Each of these lights can be at a different intensity from 0 (none) to 255 (full intensity). In graphics programs, you can identify the RGB values of the colours you want, and can even create the colours by entering the RGB values or percentages. On the web page, however, the RGB colour is translated into its hexadecimal code. The hexadecimal (hex for short) numbering system is base-16 (as opposed to base-10 for decimal). It uses the numbers 0-9 and characters A-F (to represent 10-15). It is used on the Web because it saves space. Each three-character RGB number can be represented by two hex characters.

To calculate a hex number you simply divide the RGB value by 16 – or use one of the many hex calculators or conversion tables that are available. This is then inserted in the HTML code in the order RGB. So, for example, to put a red colour with the RGB values 255,43,43 as the background in a table cell it would be converted to hexadecimal and added to the HTML tag e.g. <TD BGCOLOR="#FF2B2B">.

➥ *Background Colour, Web-Safe Colour*

LEFT: All the colours displayed on a computer monitor are a combination of three coloured lights – red, green and blue.

HOMESITE (MACROMEDIA)

Hard-coding HTML editor. Standing out among all the visual HTML editors, Macromedia's HomeSite (formerly Allaire HomeSite) concentrates not on visual design but on making the hard coding process as easy as possible. Using HomeSite, which is bundled with Dreamweaver, developers can add features like

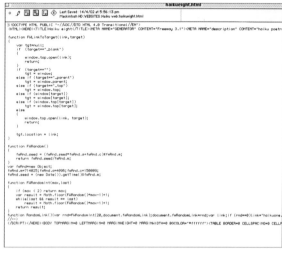

tables, frames and JavaScript elements through a wizard-based interface, and can save blocks of regularly used code for dropping into place on the page.

HomeSite does have a design view alongside its Edit source and Browser preview modes, but one click on the Design tab throws up a warning that the mode should only be used to create prototypes of your designs.

The HomeSite screen is divided into three sections: the resource window, the results window and the main window. The main window hosts the page in any of its three viewing modes. The resource window is a toolkit which shows your directory listing, a catalogue of links to and from your page, and a tag tree which shows the structure of your page.

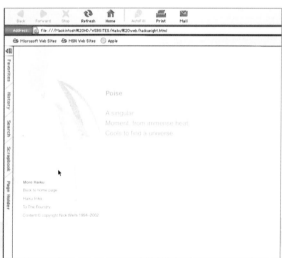

HomeSite features a comprehensive HTML checker, Codesweeper, and supports most current Web markup and scripting standards. It comes with DHTML Wizards and a utility for creating cascading style sheets called TopStyle Lite.

➡ *Codesweeper, Dreamweaver (Macromedia), HTML Editor*

HTML

Hypertext Markup Language; document markup language. HTML is the language of the Web and is used in constructing web pages. In effect, it tells the browser software how to display and handle the information or objects contained on a page. It also controls the hypertext links that enable you to click from one document to another, or from one section of a page to another.

Although the HTML specifications, or recommendations, are drafted by a standards body called the World Wide Web Consortium (W3C), they have been implemented differently by the major browser manufacturers so cross-browser compatibility is still some way off. That said, the benefit of HTML is that it is pure text (ASCII only), so it can be read by software running on any platform.

Each HTML document has two main parts the Head, which contains general information about the file and scripts that need to be run and the Body, the content that will appear in the browser window. All HTML documents are collections of tags, enclosed within less than (<) and greater than (>) brackets. Tags can be modified by attributes which allow you to specify properties such as font, size, colour etc.

➠ *HotDog, HTML, Hypertext, Netscape Composer, Web Authoring*

BELOW: Notebook is a basic web page editing program, but HTML editors, such as BBEdit, are much faster.

HTML EDITOR

Editing program for web pages. To maximize their personal control over the final look of their pages, some web designers like to hand code their HTML documents. As HTML pages are plain text files they could just use a simple text editor like Notepad.

However, if they want to speed up the process, there are HTML editors, such as HomeSite for Windows or BBEdit for the Macintosh. Unlike the 'what you see is what you get' (WYSIWYG) authoring tools, such as Macromedia's Dreamweaver, Adobe's GoLive or Microsoft's FrontPage, you can not build your page visually.

With HTML editors you need to know how to write HTML by hand, but they make the process quicker and more efficient. For instance, when they open a new document they will automatically insert the doctype declaration and the main <head> and <body> tags. There are shortcuts for inserting different types of code – scripts as well as HTML. These are displayed in different colours to make it easier for error-checking later. The HTML editor will also let you preview the page in a number of target browsers.

➠ *Dreamweaver (Macromedia), Homesite (Macromedia), HTML, HTML Tags*

HTML GOODIES (*www.htmlgoodies.com*)

HTML Goodies covers most of the technologies needed by web designers and developers today. The Goodies site goes way beyond its name. There are still the HTML tutorials in plenty, going from the basic primer

for beginners through to a full list of the HTML tags and more advanced techniques. But along with these is a series of primers and reference pieces on all the topics the aspiring web designer and developer needs to know, including a guide to server error codes and a discussion on when to use databases.

HTML Goodies looks at all the technologies that are being absorbed into web site construction today. There are sections on Stylesheets, JavaScript, Java applets, CGI scripting, ASP pages, XML and DHTML, as well as primers on PERL and CGI. But the help does not stop there. They have recently introduced the Mentor community. Here, volunteers offer their experience in each of the categories to tackle any coding queries from web designers and developers. There is also an FAQ (frequently asked questions) list with answers to the most

common queries raised in the discussion groups.

To keep abreast of all the changes at HTML Goodies and in the world of web-site design and development, there is a weekly Goodies to Go! newsletter that you can subscribe to from the site.

➡ *CGI, CSS, HTML, HTML Tags, JavaScript, Perl*

HTML TAGS

Tags are the building blocks of HTML, the most basic elements of any web page. Most developers today use graphical web editors that write the code according to which elements you place on the page and how you edit them. Even so, by understanding the function of each tag, you will be able to tweak the code by hand (hard coding) to correct or fine-tune your pages.

Everything from the title of the page to the details of a hyperlink and properties of an inline image is contained in a tag. All tags are contained in < and > brackets, and while some like <B> stand alone, most can be modified by inserting additional attributes within the brackets.

Most tags also require closing. If you italicize a word using <I>, for example, add </I> afterwards or the remainder of your page content will be italicized.

Tags are not case-sensitive, although you should be consistent within documents and writing them in upper case helps them stand out from the displayed content of the page.

<HTML></HTML>
The HTML tag is the container for an HTML document, and should form the first and last line of each page. It tells the browser that the data contained within is written in HTML.

<HEAD></HEAD>
The HEAD tag gives the browser more information about a page, and typically contains four other tags, META, STYLE, LINK and TITLE. <META> gives details of the page's content (as a reference for search engines), author and the ISO character set. <STYLE> sets stylesheet rules by containing a list of character definitions ending with the closing </STYLE> tag. External cascading stylesheet definitions are linked using the <LINK> tag as follows: <link rel="stylesheet"

href="style.css" type="text/css">. <TITLE> contains the legend that appears in the title bar of the browser. Quote the site name and a specific description as this will appear if the site is bookmarked by a user. Close with the command </TITLE>.

<BODY></BODY>

The BODY tag surrounds the entire visible content of a page, and its attributes define the colour of the document and its text content. While CSS now define text styles more efficiently, you should include TEXT and LINK attributes for users of older browsers. BGCOLOR defines a page's background colour, while BACKGROUND loads and tiles a background image. Other BODY attributes set the size of margins in pixels.

<P>, <BR>, <HR>

Standard HTML has two ways of breaking lines. The paragraph tag <P> inserts a double-line break at the end of each paragraph, while the line break tag <BR> merely turns a line at the point where the tag is added. <P> can carry the CLASS attribute, which defines a style for the whole paragraph according to an attached style sheet. Paragraphs should be closed using </P>. Extra emphasis can be given to a line break by adding a horizontal rule using the HR tag. Variables include WIDTH (in pixels or percent) and COLOR.

<B>, <I>, <U>

Basic text formatting tags embolden, italicize and underline text respectively. End formatting with a closing tag, for example </B>.

<A...></A>

Anchor or hyperlink tag. The HREF attribute specifies the destination page, while the TARGET tag places the linked page into a frame or a new window. You can use the NAME attribute elsewhere on a page to place an anchor. All the elements between the <A> and </A> tags will become an active hyperlink.

<IMG>

IMG places an inline image into a page. The location of the image is specified by the SRC attribute. The ALIGN attribute specifies the position of the image in relation to the page (LEFT, RIGHT, CENTRE) or in relation to the line of text (TOP, MIDDLE, BOTTOM). VSPACE and HSPACE define the amount of pixels placed around the image, while ALT defines text that appears until the image loads completely. HEIGHT and WIDTH can also be specified, usually to create a placeholder rather than to resize the image, unless a single-pixel spacer is used.

<TABLE><TR><TD></TD></TR></TABLE>

Table tags can be difficult to follow, especially in tabular layouts with nested tables. <TABLE> defines the position of a table, and, like an image, uses the ALIGN attribute. Its BORDER attribute sets the thickness of the bevelled border, and BGCOLOR and BACKGROUND properties work as they do for the BODY tag. Additional space can be placed between cells using the CELLSPACING and CELLPADDING attributes. Inside each TABLE tag, the beginning and end of each row is defined by TR, while each cell is contained within TD tags or, to emphasize the top line of a table, the TH tags. Cells can be merged using ROWSPAN and COLSPAN properties.

<FONT>

CSS will eventually kill off the FONT tag, but it is still worth supporting for the sake of older systems. Its primary attributes are FACE, COLOR and SIZE. FACE lets the designer insert a hierarchy of suitable fonts, for example "Arial, Helvetica, Sans-Serif" – if a computer doesn't possess the first named font, the second, then the third, will be used. COLOR over-rides the TEXT attribute of the BODY tag, while SIZE sets the relative size of the font from 1 (smallest) up to 7.

➡ *HTML, HTML Editor, Page Layout*

ABOVE: Rather like the bones of a skeleton, tags are the building blocks of HTML; combined together, they form the basic elements of any web page.

HTMLGEAR

Web site add-ons; part of the Lycos network, htmlGEAR provides a selection of free add-ons to enhance your site. To notch up your site a 'gear' the code for the add-on just needs to be put on the Web page.

There's a 'gear manager', which handles them all and there are detailed instructions at the htmlGEAR web site (htmlgear.lycos.com) for inserting the code using a number of web-authoring programs. The free gears include:

An event gear that enables you to organize parties, team events or club functions. Friends can update the event calendar independently and email notification will be sent.

The headline gear lets you choose up to 10 headlines a day on topics of your choice from Wired News.

The text gear keeps your content fresh. It takes snippets of information, such as tips, quotes, or little-known facts, and changes the item displayed each time the page is refreshed.

The feedback gear enables your site to be more interactive by letting visitors comment on the site, but to an email address that is kept private (so as to avoid the possibility of it being spammed).

The guest gear works like a traditional guestbook where visitors can leave their comments on site, but comes with a screening feature to make sure nothing objectionable is added.

➡ *Free Web Extras, Form Handling, Guestbook*

HTTP

Hyper Text Transfer Protocol; the standard set of rules, or protocol, for passing files and other information (collectively known as resources) around the Web. These resources could be HTML files, image files, query results or anything else. HTTP is usually seen at the beginning of the URL, or address, for web sites. It sets out how messages between the client (the browser) and the server are formatted and transmitted, and what actions they need to take following any commands they receive. For example, when you enter a URL in your browser's address bar this sends an HTTP command to a web server, telling it to get and send back the web page you asked for. After sending its response the server shuts down its connection, so HTTP is known as a stateless protocol. That is, it does not maintain any connection between transactions. Because it has no record of what has happened before, it is difficult to set up web sites that react to a flow of user input, but this is compensated for by newer technologies using ActiveX, Java, JavaScript and cookies.

➡ *Domain, URL*

ICON

Icons are small pictures that are used to symbolize or represent an object or program. The most common one found on the Web is the small picture of a house used to represent the homepage. Equally, an icon of a small envelope is often put next to the mailto: link to show users they can send a message from there.

In effect, they are cute buttons, some of which will be linked to an action, some not. As they are graphical images, they are inserted on the page using the <img src="icon.gif"> tag. Use the <Alt> attribute to add some text giving an explanatory title for the icon. This way, for most users, the Alt text will pop up as a tip when users mouse over the image.

On navigation bars, icons should not be used by themselves: while it may be clear to you that the fine drawing of a spanner marks the product, pages it may not be to the user. Icons should have a title alongside which immediately makes clear what the link is about. They should also be used sparingly; as they are pictures they still incur some download time. Although each individual image may not be huge, if there are several on a page, the load soon adds up.

➡ *Illustrator (Adobe), Branding and Identity, Dingbat, Freehand (Macromedia), Logo Design*

IFRAME

The iframe tag inserts an inline frame into an HTML document. Unlike regular frames, which take up a whole window and which tend to be used for navigation menus or large areas of content, inline frames are effectively small sub-windows within pages. They can be used like regular frames and are ideal holders for smaller blocks of text such as dictionary-style definitions, short news items and external images or documents.

The iframe tag can be used anywhere on an HTML page, and like the IMG image tag, can be aligned left, right or centre or assigned to a paragraph to make it stand apart from the rest of the content. The basic tag syntax defines the iframe's name, size, and tells the browser to load a page into the frame.

Iframe is only supported by the most recent browsers, and so it is good practice to enter an alternative. This could be a link to an external document, the same text formatted in regular HTML, or a message telling the reader that their browser does not support iframes. This text is inserted inside the iframe tag as follows, and will be ignored by browsers that do support iframes:

```
<iframe src="frame_content.htm" name="content">
Sorry, your browser does not support inline frames
</iframe>
```

Like an inline image, the frame can be given dimensions defined in pixels or as a percentage of the parent window. Vertical spacing can also be added around the frame. Iframes cannot be resized like regular frames but horizontal and vertical scrollbars appear automatically if the framed document is bigger than the frame.

By default, the iframe is given a prominent border, but adding border=0 to the iframe tag removes this. Matching the background of the frame to that of the framed document will give a seamless effect, and remember that you can define any attribute of the framed document in an attached style sheet.

Any kind of document can be placed in an iframe, from HTML files, GIFs and JPEGs to PDF, Microsoft Word and Excel documents (although large external documents are usually better placed in larger, full-window frames).

Inline frames can raise legal and copyright issues. Iframes make it look as though the imported copy has been produced by you and not by the actual author. Make it clear that the copyright for the imported content belongs to someone else, ask their permission to reproduce and, if at all in doubt, open the text in a new full-screen frame.

➡ *Frame, HTML*

ILLUSTRATION

Illustrations cannot take up the same proportion of space on the Web as they can in print, but used properly they can be both informative and eye-catching.

The Web offers an endless source of illustrations through clipart galleries and image libraries. Copyright-free images can be combined into montages using Photoshop or Fireworks, or if you can't find a suitable image, you can edit or create your own in Illustrator or FreeHand. If you also work in print, artwork could be scanned in for illustrative purposes.

Illustrations are best kept simple. Detailed images will not reproduce well when reduced for web use, so if you are using a large print graphic or detailed photograph, crop just one element and use that instead.

Feature illustrations should be used to complement the content, so use sparingly on a page. If you are converting a larger illustration for web use, you could slice it into smaller sections and use a different segment on each page. Choose a bright, engaging section of the image for use as a link on the homepage.

Illustrations can be used to encapsulate the spirit and subject matter of a site. On a sparse homepage, a large illustration on the left-hand side can draw the eye and add some colour to the page. Again, the rule is to keep it simple – a close-up image or basic montage with a little creative distortion will act as an eye-catching introduction to your work.

➡ *Clip Art, Graphic Design Package, Image Use*

ILLUSTRATOR (ADOBE)

Vector graphics program. Illustrator, Adobe's vector graphics software application, is a powerful illustration package that extends beyond graphic design and integrates with the firm's other products to produce high-quality web pages and internet graphics.

As well as conventional vector drawing tools, Illustrator has adopted many traditionally bitmap-only tools from Photoshop. The program supports Photoshop's extensive range of filters and plug-ins, and boasts a range of freestyle brushes normally only found in bitmap graphics software. Tools for liquifying objects and applying lens flares are new additions, and layered designs literally add another dimension to Illustrator's vector capabilities. The program's layer masks are fully exportable to Photoshop. Web-specific information like active rollovers and animations can also be exported to Photoshop, and animations can also be converted into the Flash SWF format. Image maps, which can include polygon-shaped as well as regular hotspots, can be created in Illustrator, and web images can be optimized using the program's slicing tools.

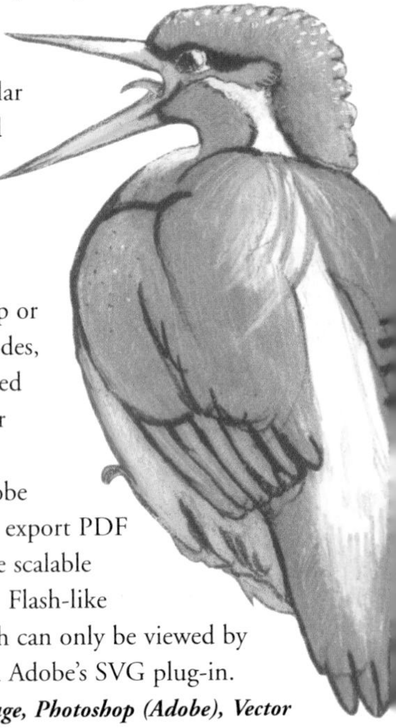

Illustrator offers 2-up or 4-up image preview modes, and can anti-alias selected text areas specifically for publishing online.

Naturally for an Adobe product, Illustrator will export PDF files, and will also create scalable vector graphics (SVGs), Flash-like interactive images which can only be viewed by browsers equipped with Adobe's SVG plug-in.

➡ *Graphic Design Package, Photoshop (Adobe), Vector*

IMAGE

Graphic file format. Images on a computer are of two types: vector graphics and bitmap images. Vector art is created by drawing programs, such as Adobe

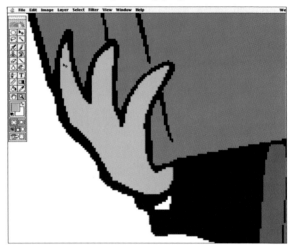

Illustrator, and uses mathematical definitions to describe shapes and lines. Consequently, the image can be rescaled or viewed at any screen resolution and not lose any of its clarity. However, to be viewed online, most vector images need to be converted to a bitmap file format and saved as a GIF or JPEG.

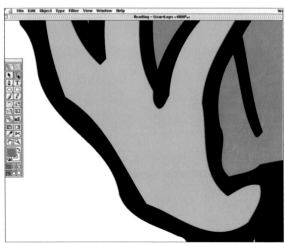

With bitmap images, also known as raster images, the graphic is made up of rows and columns of dots. Each dot of the image is mapped on screen to individual pixels. In addition, each pixel has a colour value, which is

determined by the bit depth. With black and white images one bit equals one dot, but for colours each dot is represented by several bits of data.

Consequently bitmaps are good at showing subtle shades and colours and so are used for continuous-tone images such as photographs. However, as bitmaps are represented by a fixed number of pixels they do not scale well and will appear jagged and fuzzy.

➠ *GIF, Graphic Design Package, JPEG, Pixel, Raster, Vector*

FAR LEFT AND TOP LEFT: When using illustrations on your web site it is best to keep them simple, as detailed images will not always reproduce well on a web page.

IMAGE COMPOSER (MICROSOFT)

Web graphics utility. Image Composer, bundled with Microsoft's FrontPage web editor, has been developed especially for creating graphics for the Web and for on-screen presentations; as such it is more suited to

simple image composition than high-end graphics work, but it is a useful tool for creating buttons and banners, and extends to basic image editing and animating for the Web.

Microsoft calls imported graphics 'sprites', and allows users to build composite images out of a series of sprites by defining areas of transparency. Sprites can be cropped, flipped, arranged and grouped using the program's basic interface, and text can be added and stylized.

The software comes with a range of filters for editing sprites, and art effects which can turn a scanned photo into a watercolour painting in seconds. The software is compatible with Photoshop plug-ins. Photoshop layers can also be imported as individual sprites. Ambitious

users can create their own sprites using Image Composer's range of brush types, and an animation utility lets you export a series of sprites as an animated GIF.

Image Composer can be accessed directly from FrontPage by double-clicking on the image you want to edit, and elements can be pasted from the software to and from other programs in Microsoft's Office suite.

➠ *FrontPage (Microsoft), Graphic Design Package*

IMAGE COMPRESSION

Reducing file sizes safely. Inline images have to be as small as possible. Large images can slow download times for dial-up users, and cause bandwidth charges to mount, turning a hobby into an expensive pastime.

The three major web image formats – GIF, JPEG and PNG – are all highly compressable, and all three formats allow designers to balance image size and quality with an array of compression techniques.

Image compression tools are usually applied when a file is being exported into its web format. Programs like

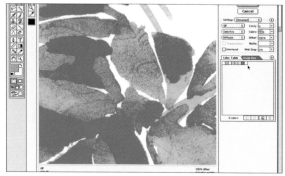

Fireworks and Photoshop can display the original image alongside a number of previews so that you can try out different degrees of compression on an image and compare the results side-by-side before committing.

Shareware tools such as GIF Blast for the Mac and Image Optimizer for Windows are available from software libraries, and dedicated applications such as Ulead SmartSaver Pro have been created with compression in mind. There are also web sites and services that compress your image files automatically. OptiView (www.optiview.com) will gauge all the images on your site and, if required, send you compressed alternatives for uploading.

When compressing images manually, the different formats compress in different ways. GIFs are compressed by a reduction in the number of colours contained in the image. Graphics editors let you specify the palette size, and some let you apply a degree of compression which reduces the colour depth automatically. You can opt to dither colours when saving a GIF, although this can increase image size and reduces image quality, so use carefully.

Graphics editors compress JPEGs by removing pixels that the eye is unlikely to miss. Just how many pixels are combined with their neighbours is determined by the degree of compression the editor applies. This is usually expressed on a sliding scale between 1 and 99, where 99 is almost uncompressed and 1 would be little more than a blur. Every image reacts differently to compression (smoothly graduated areas in particular break up badly), so the export preview should come in useful as you try various points on the scale.

PNGs compress similarly to GIFs, except that they can be saved in 8-, 24- or 32-bit formats. The size of a 32-bit PNG file is probably too big for web use, so if you do use PNGs, stick to 8-bit for low-colour, GIF-style graphics and 24-bit for photographic images. Dithering also has a less detrimental effect on PNGs than on GIFs.

➡ *File Size, Dithering, Graphic Design Package, Optimizing Images*

FAR LEFT: The program Image Composer features art effects which can miraculously turn a scanned photo into a watercolour painting.

IMAGE ENHANCEMENT TECHNIQUES

Scanned images or pictures captured with a digital camera will rarely be perfect; whichever automatic settings you apply, slight variations in focus and lighting can effect the output. Graphics packages offer a range of filters for enhancing such images into sharp, bright, colourful pictures that leap out of a web page.

The most familiar enhancement tools are the contrast and brightness filters. Increasing the contrast makes light colours lighter and dark colours darker, and such increased definition brings out the detail in most images. It's a good idea to adjust the brightness level as you tweak the contrast.

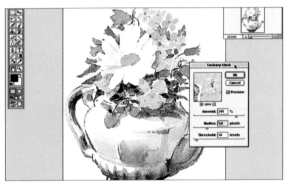

The danger with using contrast and brightness filters is that the dark and light tones can become too exaggerated, as lightening one area of an image can cause another part of the picture to wash out. The Levels tool brings out details without sacrificing definition elsewhere.

The colours contained in every image fall into three categories: light (highlights), dark (shadows) and midtones. An ideal image will have an even number of pixels in all three categories. Too many highlights and a picture will look washed out, too much shadow obscures the finer details, while an over-concentration of midtones looks bland. You can alter all three settings, but for subtle enhancement, it is best only to tweak the midtones. Add some depth to a washed-out photo, for instance, by darkening the midtones.

Even after altering the midtones, an image can look washed out if its colour balance is wrong. The Levels tool should let you split the image into red, green and blue composites so you can alter their tonal ranges independently.

Altering the hue and saturation increases the tone and intensity of an image. Every image has a subtle underlying colour, and if it is incorrect – skin tones might have a blue tint, for instance – tweaking the hue can correct it. Saturation refers to the volume of colour in an image. If an image looks cold and colourless, increasing the saturation gives warmth.

Finally, sharpen the image. Scanning and reducing images tends to soften hard edges, but the Unsharp Mask tool sharpens those areas where colours meet.

Image enhancement involves a great deal of trial and error, but combining the tools correctly will produce the desired result. To avoid having to switch between filters, Extensis' Intellihance Pro for Photoshop lets you mix effects and view up to 25 previews at a time. Successful combinations can then be saved for automatic and batch processing.

➡ *Filter, Optimizing Images*

IMAGE LICENSING

Terms of use for graphics; whether images are bought individually, by subscription or in a collection, it is important to check the details of the licensing agreement.

Photo libraries license use of their images in different ways. Most have very specific, individual agreements which you should read carefully before purchasing any artwork. Generally, though, pictures are licensed for one-time use on a specific project or are offered as part of a royalty free collection and can be used many times on many projects.

An example of the royalty free method is ArtToday (www.arttoday.com), which works on a subscription basis. Once you pay your weekly or monthly fee you can download and use as many images as you want. Like all royalty free graphics there are still restrictions, such as the images not being used for 'obscene' or 'scandalous' works.

More traditional photo libraries sell a license to use their images. The price will vary depending on where and when the image will be used, how big it will be reproduced and what its intended purpose is. Note that some image libraries, such as Corbis (www.corbis.com) charge a lower fee if the picture is for editorial use (in a magazine or on a web site) rather than being used commercially for advertising or promotional purposes.

➡ *Graphic Design Packages, Stock Photo Suppliers*

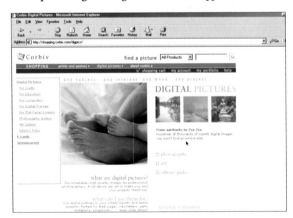

FAR LEFT: These two versions of the same image demonstrate the effect that image enhancement can have upon a picture.

IMAGE MANIPULATION

With the power of web-graphics editors, a basic image doesn't need to stay basic for long. It can be significantly improved by a relatively simple addition, such as a coloured border. While most graphics packages have a range of borders that can be used, they need to be applied to a flattened image. If your graphic has more than one layer it needs to be flattened before the border is applied.

There are a number of tools which enable you to gloss over any faults on the image. Using the Clone brush, you can copy (clone) from one part of an image to another to cover any flaw in the background. A Retouch tool enables you to apply special effects to a section of an image rather than to the entire graphic. It is useful if you want to lighten colours or emboss a part of the image. More

fundamentally, you can alter the orientation of an image by flipping it (reversing an image along its vertical axis) or mirroring it; that is reversing it horizontally so what was on the left side becomes the right and what was on the right appears on the left.

Colour information about images are stored in channels. These channels can be split in different ways, such as HSL (Hue, Saturation and Light) or RGB and CYMK. Filters or masks can be applied to the individual channels to create interesting effects, and the channels recombined. When you split an image into its channels it creates new images, so the original is unaffected by any changes.

To create the brown sepia effect of old photographs you use a colourize command, which provides a uniform level of hue and saturation while leaving the lightness values unchanged. Alternatively, the posterize effect gives

an image a flatter look with bands of colour rather than a smooth gradient, achieved by reducing the number of bits per colour channel. It is also possible to generate a 'negative image' using the function that replaces each pixel colour with its opposite on the colour wheel. So if the brightness value of the pixel is 30, its negative is 225.

Most graphics programs also come with a set of special effects that can be applied to distort your picture, give it a textured look, or appear in 3D. Similarly you can blur or soften an image by applying filters that smooth the transitions and alter the contrast around the edges by averaging the pixel colours. Alternatively, you can apply different filters to enhance the edges of an image by increasing the contrast.

➧ *Artful Distortion, Graphic Design Packages, Resizing Images*

IMAGE MAP

Graphical navigation tool. Image maps are inline graphics encoded with hotspots that act as hyperlinks. They are used where a graphical menu aids navigation – a map of the UK could be split into hotspots to display a company's regional offices, for instance – or simply to liven up introductory index pages.

The original image maps were server-side elements, where the browser would have to refer to a CGI script and a separate MAP file before opening the destination URL. Today client image maps are supported by all browsers, giving the designer more control over the mapping process and speeding up page access.

Hotspots can be rectangular or elliptical, or can consist of polygons with any number of sides. Regular shaped hotspots are easy to apply in standard hard-coded HTML. Having added the ISMAP USEMAP instruction to the IMG tag, state whether the hotspot is a rectangle, a circle or a polygon, and express the left-hand corner of a hotspot as x, y co-ordinates relative of the image followed by the x, y co-ordinates of the right-hand corner of the hotspot. Add a destination URL and your image map is complete.

As you can probably tell, calculating hotspots' co-ordinates down to a precise pixel is difficult, and expressing a polygon hotspot is even harder. Fortunately, there are many shareware and freeware tools available that make the job easier by letting you import the image to be

mapped, adding the hotspots using conventional drawing tools and creating the accompanying HTML for pasting into the page.

Image mapping utilities for Windows such as Imapper Studios, Image Mapper and GlobalScape's CuteMap are available from all good software download libraries, while Mac users will find Mapedit at www.boutell.com/mapedit serves their image mapping needs.

Professional web graphics packages like Fireworks and Photoshop make it even easier, incorporating image maps into entire pages. They will also split a larger image map into a series of smaller images and generate HTML table code to put the sliced elements back together. This serves two useful purposes: firstly, image maps are by their very nature large images, so slicing them into smaller components using a graphics package speeds up loading; secondly, using a web-graphics tool lets you apply JavaScript rollovers to an image map to add an extra dimension of interactivity.

If you do use image maps, consider those still using older browsers or who may not want to wait for slow-loading images, and add a list of text-based equivalent links beneath the map.

➧ *Client-Side, Link, Fireworks (Macromedia), JavaScript, Photoshop (Adobe), Server-Side*

LEFT: Use image manipulation to successfully re-create the brown sepia effect of old photographs.

IMAGE MODE

File format. Images can be saved in several formats, or modes. For example, when you open an image in Photoshop, go to the Image Menu, select Mode and you will see by the tick mark what format the image is saved in. It could be stored in indexed colour mode, RGB or CMYK.

Within Photoshop there are Actions – recorded sequences of commands and photo-editing functions that can be applied to an image or a batch of images. For example, one action could be used to convert several images to a different file format, or image mode. A particularly powerful action is the Conditional Mode Change. Through one dialog box setting you can run a sequence of complicated commands that ensure that all the files being processed end up in the image mode you want. It is accessed from the Automate command on the File menu. From the dialog box you select the original file image mode, i.e. bitmapped, indexed colour, CMYK etc., and then choose from a drop down menu the image mode you would like it converted to.

➠ *CMYK, Greyscale, Graphic Design Package, RGB*

IMAGE RESOLUTION

Image Resolution is a measure of how sharp and clear an image is. Normally it is measured in terms of pixels per inch (ppi) or for printed images, in dots per inch (dpi), although often the two terms are used interchangeably.

The ideal resolution for an image often depends on where it will be displayed. If the image is going to be printed out, it would typically be around 300 dpi. On the Web, there is no need for it to be such high resolution. All images should be low resolution as they will ultimately be viewed on low-res screens.

Traditionally, the highest resolution on a monitor was in the region of 72 dpi, and although newer monitors have a wider range it is still standard practice to create images at 72 dpi. In fact, it is not so much the number of pixels per inch that's important, but the number of pixels in total. On the Web, graphics map one-on-one with the screen pixels so no matter what the resolution, a 600 pixel-wide banner will fit 600 pixels. On a high-resolution monitor this will appear smaller than on a lower-resolution monitor.

➠ *File Size, GIF, JPEG, Pixel, Raster, Vector*

IMAGE USE

Web images are usually in one of two formats, GIF or JPEG. GIFs are best used for line art and well-defined vector images like buttons and logos, while JPEGs are suited to photography and full-colour imagery.

Images should be compressed as much as possible so that they load quickly, and web-safe colours ensure that images can be viewed across all platforms. Interlacing gives the impression that images are loading faster, even though they are not. Always include the ALT attribute to give an alternative text description of each image. It is useful to specify the width and height attributes of any images, giving the exact dimensions in pixels, as this will allow browsers to reserve the proper amount of space for

the image, and continue to render the rest of the document (giving the appearance of a faster-loading page).

Animated graphics can be used to catch the reader's

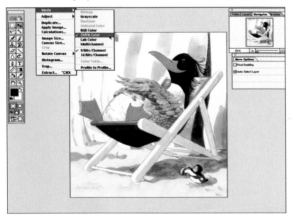

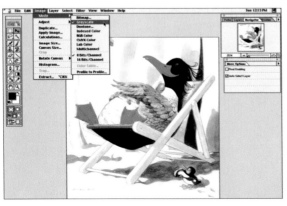

eye, but beware animation overload, as it can become confusing, and avoid hackneyed clipart movies as they are likely to annoy rather than amuse.

Graphics can be used in place of HTML text where a precise font or font spacing is required, but use sparingly – it is not needed with paragraphs as CSS offers enough control over typography.

Images should complement the content of a site, not just be there for their own sake. Do not make illustrations too large so that they dominate the page and avoid neat but boring over-alignment – instead, balance images in the space around them.

➥ *Design Basics, GIF, Illustration, JPEG*

INCORPORATING FLASH FILES

Once converted from the .fla project format into the browser-compliant .swf movie format, Flash animations are placed on the page using the OBJECT and EMBED tags. OBJECT defines the size and name of a movie and the version of Flash that was used to create it; the EMBED tag includes its display attributes and the filename and location of the movie.

Your web editor should let you import Flash files just as you would graphics, and in fact the two elements share common attributes. You can set height, width and alignment, and specify the amount of white space to leave around the object.

Flash-specific attributes can be set as parameters. These include background colour – useful if you want your animation or button to blend into its environment – and a quality setting (low quality calls on less processing power to render but obviously degrades the image). Parameters also include the movie's autoplay and loop settings. If autoplay is on, the movie will run as soon as it loads (making it essential for buttons and banners). If it is off, the user will have to right-click on the movie and click the Play option. A more user-friendly option would be to build VCR-style play and stop buttons into the original Flash project.

➥ *Animation using Flash, Flash (Macromedia), HTML*

ABOVE LEFT: Autoplay ensures your movie will run as soon as it loads, and there is no need for cumbersome reels of film.

INTERACTIVITY

Interactivity on the Web enables users to customize what they see, what they do and even what they buy. When a web page is posted on the Net it is said to be published. But what separates the Web from most other types of publication is the degree of interaction there is. This exchange is not only between the site and the users but also between users themselves, particularly with online games and chat.

At the most basic level, interaction comes simply by clicking on a link that takes you from one page to another. Equally, that link can move you from one site to another half way across the world.

Client-side scripting, such as JavaScript, and DHTML will change what's on view in response to a mouse click or the position of the cursor. Click on a mailto: link and it launches your email client for instant feedback.

More fundamentally, a front-end form can gather all sorts of information from the user that can then be used for many kinds of interaction. It can be posted to a database, alter the information the user sees next, or even lead to the purchase of some item as part of an online store.
➠ *DHTML, Flash (Macromedia), Functionality, JavaScript, Links, Multimedia*

INTERFACE

Visual presentation of a site which enables users to interact with it. The interface is how the logical structure of the site is presented visually to the user. As such it shows what information is available and provides the navigational tools for getting around the site.

Because most web sites offer so much information they have to be grouped together into manageable units. These units can be represented graphically, such as by a different tab, or coloured button, or a different colour, for each section. However, colour alone should not be the only way of differentiating content, it should also be backed up by clear labelling. While it may seem clear to you that product pages are blue and corporate information is grey it will not necessarily automatically register as such with the users.

Some designers believe that there should be no more than seven different sections – or choices – at any one time, or users will get confused. This is probably based on research which says that seven is the number of items that the short-term memory can comfortably hold. However, the different options do not need to be retained in the memory, they are visible on the page so the figure seven is perhaps unnecessarily restrictive. What is needed is a clear, consistent and logical design.
➠ *Consistency, Page Layout, Site Navigation, User Interface*

INTERLACED IMAGE

Display method for images by which they are downloaded in several passes so that users get a rough idea of what's coming before they complete.

Ever had to wait a long time for an image to download – and then not wanted to view it anyway? An interlaced image won't try your patience in this way. What it does, in effect, is to download the image in several passes. With each pass the picture gets clearer and more detailed.

Consequently, you can decide whether it's worth the wait. If the graphic is an image map, you can click on the link that interests you and move on before it downloads completely.

If the image wasn't interlaced it would appear a few rows at a time or, more likely, all at once after it had been fully downloaded. While interlacing isn't worthwhile for small graphics it is for larger images and image maps.

The effect is achieved differently according to which file format you use. An interlaced GIF would normally take four passes to display the full image, while the PNG will appear up to eight times faster. That's because on each pass it adds information in both rows and columns, whereas only rows are filled in on the traditional GIF.

Progressive JPEGs are similar to interlaced GIFs in that a blurred, very low resolution version of the image is downloaded that is gradually completed in a series of passes.

➠ *Image Compression, Page Loading Time*

INTERNET EXPLORER (MICROSOFT)

Web browser. Set at the heart of the Windows operating system, Microsoft Internet Explorer (IE) is the most widely used browser on the Internet today. Customized versions of IE are supplied free with most ISP accounts and by proprietary service providers like AOL, and the software is available free from www.microsoft.com/windows/ie.

Browser technology has slowed down since constant changes to HTML and Microsoft-Netscape competition

led to a rapid series of updates in the mid-1990s. Subsequent updates have concentrated on the experience of browsing, and the latest version – version 6 – is no exception.

On the technical side, the latest HTML, Java and XML standards are supported, backed up by enhanced

DHTML features and CSS1 support. More obvious enhancements for users come in the form of media handlers. A new image toolbar appears when a user points at an inline image, and shows four buttons that let you save, print and email images direct from the page. If an image is too large to fit in a browser window, it can be resized to fit automatically.

Rich media is handled by the Media Bar, which offers an interface to search the web for and play music clips, videos and movie trailers. Extras include email and newsgroup software Outlook Express, and Macromedia's Flash Player.

➡ *Browser, Netscape Navigator*

INTRANET

Secure internal web site; only open to those within a particular company or organization. An intranet can have all the features of any web site: useful information, company forms, an organization-wide address book, details of company procedures, discussion groups, virtual meeting rooms, even instant messaging. However, its use is restricted to people inside a company or organization, or those who are authorized. Access to all others is prevented by a firewall. Consequently, an intranet is great for companies where teams need to share

information but are
spread over large
geographic areas and
across different time
zones. A company
wide intranet also
makes it easier for
road warriors to keep
in touch wherever
they may be.

In fact, intranets
are one of the fastest
growing areas of
the Internet. As
a company wide
resource to aid
communication and
workflow they are
much cheaper to
build and maintain
than setting up a
private network based on proprietary equipment.
Intranets may also be accessed by trusted outsiders, like
suppliers who have been given the necessary authorization.
In such cases the sites are known as an extranets.

JAVA

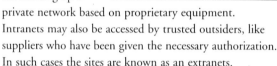 High-level programming language. Java was
originally designed as a programming language and
operating system for the consumer electronics market, to
control everything from TV sets to toasters. Although it
did not succeed there, it had a number of features which

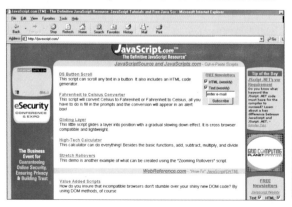

made it ideal for the Web. It is small (as it was designed
to fit into items with little memory), can be transferred
quickly, and is platform-independent.

It is now essential in web design, and achieves this by
being an interpreted rather than a compiled language.
Unlike C++ – on which it is based – it is not compiled
into code for a specific platform, such as the PC; instead,
it is put into a single compiled version called Java
bytecode. On the Web, this is interpreted by a virtual
machine, usually running within the browser, on
whichever platform is being used.

Although it is a fully-fledged programming language,
Java is mainly used on the Web to create applets – which
can be embedded on a page. These programs, which have
the extension .class, can add all sorts of interactive
features to a site as well as enable multimedia animations
and database integration.

➟ *Applet, Functionality*

*ABOVE: Java was originally designed as a programming language and operating
system for consumer electronic products, such as TV sets. It is now essential in
web design.*

JAVA APPLET

Small programs designed to add interaction to your Web site. Applets are easy to come by and secure, and will run on any platform through a Java-enabled browser.

When Java programs are run within a browser they are known as applets. They can do pretty well anything: present news ticker-tape style, launch interactive games, or serve up a complete multimedia show. They are similar to ActiveX controls, which are also mini-applications downloaded to the computer to run. When you visit a web site that has a Java applet on it, it is automatically loaded from the server before being run in any Java-enabled web browser. Being small, the applets download quickly. Unlike ActiveX controls which can access the user's hard drive, applets operate in a 'sandbox' within the browser – in the Java virtual machine. As well as being more secure, this means applets can run on any platform without needing a proprietary plug-in installed.

They are a good way to add interactivity to your site and there are several places, such as www.javaboutique.internet.com, where you can download applets to use. To add the applet to your page, use either the <applet> or <object> HTML tag and follow any special instructions provided.

➡ *Functionality, Java*

JAVASCRIPT

Client-side scripting language that can add animation and interactive effects to web sites without demanding the programming skills of server-side programs. Despite the name, JavaScript is not related to Java. Originally developed for Netscape Navigator, it is a client-side scripting language designed to bring some

basic interactivity to web pages. It enables designers to control different elements.

JavaScript is easier to learn than Java and is commonly used for providing animation, dynamically changing content, creating rollover effects and navigational aids, opening new windows and verifying that information is entered into forms in a valid format.

A scripting language like JavaScript is somewhere between a markup language like HTML and a fully-fledged programming language like Java. The advantage of JavaScript is that it requires few programming skills. Basic animation and special effects can be added to web pages without the complication of server-side programming such as CGI.

The extra functionality JavaScript supplies is added through short snippets of code that are written directly within the HTML code on a web page. It is enclosed within the <SCRIPT> tag to tell the browser to run it as a JavaScript program. <SCRIPT> tags are most commonly put in the <HEAD> section as it means the script can start running while the rest of the page is downloading. However, scripts that write text to the screen or HTML are usually best placed within the <BODY> section.

You do not have to write your own JavaScript at all. There are programs like Macromedia's Dreamweaver which do the coding for you, adding their built-in 'behaviors' (JavaScript) to the HTML. There are also sites where you can freely download scripts to add to your page, such as the JavaScript source (www.javascriptsource.com). However, as it runs on the client, JavaScript does need to be supported by the browser. Unfortunately, not only do different browsers interpret JavaScript in different ways, but so do different versions of the same browser. If there is a script on your page that the browser does not understand, it will be interpreted as straight text and look strange on-screen, or worse – generate an error message and crash the user's browser.

One way to sidestep the problem is to use a script which checks which browser version is being used. It will serve the script if it is supported, but run a different version of the page for users whose browsers do not support that feature.

➡ *Client-Side, Functionality, Manipulating JavaScript, Utilizing JavaScript, Webmonkey*

JHTML

Server-side technology, similar to Microsoft's Active Server Pages, but which has the advantage of separating dynamic elements on the page from the static HTML. JHTML was the earlier method for including a Java program as part of a web page. It has now been replaced by JavaServer Pages (JSP). This is a server-side technology that, together with Java servlets which bring dynamic content to the Web, were developed by Sun as an alternative to Microsoft's Active Server Pages (ASP).

The advantage of JSPs is that they separate the static HTML elements on the page – the actual design and display of the page – from the dynamically generated HTML. It has the advantage over pure server-side applications like CGI in that it does not generate the entire page each time, even when most of it is the same. As a result, designers can change the look and feel of the page without compromising any of the back-end coding. They simply leave places where servlet programmers can insert the dynamic content. Servlets are Java applets running on a web server and are becoming increasingly common as an alternative to CGI applications. Because servlets are written in Java, with its 'write once, run anywhere' philosophy, they have the bonus of being platform-independent.

➡ *Functionality*

LEFT: Javascript can be used to animate your web page.

JPEG

Graphics file format. The best file format for images with lots of subtle colours, JPEG compression does involve a trade off between image quality and file size.

JPEG is the best format to use for images, such as photographs, which have lots of subtle colours, blended together. It is also good with greyscale images. The format is named after the Joint Photographic Experts Group, the standards body that developed it. The file extension is .jpg or .jpeg.

Because they support 24-bit colour, JPEGs can contain millions of colours, compared to the GIF which is restricted to a palette of 256 colours. JPEGs are widely used on the Web because the compression algorithm they use can reduce file sizes significantly and shorten download time. The technique involved is called 'lossy compression', whereby redundant information is removed. As a result, when an image is heavily compressed quite a lot of the detail is lost and blotchy squares of colours, referred to as artifacts, may appear.

The lossy compression technique also means that once image quality is reduced it cannot be replaced. So, if you resave a JPEG as another JPEG you lose even more image quality. For that reason, it is better to keep the original version intact and when you want to change something, go back to that and save it as a JPEG.

As with most images on the Web, there is a trade-off between the quality of the image and having a small file that will download quickly.

With JPEGs the more you compress the file, the worse the image looks. However, it is better at compressing smooth, even blurred images than those with sharp edges. You can use this to your advantage when optimizing graphics by opening the image in your picture editor and softening it. You do this by applying the Gaussian Blur filter, or in Fireworks the Smoothing tool. As always you need to be careful that you don't trade too much image quality for better compression and a smaller file size.

JPEGs can also be downloaded in sections, in the same way as interlaced GIFs. In progressive JPEGs, a blurred, very low resolution version of the image is downloaded that gradually becomes clearer and more detailed. With some graphics programs you can set how many passes it takes to complete the image. For viewers it has the advantage that they see a rough version of the graphic before it fully downloads. Unfortunately, some of the earlier browsers do not support progressive JPEGs.

➡ *File Type, GIF, Photography, Raster*

KILLERSITES.COM *(www.killersites.com)*

Although visitors to this site would benefit from reading the book it is linked to (Creating Killer Web Sites by David Siegel) it can stand by itself. Not only does the web site follow some of the example sites used in the book, it also offers a number of design tips – from the difference anti-aliasing makes, to reducing the number of intermediate colours used in text images. It also gives updated information on creating cross-browser-compliant designs and offers some HTML tips and tricks. While the book itself offers a primer on cascading style sheets (CSS) the web site links through to a number of CSS resources, including the web standards body W3.org. There are also links to a number of

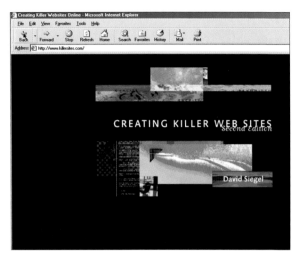

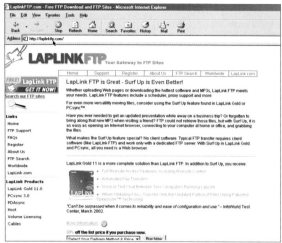

freeware and shareware sites that have the web-building tools that Siegel believes are necessary to make killer sites.

The site also introduces what is a common theme in the second edition of the book – the evolution of web building to third-generation sites. These 3G sites use

similar layout tools to those employed by print designers that give much closer control of the layout. As a result, 3G sites are better able to use metaphors and visual themes to guide surfers round the site.

➡ *Design Basics, Page Layout*

LAPLINKFTP *(www.laplinkftp.com)*

LapLinkFTP is fully featured client software that enables you to connect your PC to a remote server and transfer files. FTP is the standard method of moving

files (particularly large files) between computers, especially when they are connected via the Internet. And there are several software programs that use this protocol to enable you to download files from the Internet, or to load your pages to a web server.

LapLinkFTP is client software that connects your PC to the remote FTP server. It displays a directory of each computer in separate windows, rather like Windows Explorer. Transferring files is simply a case of dragging and dropping the files where you want to move them. To speed up transfers LapLinkFTP lets you connect to several remote sites at the same time. Should the connection be broken you can automatically resume transfers where you left off. The program is also integrated with LapLink's online FTPSearch, a huge index of the millions of files available on FTP servers around the world. Although the program is freeware, it is ad-supported and requires an email address for the free registration code. Alternatively, you can buy an ad-free version.

➡ *Anonymous FTP, CuteFTP, FTP, Server, Uploading a Web Site*

FAR LEFT: While JPEGs may contain millions of colours, GIFs are restricted to a palette of 256 colours.

LAUNCHING NEW BROWSER WINDOWS WITH HTML

New Window. Links can be launched in a new pop-up window using HTML, but there are some features, such as its size, that can't be controlled. Seemingly irremovable advert pop-ups can be extremely irritating, but if you want to link your readers to another site without losing them completely, a pop-up could be the answer. It is simply a second browser window which is opened to display the contents of a link, while the existing page stays on screen.

There are two basic methods to launch a new browser window using HTML. In both cases you add the target attribute to the anchor tag. Although you cannot alter the size of the new window it will usually be similar to the one already open.

With the first method, setting the Target to '_blank' opens a new window when you click a link. Use this on several links and you will soon have a screen full of open windows. The alternative method is to give the target window a name – such as 'showcase', which is used as a target for each link. This way any link that is clicked will open in the same second window. (e.g. <a href="http://www.yahoo.com" target="showcase">...</a>)

➡ *Frame, HTML, Target*

LAUNCHING NEW BROWSER WINDOWS WITH JAVASCRIPT

Gain control over pop-up windows. The Target="_new", or TARGET="_blank", tags in HTML are good for opening secondary, external browser windows, but using JavaScript commands can give more control over the size and appearance of your pop-up window.

JavaScript's window.open method is easy to use alongside regular A HREF tags and equally easy to customize. To open a new window, simply add the onClick method to the hyperlink tag as follows:

page, using the same window name would place the new link into the same open window. Changing the window name would open a further pop-up window.

The window_options entry is where JavaScript pop-ups really come into their own. Each window has nine variables that can be switched on and off to govern the size and position of the new window and determine which elements of browser furniture are featured in the pop-up. All the variables are switched off by default, but can be added to a window simply by entering the keyword into the window_options variable, separated by commas.

The control options are: toolbar (which displays the row of buttons at the top of a regular browser window), directories (single-click bookmarks), location (address bar), status (the status bar at the bottom of the browser window), menu bar, resizable (which determines whether a window can be dragged out) and scrollbars.

To specify a window size, add height=xx and width=xx into the window_options area, bearing in mind that the size specified is for the browser's whole interface and not just the page display area.

Finally, you can specify where you want the new window to appear on-screen with the top=xx and left=xx values. These tell the browser how many pixels from the top and from the left-hand side of the screen the top-left corner of the new window should be positioned.

If we wanted a 300 x 300-pixel resizeable window with a toolbar and status bar placed 150 pixels from the top of the screen, then, our link would read:

```
<a href="URL" onClick="window.open('URL',
'window_name',
'resizable,toolbar,status,height=300,width=300,top=150');
return false">link_here</a>
```

➡ *JavaScript, Launching New Browser Windows with HTML, Navigation, Pop-Up*

```
<a href="URL" onClick="window.open('URL',
'window_name', 'window_options'); return
false">link_here</a>
```

The destination URL is included twice. This is because older browsers that do not support onClick will ignore the JavaScript code and interpret the line as a straight hyperlink. Remember to include the full URL (including http://) if you are linking to an external site.

The window_name variable gives the pop-up window a name. If you add another pop-up link further down the

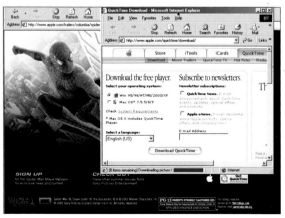

LEFT: Pop-up adverts, like print adverts are most effective when well-designed and carefully placed for a target audience.

LINKS

 Web page connections. Links are the essence of the interconnectivity of the Internet. Within one web site there will be several different kinds of links. These include:

Internal Links

These are the starting points to other pages on the same web site and are also known as local or page links. Crucial to linking is the anchor tag <A> which is wrapped around any text or graphic you want linked. To tell the browser what page to link to, add the HREF attribute with the address, or URL, of the page. This link is usually to a web page, but it could equally be a sound file or a video clip. For internal links this a relative URL, i.e. the page or file is on the same server as your site. Consequently you do not need the initial http:// but you do need to direct the browser to the directory where the document is, by giving the pathname. Each directory is separated by a forward slash. If the file is in the same directory you only need to give the filename. So to link from your homepage to a content page stored in the same directory would be:

<A HREF="products.html"> Product information</A>.
To a file in a different directory it would be:
<A HREF="gliders/accessories.html">Glider wheels</A>

External Links

These take the user to pages on a different web
site and are sometimes referred to as remote links.
To take advantage of these you need to provide the full
(absolute) URL including the initial http://. For example,
to link your site through to Amazon.com would be:
<A HREF="http://www.amazon.co.uk">Amazon</A>

Anchors

Typically these take a user to a particular section on a
web page. They are also good for jumping to a specific
point on another web page or for going back to the top of
a page with a single click. Linking is a two-part process.
First you need to give the anchor point (the point to
which you are jumping) a name and then you make
a link to it.

Imagemaps

This is a single graphic that has several hotspots or
links within it. Most web-authoring tools enable you
to generate the image map needed to set up the links
within the graphic.

Email Links

Instead of linking to a web page there are other useful
connections, such as the 'mailto' link. Click on this
and up pops a new email message, complete with the
specified address. e.g. <A HREF=mailto:yourname
@isp.com>Contact name</A>
➟ *Anchor, Graphical Links, Interactivity, Target*

LISTS

Ways to itemize information. Just as in any letter
or document, it can be clearer to structure
information on your web page in a list. There are basically
three types of list that can be defined within HTML:
ordered lists (also called numbered lists); unordered
(bulleted) lists; and definition lists (which itemize terms
and their definitions). An ordered list is good for a recipe,
where the sequence of items is important. A number is
automatically inserted before each
item. Equally usefully, the list will be automatically
renumbered if you delete or insert an item. An ordered
list is shown by the container tag <OL>…</OL> with
<LI> and the optional closing tag </LI> for each item.
You can also change the style of numbering to letters or
roman numerals using the
TYPE attribute.

With unordered lists (marked by the <UL>…</UL>
container tag) each list item <LI> has a bullet added
automatically. The default black dot bullet can again be
changed using the TYPE attribute.

With definition lists, items are displayed followed by
blocks of descriptive text, dictionary style. Consequently,
they are also known as dictionary lists. They are marked
with the container tag <DL>…</DL> while each term is
marked by <DT> tag (dictionary term) followed by
<DD> for dictionary definition. One type of list can also
be nested within any other list.
➟ *Bullets, Page Layout, Site Layout*

*LEFT: Points in a list are automatically numbered, but you can choose the style
of the numbers to suit your web site, for example roman numerals can be used.*

LOGO DESIGN

 A site's logo is the first thing most visitors will see on a homepage. As first impressions count, the logo has to be eye-catching, engaging, bold and clear. Most of all, it has to say something positive about the company or person who has created the site.

There are three basic elements that go into creating a good logo: shape, colour and typography. Web-graphics software supplies you with all the tools – apart from the inspiration – needed to create a stand-out logo.

Most modern web logos consist of a graphical motif and the company name. As photographic images are best avoided, the shape should be an abstract representation of what the site is all about. A bookshop might use a simple book motif, a communications company could opt for a series of concentric circles, while a site for music reviews

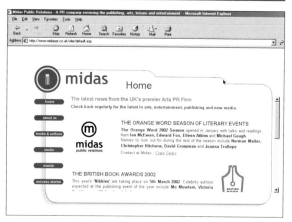

might use an angled ellipse to represent a CD. The motif could even be a play on an unusual company name.

Make the motif natural, as the eye will soon spot irregular dynamics. Any implied movement should be from left to right, and items should appear to rest on an invisible surface – the CD, for instance, should appear to 'sit' on its right-hand side, leaning back to the left. A second ellipse, acting as a shadow, can help emphasize this effect.

Colours should be kept simple and realistic. The CD's

'shadow', for instance, should be a darker shade of the colour of the main motif. Choose three or four complementary colours and tie these in with the overall theme of your site. Be natural with colours too – if your logo is a stylized tree, don't shade it blue unless you have good reason (if the company name is Bluetree, for instance).

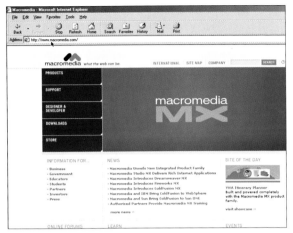

illustrations, Java applications and database-linked systems. Dreamweaver is the world's most popular professional web editor, and its Fireworks sibling provides the tools to let anyone create professional web graphics. FreeHand is the company's vector graphics program for web or high-end print work. The company has created a web standard with its Flash animation format. Flash Player comes bundled with all browsers, and Macromedia supplies the software to create the clips. While it is less widespread, Shockwave expands on Flash to create interactive presentations for the web, CD and DVD.

➥ *Dreamweaver (Macromedia), Fireworks (Macromedia), Flash (Macromedia), FreeHand (Macromedia), HomeSite (Macromedia)*

The final element of your logo should be the company's name. Indeed, this may be the only element if you opt for a stylized name or monogram, in which case the rules governing shape and colour still apply (the name would stand out more if placed inside an ellipse or square, for instance).

Use all upper or all lower case, and choose a font you like from your library. Don't use elaborate script or display fonts as they will lose their clarity once shrunk to button size. Place the name to the right or underneath the motif to conform to natural eye flow.

Finally, add some special effects. Drop shadows, highlights and gradients are common, but use sparingly as they could spoil a logo's simplicity and, when the logo is reduced, the effect will be lost altogether. Some characters lend themselves well to stylization – the dot on the 'i' is commonly tweaked by designers, for instance.

Rather than resizing the same image for use on banners or buttons, create different versions for different sizes. The difference could be as little as a slight change of colour to emphasis the motif or company name, or repositioning the name to the right of the image and making both elements the same height.

➥ *Branding and Identity, Eye Flow, Geometric Shapes, Graphic Design Package*

MACROMEDIA

Web creation software giant. Macromedia's range of web packages can take developers from creating simple graphics and single web pages to complex

MAILTO

Email link. While most links are to other web pages, or sound and video files, they can also be used to set up mail messages. Instead of the http protocol, the mailto protocol inside the anchor tag automatically opens a new email message, ready to send to a specified address, using the viewer's email client.

The browser does have to be configured to use this tag. Most are, but it will not work for all users. One way to ensure that no one misses out is to use the email address as the text for the link. As well as the address of the recipient of the email you can also automatically add the subject line or names in the cc or bcc field etc. However, these functions are only supported by more recent browsers, so are not universally accessible. For instance, <aHREF=mailto:yourname@isp.com?subject="Special%20Offer">Special Offer</A> would write Special offer in the subject line of an email addressed to Yourname. Note that spaces in the subject lines are written as %20 which is the space character in hexadecimal notation.

It is as well to bear in mind, however, that putting an email address on a web page is likely to attract spam (unsolicited email) as spammers use automated programs to search for email addresses to add to their lists.

➥ *HTML*

ABOVE FAR LEFT: A company or site logo is particularly important in web design; it must be simple yet eye-catching.

MAINTAINING A WEB SITE

Designing and publishing a web site is only the start of the work. Once a site is uploaded and has started pulling in readers, the work of keeping the site up-to-date and running smoothly really begins. An out-of-date web site full of broken links has little credibility and will soon start leaking visitors.

1. The instant nature of web publishing means that few web sites are truly up to date, as there is always new information to be added. The subject matter of some sites lends itself more to regular updates than other topics, but take a look at a rival site and try to update as often as they do.

2. If you have no new content to post on the site, make the most of your initial hard work and feature links to different permanent areas of the site from the front page. Many users may not have discovered those sections and a simple button will make it look as though you have added a new section.

3. All web sites are 'under construction', so avoid using the phrase and don't upload sections unless they are complete. If you think a site won't be updated very often, don't put a 'Last updated …' notice on the site. Instead, you can add a simple JavaScript that displays today's date automatically.

4. Check any external links at least once a month. Sites can be taken down or their URLs changed, and Not Found links look sloppy.

5. Run regular checks to ensure your own site is working properly and that all links and images are valid using a diagnostic tool like Web Site Garage's Tune Up (from http://websitegarage.netscape.com).

6. Get users' feedback about the site and respond with words and actions. Feedback could be through emails or contact forms, through surveys (available through sites like Sparklit.com) or through the site's own message board. Contribute to the board to help build and maintain the community and always respond to emails personally, and not with a computer-generated message.

7. Monitor the site logs using a free page counter from webstat.com, freewebcounter.net or GoStats.com. These will tell you a lot about how users read the site, and which pages are most popular. You can then prioritize sections to update ahead of others.

8. HTML is always evolving, so consider redesigning the site every 18–24 months, starting from scratch. Adapt older content to the new design and don't take the old site down for a day or two before relaunching.
➠ *Links, Maintaining Web Site Interest*

MAINTAINING WEB SITE INTEREST

Whether a site is created to promote a business or to share one's leisure interests with the world, webmasters like to see healthy visitor numbers. And whether those are in the hundreds or the millions, the site owner will want the figures to continue climbing. As well as creating interesting and diverting content, there is a lot

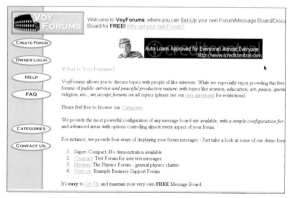

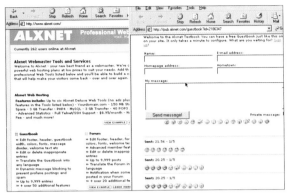

hosting the site. Voy.com (www.voy.com) and BeSeen (www.beseen.com) are good examples of free guestbooks.

Users will also return time and again to monitor topical polls. Sparklit (www.sparklit.com) and Alxnet (www.alxnet.com) offer free polls that can be incorporated into the design of any site, and again, packaged poll solutions are available for business sites.

Entertainment is another winning formula, and if you have the talent and the resources, basic games created in Flash or Shockwave can keep visitors coming back, especially if you can add a high-score leaderboard to keep the challenge going. Competition prizes – no matter how small – also draw users back.

Finally, spread the word about your site. Regular users will download and install branded screensavers and desktop wallpaper, and this might catch the eye of friends or office colleagues. Businesses should advertise their URL on all stationery, and have enough diverting content on the site to keep them coming back time and again.

➡ **Content, Maintaining a Web Site, Promoting a Web Site**

webmasters can do to keep visitors coming back.

Regular updates are vital. The Web has become the first port of call for users seeking the latest information and news, and your site will soon be overlooked if the most interesting thing on the front page is a legend reading 'Last updated January 1999'. This is even more important for corporate sites, where images of long-retired chief executives and outdated phone numbers will not only turn visitors away from your site, but will lose you business.

To make the most of any updates, why not shout about it by listing and linking to the newly updated areas on the front page. Visitors will not only be able to find the freshest content quickly, they will also be impressed by the topicality of the site and are more likely to return regularly.

You can take this a degree further by sending out daily or weekly updates to subscribers. List managers like Bcentral's at www.bcentral.com/services/lb and the MSN Communities service at http://communities.msn.com allow users to send their email addresses to a secure server. Webmasters can then send out an email to thousands of users at once announcing site updates and featuring links back to the site. The trick here, especially if you are running a news-based site, is not to send out entire stories, but teaser paragraphs that will tempt the subscribers back to the site.

Sometimes there may be no new content to upload, at which point why not let the readers add to the site's content themselves? A lot of web sites host chat forums and message boards which webmasters can customize to their own page design, and not worry about managing or

ABOVE: Competitions are a great way to maintain web site interest and the prizes don't necessarily have to be worth millions!

MARQUEE

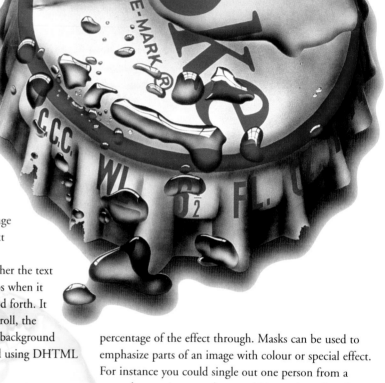

A marquee can refer either to a selection tool in a graphics editing program or to scrolling text on a web page. In graphics editing software, the marquee tool is the frame you drag over a bitmapped image to select the pixels on which you want to work. The marquee tool is usually rectangular, but can also be elliptical. The selection is usually shown by a moving dashed line, which is where the name comes from. The dashed lines look like the traditional flashing lights around a circus marquee.

On the Web, a marquee is a scrolling area of text, also sometimes referred to as a ticker-tape. The <Marquee> HTML tag was introduced in Version 2 of the Internet Explorer browser but has not been supported by Netscape. It is a shame as it is a useful tag. You can change a number of features of the scrolling text by adding attributes to the tag.

The Behavior attribute dictates whether the text scrolls from one side to another; or stops when it reaches one margin; or bounces back and forth. It is also possible to set the speed of the scroll, the number of times the text loops and the background colour. Scrolling text can also be created using DHTML and Java applets.

➠ *Dynamic Web Pages, HTML*

MASKS

Masks are a feature of most graphics design programs. They act like virtual masking tape, covering up areas of images so that you can apply dramatic effects to the unmasked areas.

Just like images in Photoshop or Fireworks, masks can be created or imported as vector or bitmap objects and are effectively greyscale graphics – black areas block part of the image, while white areas leave an area clear to work on. Like an acetate mask, the grey areas only let a

percentage of the effect through. Masks can be used to emphasize parts of an image with colour or special effect. For instance you could single out one person from a group by creating a mask around him and turning the rest of the image to greyscale.

If a pattern is applied to a mask, effects can be pasted over parts of an image. A textured effect, for instance, can be overlaid on every picture on a site and also on to the page's background to create a stylish site-wide theme. You could do the same with a company logo.

Macromedia's Flash uses animated masks. Arranged cleverly across an animation's layers, these could be used to create engaging effects, such as a searchlight that gradually reveals a page title.

➠ *Graphic Design Package, Image Manipulation*

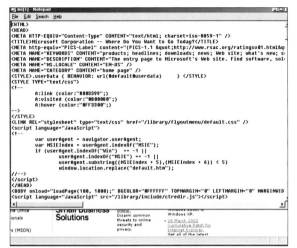

META TAG

Document information tag; a way of including information about a document and the content it contains that is particularly used by search engines to describe and categorize web pages. Meta tags, which must be nested inside the head of a web page, hold hidden information about the document. Invisible to the reader, this is picked up by servers, browsers or search engines and acted on.

There are two main types of tag, the Http-equiv and Name. Information provided by the Http-equiv generally affects the way your browser deals with a document. So it can be used to reload a page after a certain time delay (in which case it would be linked to information that is being updated by the server) or to redirect users to a different URL.

The Name attribute normally contains information about the content of the page, such as the author's name and details of the copyright as well as two tags – description and keyword – that are used by many search engines for categorizing and indexing documents.

Text put within the description tag describes the content of your web page. If the tag is recognized by the search engine the description will appear on the search results page. As some engines only display around 20 word descriptions you need to put the important information early on. With the keyword tag you can provide a comma-separated list of words to help search engines index your document.

➡ *Cross-Browser Compatibility, HTML, Promoting a Web Site, Search Engine*

MICROSOFT

Microsoft is without doubt the biggest desktop software company on Earth, and after a slow start in web software, its Internet Explorer is now the dominant browser, and the accompanying Outlook is the de facto standard email tool.

Microsoft also produces software to manage the servers that many web sites sit on, and the Windows operating systems are fully internet-enabled.

FrontPage, the company's web editor, uses the familiar Office interface to ease the user's path to creating web sites, and while it is something of a low-end package, comes with a comprehensive set of page templates and site-management tools. It also includes a graphics editor.

➡ *Internet Explorer*

FAR LEFT: Masks are used to give images special effects, for example a textured effect or the impression of water as shown on this bottle top.

MONITOR CALIBRATION

Colour differences between screens. Calibration differences mean that colours viewed on one monitor look different when viewed on another. The differences are not only from computer to computer, but also from platform to platform.

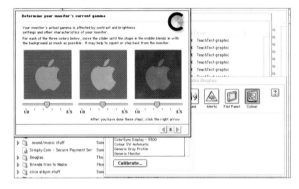

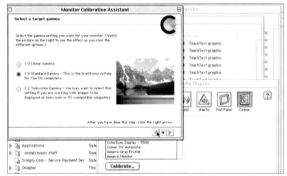

At the end of the day your web pages will be viewed on screen and even if everything else was perfectly compatible, colours on one monitor are going to look different to colours on another. Not only is it the type of monitor or video card that makes the difference, it is also the number of colours it supports, the resolution at which it is viewed, and the level of gamma correction (that is the overall brightness).

Even in design companies few monitors are calibrated accurately to one another with the result that shades of colour look drastically different on different machines. The differences are not only noticeable between the different platforms but also between individual PCs.

Particularly noticeable as a cross-platform issue is the gamma difference. Gamma levels control the brightness and contrast of your computer monitor, however they are set differently on the Mac to the PC or UNIX. As a result images generally appear darker on the Mac, while those taken from a PC appear washed out on a Mac.

➥ *Colour*

MULTIMEDIA

The Web is a potential multimedia paradise, as it can combine animation, sound, graphics and video as well as text. What holds it back are many of the issues that affect the design of web sites. There are no standard formats, there is mixed browser support for multimedia and with current bandwidth levels it takes a while to download sound and video files. However, there are technologies attempting to solve these problems. For example, most multimedia players, such as RealVideo or Windows Media Player, support streaming technologies where only part of a file needs to be downloaded before it starts playing. More fundamental are applications, such as Macromedia's Flash, that reduce the multimedia file size altogether. They use vector-based graphics animations that are constructed on the user's computer from a small segment of code. They do not need to be built up from a heavy bandwidth load of several graphics files. Flash is even used as an interactive interface for navigating a web site, but it does have the drawback that it needs a plug-in to play through the browser.

Adobe's LiveMotion can also produce Flash files, while Macromedia's Director, which was originally mainly used to produce presentations for CD-ROMs, can now produce highly-sophisticated multimedia movies on the Web.

➥ *Flash (Macromedia)*

NAMING CONVENTION

It is important when planning your site to take care over the naming of your files to ensure they conform to the naming conventions for your web server's operating system. Each operating system differs in the number of characters it allows in a filename, which characters can be used, and whether it is sensitive to uppercase and lowercase letters. For example, a UNIX server is sensitive to case – so a link to Image.gif is not the same as image.gif, while Windows and Mac-based servers are not. Similarly UNIX servers do not accept spaces in filenames, so links to my file.html will not work although they will on Windows and Mac servers. Servers are also sensitive to file extensions and the correct one has to be used or the server will not recognize the page.

To avoid any problems some people adopt the ISO (International Standards Organization) convention for file names of a maximum of eight letters, followed by a period and a three-letter extension. No spaces or special characters are allowed in names except for the underscore.

➠ *File Organization, Asset Management*

NAVIGATION

Moving round a web site. Site users need navigation tools to show them where they are, where they can go and how they can find their way back.

Just as anyone circumnavigating the globe needs directions, navigation on a web site provides the signposts to help you find your way around. It may be the site map, which gives an overview of all that is available, or it may be the navigation bar, buttons, and other links. The aims of a navigation system are to let users know where they are, where they can go, and how they can get back.

How we navigate the information available on a site will depend in part on how it is structured and organized (that is, its information design). This requires identifying the content available and giving it a shape. That can be a traditional hierarchical structure, starting with the homepage, where there is a choice of sections, from which in turn you can select further subsections, and so on. It could also be linear, like a company history where pages are viewed in a set order.

One of the complications of the Web is that all not all users start at the same place. If they are clicking a link from another site or a search engine they can enter your site at any point and not just the homepage. Consequently, every page needs to clearly identify the site and have the navigational elements to take users around the site. These elements should look like navigational tools, i.e. buttons should be labelled clearly to show what they are (Home, Products, Shop etc). It is also a good

TOP RIGHT: A web site navigation system should include a site map, showing the user where they are, where they can go and how they can get back.

idea to link to the homepage from every page on your site.

Similarly, there may be some pages that you will want to be able to access from anywhere – such as the search box, a help file, a mailto: link etc. Usually these will form part of the navigation bar. The nav bar will typically be at the top of the page and is often set in a frame so it is always available. It may also be along the side or bottom of a page.

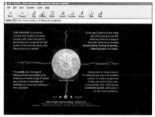

Instead of a nav bar some sites use navigational tabs for each section but these can get very cluttered for big sites (e.g. amazon.com). If there are a large number of links to fit into a nav bar then a drop down menu or a flyout menu save on screen space.

➠ *DHTML, Eye Flow, Interface, JavaScript, Page Layout, Rollover*

NETSCAPE NAVIGATOR AND COMMUNICATOR

The Netscape suite integrates the company's Navigator browser with its email, instant messaging, address book and web editing utilities. A set of third-party rich media players are also included.

As the browser, Navigator is the core of the collection, and lets you search for and view information across the Web. It supports all current standard HTML tags, as well as JavaScript and cascading style sheets. It is particularly strong on usability – its bookmark management lets users find pages based on their name, URL or other attributes, and the History palette files visited pages according to the day they were last visited.

Netscape lets you integrate your favourite search engine into Navigator and search directly from the URL bar. You can alter the program's appearance by selecting one of a range of themes which can be downloaded from the firm's own web site. Businesses can create their own branded themes.

Netscape's My Sidebar feature, which sits on the left-hand side of the screen, gives convenient access to important information. Netscape offers almost 600 tabs which can be added to the sidebar so that users can keep in touch with topics like the news, share prices and music, all supplied by content providers like CBS and CNN. Webmasters can use Netscape tools to create My Sidebar tabs for their own sites.

My Sidebar also integrates with the application's other utilities for seamless communications. The Buddy List from AOL's Instant Messenger (IM) is tabbed so you see whether colleagues or friends are online with one click. You can then exchange short messages with them in real time.

Netscape Mail gives access to multiple mail accounts, and on Windows PCs lets you send office documents without leaving the application. The Composer web editor does not hit the heights of professional tools, but is easy to use and supports all standard HTML tags. It also includes a basic image editor. Rich media is handled by the Nullsoft Winamp audio player, RealPlayer 8 for streaming media and the Macromedia Flash Player.

The Netscape suite is available from www.netscape.com/browsers, and you can also download the standalone Navigator browser without the email utility. This is advisable for designers who want to check the consistency of their designs across all browsers.

Netscape also offers a larger suite, Netscape Communicator, which includes all the components of the Netscape suite along with the enterprise-class Messenger email client, the Netscape Radio service, which broadcasts 10 channels of streaming music, and single-click access to the Shop@Netscape e-commerce channel.

➡ *Browser, Cross-Browser Compatibility, Internet Explorer (Microsoft)*

NON-LINEAR ANIMATION

Realistic and engaging animation techniques. Movement in the form of Flash of GIF animations can catch a web surfer's eye, but will not keep their

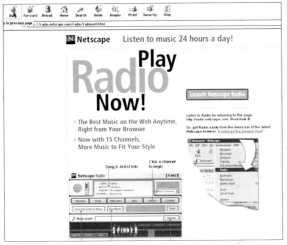

line at a constant speed. In reality, people accelerate and decelerate as they walk. When an animated object starts moving, let it pick up speed gradually and slow it down before stopping or turning. If you must include a linear, constant, straight-line motion in the middle, keep it as short as possible.

Linearity can be decreased by adding a third dimension to an animation. This needn't mean developing complex 3D graphics, just enlarging or reducing an object gradually to give the impression of it coming towards or moving away from the viewer. This can be combined with shading effects – lightening the sprite as it approaches, darkening as it moves away – to give the impression of it approaching a light source. Similarly, placing an exaggerated light source on a single area of an animation prevents linearity with a simple twist.

As well as adding a dose of reality, non-linearity also means surprising the viewer. Although they have been over-used online, morphing sequences still fascinate and amuse, and morphing utilities are available online. Flash itself offers a Shape Tweening control that slowly morphs one image into another.

➡ *Animated GIF, Animation Using Flash, Flash (Macromedia)*

attention for long if the motion within the animation is monotonous and linear. Real objects rarely move in an absolutely straight line with no regard for the laws of motion or gravity, so why should their animated equivalents? Adding such variation to sequences is termed 'non-linear' animation.

If a character in an animation – an aeroplane, for instance – moves from one side of the screen to the other in a straight line before bouncing back again, it isn't going to engage the viewer for more than a second or two. The most basic non-linear animation you could add is to run the character through a twisting, curving path.

Flash lets you create Bézier curves and run a sprite along the length of the curve with its Motion Guide Tweening feature. Realistically, the plane would also dip and rise as it followed its wavy path, and the Orient to Path Direction option does this by sending an object on its way 'nose first' over the path. Even if you must run an object over a straight line, try twisting it slightly back and forth as it moves for another non-linear, realistic touch.

Too often, objects in animations travel in a straight

ABOVE LEFT: An example of non-linear animation is an aeroplane moving from one side of the screen to the other. A simple animation such as this will add visual appeal to your web page.

NON-LINEAR DESIGN

There can be a tendency, particularly in table-based page design, to use sharp, positive delineation between areas of a web page – a big horizontal block for a header, a solid rectangular menu on the left and the main content area sliced up like a Neapolitan ice cream. While this may seem orderly, on a subconscious level it is far from engaging, and by adding non-linear elements like

curved lines and patterns you can eliminate the impression of an austere grid and draw the user in towards the more important parts of the site.

Rather than separating the header from the rest of the page with a sharp horizontal line, divide the elements using a slight wave using your graphic package's Bézier curve tool and apply a gentle drop shadow. This gives the impression of three-dimensional non-linearity by making it look as though the header is sitting slightly above the flat surface of the page.

The same effect works by dividing left-hand menu bars from the main content area with a vertical curve. You can combine the two using a framed effect, where the content area sits in a round-edged panel shadowed or bevelled to sit above or below a coloured frame which unites the header and the menu.

Curves can be used to guide the reader's eye towards the most important element of the page by using a deeper curve as a gentle but persuasive pointing device. In either case, contrast the colour of the menu or header with the page background for increased effectiveness.

Long swathes of paragraphs can seem unappealing to readers, but you can use non-linear elements to break up the page here too. Incorporate lightly shaded curves or ellipses into a page background, but keep them large so as not to create a distracting tiled effect.

➡ *Curvature Range and Bézier Curves, Geometric Shapes*

OPTIMIZING GRAPHICS

Getting the most out of online images. Images bring the Web to life, but if colourful logos and stunning photographs take a long time to download, a visitor might give up and browse another site instead. By using graphics properly and understanding the finer points of HTML, you can ensure your page downloads quickly and still looks good.

One of the most common mistakes which leads to overly large images is the use of the wrong image format. Your choice is largely between GIFs and JPEGs (though PNGs are starting to gain support across the Web). Use GIFs for the majority of your images, especially for small icons, little blocks of text, buttons and line drawings. That the JPEG format was created by the Joint

Photographic Experts Group suggests its best usage – for photographs and other detailed graphics where little of the image would be lost in compression.

If your program allows it, save GIFs as interlaced and JPEGs as progressive. That way they will load gradually from a low-resolution image to the final graphic, and not in the seemingly slower (but in fact just as fast) line-by-line manner. It is worth noting, however, that file sizes for interlaced files are usually larger than for non-interlaced images, and that some of the older browsers are unable to support progressive JPGs.

When editing images, crop in as tightly as you can to get rid of extraneous detail. This is common practice in print publishing, and on the Web it has the extra advantage of reducing file size. Make sure, too, that the resolution of every image is 72 dpi. This is the most common screen resolution, and saving at a higher resolution will only increase file size and not image quality.

When placing graphics on the web page, specify the width and height of each image. Some web-editing packages do this automatically, while others leave the relevant fields blank for you to fill in. When a browser loads the HTML page, it will then leave a space for the graphic and continue loading the rest of the page – and specifically the text – first. That way a visitor can get on with reading the page content while the image loads. Do not, however, use the width and height tags to shrink an image on-screen. As the source image is still the same, download times will be no quicker and the image itself may lose quality. Instead, reduce the file size in a graphics package. With very simple images though, it can be good practice to enlarge GIFs using the width and height tags. Three pixels of green, white

BELOW LEFT: Ensure that your web site has non-linear elements (curves and patterns) to avoid the impression of an austere grid.

and orange, for instance, weigh in at just a few bytes, but enlarged to 200 x 140 pixels produce a passable Irish flag.

Another good practice is to give each image a text alternative using the ALT= attribute of the IMAGE tag. The alternative text appears inside the graphic's placeholder frame until the image is loaded.

If you use large images such as photo galleries, create a page of thumbnails that link to the full-size images. FrontPage creates thumbnails automatically, and several graphics packages have batch conversion processes that will reduce a portfolio to thumbnails in seconds.

➠ *File Size, Graphic Design Package, Image Compression, Image Resolution, Thumbnails*

OVERLAYING IMAGES

Image manipulation. Sometimes you can achieve a dramatic effect by taking the subject from one photo and overlaying the image on to another. Such composite images can disguise your travels. Take a picture of the children in the living room and they can soon be standing in front of Ayer's rock without moving an inch. The key to doing it, using a photo editor such as Adobe's Photoshop, is the Extract command. This is a powerful tool that permanently removes pixels, so it is best to work on a copy of the layer you want rather than the original. With the edge highlighter select the brush size and draw along the edge of the area you want to extract (if smart highlighting is selected the highlighter will automatically follow the edge as you drag the tool). You can tidy up the extraction with the cleanup tool.

To combine the two images simply use the Move tool to drag and drop the new background on to the extracted image. To arrange the layers, go to the Layers palette and move the imported layer under the extracted layer. You can then use the normal tools to position the images, scale the background, or give it a softer look by blurring the image.

➠ *Graphic Design Package, Image Manipulation, Photoshop (Adobe)*

PAGE LAYOUT

Online design. Web page layout has come a long way from the early days when each element lined up left in the window, one under another. Today, it can be an immense multimedia experience that, at its best, can rival TV. And this evolution has taken place in a relatively short period of time.

HTML's table tags have added tools for creating grids that can align objects and include the designer's best friend – white space. The arrival of style sheets has meant that designers also have much fuller control over the look and feel of a page. Along the way some tags have been

lost – such as Netscape's <blink> for blinking text – but generally the designer has gained a lot more. For instance, table tags, originally designed to hold traditional statistical data, have been adapted; now they hold text, graphics, even other nested tables, and are a powerful way to break up a page both horizontally and vertically. Tables also provide a basic design grid similar to, although less flexible than, page layout programs like QuarkXPress.

Like tables, frames enable a designer to split the browser window into a number of different rows and columns. However, unlike tables, each frame can hold a separate HTML page, that can also be scrolled separately. Clicking in one frame can load a different page in another; this makes frames a natural structure for holding navigation controls. The navigation bar, whether at the top or side of the page, can be permanently on view in one frame. Clicking one of its links then loads a different page in a separate frame.

Stylesheets provide a centrally stored set of definitions for different layout attributes, such as text size, line spacing or indents. A single definition can be applied site-wide so changes can be done in one hit rather than being applied to each specific instance.

As a layout tool, CSS treats each element as an object, or box. So, rather like the table cell, you can add a background colour, borders, extra padding, etc. With CSS positioning, you can also tell the browser the exact place on screen that you want the 'box' placed. This can either be a pixel-precise co-ordinate (absolute) or relative to some other box or the top left of the browser (relative). It is this positioning that is at the heart of DHTML and can be used with JavaScript for animation and interactivity. However, browser support for DHTML is still variable.

➠ *Content, Eye Flow, HTML, Image Usage, Navigation, Readability*

PAGE LOADING TIME

Download time. The secret to minimizing page download time is controlling graphics. That does not mean avoiding them altogether, but carefully preparing them in the right format and using HTML controls to speed up their download.

Firstly, images are cached, so once downloaded they can be used again with little overhead. This can be useful for constructing navigation aids where just one element changes between pages. Reducing the number of colours in an image can also significantly reduce file size. You can also speed up download time making sure your images are in the right format – GIF for flat colour images and JPEG for photographs. Make sure that the HTML code contains the height and width of the image together with alternative text. That way users can check out whether they want to wait for the image to download or can click on a link to another page.

Similarly, you can save user time (and patience) by using interlaced GIFs or progressive JPEGs, where a rough version of the picture appears before it is fully downloaded. In the same way, a fast-loading low resolution version of a graphic can be used as a placeholder, while the higher resolution image loads.

➠ *Bandwidth, File Size*

LEFT: Overlaying several images can be a good way to achieve a dramatic effect or emphasize a point.

PAINT SHOP PRO (JASC)

Graphic design package. Jasc's Paint Shop Pro (PSP) is a photo-editing and drawing package for users who may not have the budget for something as complex as Adobe Photoshop but who want more than the limited hand-holding alternatives offered by sub-£50 packages.

Although it carries a low price tag of around £75, PSP shares many features with the more expensive rival. Images are created on transparent layers, and the program works with Photoshop-compatible plug-ins and filters, and has a wide range of special effects and filters of its own.

PSP has a good selection of textures and gradient fills, and its Picture Tube tool lets you paint with patterns. It also boasts special enhanced filters for cleaning up photos – tools like the red-eye remover will prove useful to webmasters whose sites feature regular photo galleries.

Web functionality comes in the shape of Animation Shop 3, which is bundled free with PSP. The utility features an image optimizer for JPEG, GIF and PNG files, and an image slicing tool that speeds up download times by cutting up large images.

Image maps are easier to create than with many more expensive packages, and rollover graphics can be exported along with the JavaScript that binds the sequence together.

➡ *Graphic Design Package, Image Enhancement Techniques*

PDF

Portable Document Format; document format system. PDF is a file format that enables documents to be presented just as they originally looked, regardless of what type of computer or platform they are viewed on. Because the document keeps its original formatting it is very popular with companies that want to put forward a consistent corporate brand across all their publications. It is also a natural for the Web, as it works cross-platform; consequently, most white papers, instruction manuals and other documents viewed or downloaded, whether on the Internet or the company intranet, are saved as PDF files (file extension .pdf).

In order to view a PDF file in your browser you need the special Adobe Acrobat reader free from

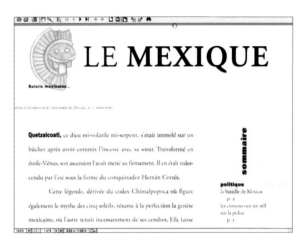

www.adobe.com. Within the viewer it is possible to navigate long documents through thumbnails, enlarge the view, print the pages or even add comments. The ease of navigation and consistent formatting makes it particularly popular for e-books, especially through new security features such as digital watermarks, which help designers, writers and publishers protect their copyright.

➡ *Acrobat (Adobe), File Type*

PERL

CGI scripting language. Not as flawless as its name suggests, Perl stands for Practical Extraction and Report Language. Because it is good at processing text it has become one of the most popular languages for writing CGI scripts, particularly on UNIX machines. It has the

advantage over CGI programs written in other languages, such as C or C++, in that it does not need to be compiled, which makes it easier to debug, modify and maintain.

While you would need programming experience to write a Perl script from scratch there are plenty of ready-made scripts available. They include scripts to help process forms and send their contents as emails. Many web-hosting companies have a set of standard scripts already installed that you can use simply by linking to them. Others allow you to upload your own. There are also archives on the Web, such as www.scriptsearch.com/perl.

Even so, it is important to follow any instructions that come with it. As Perl is an interpreted language, make sure there is a Perl interpreter installed on the server to enable the script to work. You will also need to know the exact pathname to the script.

➡ *Functionality, Script*

PHOTODISC (*www.photodisc.com*)

Photodisc is the main CD image collection section of Getty Images. Each CD has a theme: some are self-explanatory – such as Work, Men, Women and Teenagers; others are more abstract, including Momentum, Juxtapose, or Find Found which promises to unveil the 'newest trends in living, working, thinking and expressing'. If you prefer to see the images in print then catalogues are available, or there are low-cost CD versions which come with a thumbnail index.

The Photodisc collections house about 100 images per CD and cost around $400. The maximum file size is 48 MB, which is obviously not ideal for a homepage. To see which collection you want you can view thumbnails of each picture online. Clicking on the image shows

a bigger version, along with pricing information if you want to buy a single image for immediate download. The images are royalty free, they can be used for multiple projects, but cost is related to the size at which the picture is used. If you register you can access low resolution, non-watermarked copies of the picture to check out before you decide to buy.

If you don't register the photo has a 'gettyimages' watermark across the middle.

➡ *CorbisImages, GettyOne Images, Image Licensing, Stock Photo Suppliers*

RIGHT: An image from photodisc.com, a collection specializing in royalty free lifestyle images.

PHOTOGRAPHIC IMAGES

There are two main file formats for photographic images on the Web – GIF and JPEG. GIF is the format of choice for images that have only a few, mainly solid colours. You also need to use it if you want the web page background to show through transparent areas of the picture. However, a GIF can only save a maximum of 256 colours, which can radically alter the look of a photo with a range of subtle colours.

For a full-colour photo it is better to save the file as a JPEG. As a format this still reduces download time by compressing the image. It does so by a process of lossy compression – in which bits of the image data are thrown away – which can affect image quality if carried too far.

There is a third picture format emerging, called PNG, that combines the qualities of the other two. Like JPEG it supports millions of colours but still compresses files smaller than the GIF; however it is not yet widely supported.

➥ *File Size, JPEG, Image Usage, Raster*

PHOTOIMPACT (ULEAD)

Graphic design package. PhotoImpact is Ulead's image editing, vector creation and 3D drawing suite. Priced at around £50, it also offers a web editor, image optimization tools and utilities for creating dynamic rollovers, image maps and animations.

Ulead's digital image editor boasts a range of tools for photo enhancement and retouching, and can even correct distortion in scanned images. Photo sharing tools include an album management feature and a utility that converts image libraries into web-based presentations. Vector tools let you shade and contour text and wrap it round Bézier curves, and 3D graphics can be created in a matter of clicks using textures like plastic or glass.

PhotoImpact's WYSIWYG web editor requires no knowledge of HTML, and supports cascading style sheets and rich media like Flash and digital video. Dynamic rollovers and image maps can be created easily, and images can be optimized and exported in GIF, JPEG and PNG formats.

The program comes with a set of JavaScript elements, making it easy to create pop-up menus, distance rollovers and dynamic text effects. Animations are also catered for

with the inclusion of Ulead's GIF Animator. This creates animated GIFs and digital movies from Photoshop layers or your own compositions, optimizing them for fast download from the web.

➥ *Animation, Graphic Design Package*

PHOTOSHOP (ADOBE)

Image editing application. Adobe's Photoshop has been the high-end image-editing package of choice for designers for some 10 years, and though it carries a high-end price tag to match, it fully justifies this with a comprehensive collection of tools that include web-optimization software and vector-style drawing tools.

Photoshop's import and export filters can handle every common graphic format as well as plenty of obscure ones, including the native PSD format, which can be imported from its sister program, Illustrator.

The Photoshop interface consists of a toolbox and a collection of tabbed context-sensitive dialog boxes that control the attributes of each tool. Brush, airbrush and pencil tools are available to create new bitmap images, and editing tools like burn, smudge and sharpen can be applied to selected areas of imported or scanned images. As well as the usual brightness, contrast and colour adjusting filters, an ever-expanding range of art and special effects (warps, radial blurs and a new liquify command) can transform images into professional compositions for print or the web.

New vector tools mark a diversion for image-editing applications, and let Photoshop users create cleaner, crisp-edged shapes which are ideal for the web. More complex vector graphics can be imported from Illustrator.

All images are created as a series of layers, so that different elements of a composition can be edited

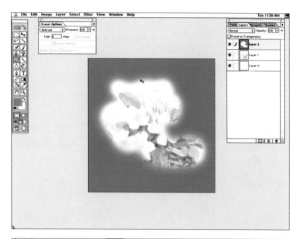

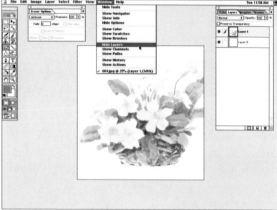

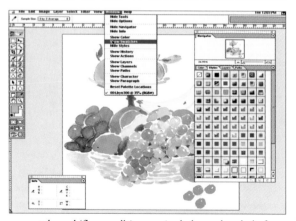

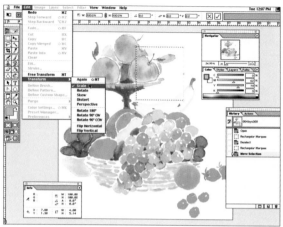

Photoshop's web graphic optimization tools come in the form of the integrated ImageReady utility, which is available in addition to Photoshop's own optimization facilities. ImageReady, which is not available separately, lets you preview images before exporting and assemble animations before fine-tuning the graphics.

Clicking a button at the foot of the Photoshop toolbar invokes ImageReady. In its simplest mode, you can preview images side-by-side, two or four samples at a time and experiment with settings, formats and palettes before committing to a final file.

ImageReady simplifies the creation of animated GIFs, and rollovers and image maps can be created and exported with automatically generated HTML and JavaScript code. Larger images can be sliced by the user or automatically along the lines of layered elements, and different optimization settings can be applied to the various slices.

All these creations can be previewed in a browser before saving in GIF, JPEG or PNG format, with ImageReady adding a panel displaying the image's dimensions, file size and palette and compression settings beneath.

➡ *Graphic Design Package, Image Compression, Optimization*

separately and 'flattened' into a single layer shortly before exporting to a publishable format. Text elements sit on separate layers, and paragraph styles can be applied to each block of text.

FAR LEFT: Adobe Photoshop features an ever-increasing range of art and special effects to help make your web site a masterpiece.

PIXEL

A single point on-screen, whose colour or brightness can be altered to reproduce an image or text. A pixel is the smallest element on screen that can be individually controlled. These pixels are arranged on a grid over the screen; each pixel (short for picture elements) on-screen is made up of a set of three individual dots (red, green and blue) which are combined to create a particular colour. Although the dots are separate they are close enough to appear as a single blended colour – or virtual pixel – to the human eye.

When you open an image, web page or program, the computer changes the colour and brightness of each pixel to reproduce the image or text etc. The amount of colours shown depends on the the the number of bits used to send information to each pixel. With a 1-bit monitor it is quite simple, the pixel is either off or on. When the colour depth (also known as pixel depth) is 8-bits, greater variety is possible. The pixel can handle 8 bits of information at once which gives 256 possible combinations. 24-bit monitors or images can display up to 16.7 million colours.

➟ *Bitmap, Image Resolution*

PLUG-IN

A mini-program that runs within the browser to add extra features, such as a multimedia player. Plug-ins take the idea of helper applications one stage further. Whereas a helper application is an external program, like the compression tool WinZip, that runs outside of the browser, plug-ins are better integrated. They run within the browser and extend the browser's capabilities, such as the Flash plug-in that runs the Flash-created animations used on some web pages. Similarly, the Adobe Acrobat plug-in lets you view PDF files in your browser, rather than having to download the files and launch a separate program to read them.

There are drawbacks with plug-ins. Users have to locate the plug-ins they need and install them, sometimes having to restart the PC before they operate. To compensate, later versions are self-installing and browsers now come with a set of plug-ins as standard. Most are geared towards multimedia players, such as Flash and Shockwave, QuickTime, RealVideo and RealAudio. Even so, updates are constantly emerging and it may be that although you have the plug-in, you still need to download a newer version to play the file. Design-wise plug-ins can easily be included on the web page using the <embed> tag, or the more favoured <object> tag.

➟ *Acrobat (Adobe), Browser*

PNG

Portable Network Graphic; graphics file format. Although not yet widely accepted, PNGs combine many of the best features of GIFs and JPEGs.

In many ways the PNG (pronounced 'ping') format combines most of the best features of its rivals GIF and JPEG. It was especially designed as an open standard for web graphics back in the mid-1990s, but despite its many attractive features the Portable Network Graphic (PNG) format has been slow to take off, largely because it is not widely supported by browsers. That said, most of the well-known graphics programs do allow you to save files in the PNG format.

Although, like JPEGs, PNG can support millions of colours it uses a lossless compression technique. Consequently, it will invariably create bigger files than

JPEG's lossy compression when used on the same image.

PNGs are more usually seen as a substitute for GIFs. The compression is better, resulting in smaller file sizes.

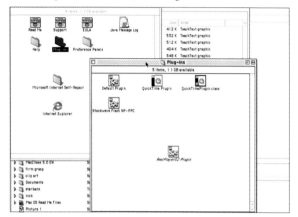

They support interlacing, and images will appear up to eight times faster than with traditional GIFs. This is because they fill in information in two dimensions (both rows and columns) as opposed to one with GIFs. They also allow for transparent backgrounds and it is even possible to vary the level of transparency for special transition effects.

➟ *File Type*

POP-UP

New window link. A Pop-up is a Graphical User Interface display area, usually a small window, that suddenlys up in the foreground of the visual interface. A pop-up window should be smaller than the background window or interface, otherwise it is a replacement interface.

While it is good to have links on your page if people follow them – particularly to external sites – they might not come back. One solution to this problem is to open a linked page in a new browser window that will pop-up (hence its name) on screen while your existing page remains underneath. Pop-ups are also useful for presenting extra information (such as terms and conditions, or product descriptions) that may not need an entire new page.

There are two ways to create a pop-up window: one uses HTML but has the drawback that you cannot control the size of the window; the other, more flexible

but also more complicated, is to use JavaScript. (Strictly speaking pop-up windows created by HTML are not pop-ups at all, but targets. True pop-ups are the ones controlled by Javascript.)

In HTML the way to create a pop-up window is to add the target attribute to the anchor tag. This opens a separate window to the one displaying the current document. You cannot alter the dimensions of the new window, but it is usually a similar size to the one already open.

If you set the Target to "_blank" clicking on the link will open a new window. If you use this on several links you could soon have enough windows to set up a double-glazing factory. The solution is to give the target window a name – such as "gallery" – which can be used as a target for each link. This way, each link will open in the same "gallery" window (e.g. <a href="http://www.msn.com" target="gallery">...</a>).

To go one step further and control the size of the pop-up window and other features, you need to use JavaScript. The script itself goes in the <head> of the document. It's enclosed in comment tags <– ... //–> so older browsers that don't support JavaScript will ignore it.

In the <body> of the page, before the URL of the link, there is a reference to the fact it is JavaScript and the function that's involved (here, that is the window.open( ) method).

Within the script itself you can specify the height and width of the window in pixels. By setting the values to either yes or no you can also switch on or off other features, such as whether the new window has a toolbar, status bar, or scrollbars, and whether the user can resize it. Several web-authoring tools will automatically generate the code for pop-up windows for you. Alternatively there are several free scripts available online that can be copied, and with a little customization, used on your own pages.

➟ *HTML, JavaScript, Launching New Browser Windows with HTML, Launching New Browser Windows with JavaScript*

ABOVE LEFT: The work of the pointillist artist George Seurat consists of thousands of dots which all combine to form an image. Images on a computer screen are created in the same way; the dots are called pixels.

PORTAL

Portals are information gateways to the Web. They also contain a wealth of material of their own that they hope will keep visitors on their site and make them want to return.

As gateways to the riches of the Internet, portals provide their own wealth of services and information. They are not always, although they may be, the web site for the service provider you use to connect to the Web. Although they are your jumping-off point to the web, portals have a range of services of their own that they hope will improve their 'stickiness' and keep you on their site. Typically, the content will cover news channels, shopping, relationships, health, etc., along with email, chat and discussion groups.

Generally, there are three types of portal: the big search engines and directory lists, like Yahoo! and AltaVista; more general commercial gateways like MSN and AOL, which provide a lot of branded material as well as messaging services and forums; and specialist portals, like www.theitportal.com which concentrates on the IT industry. Gateways like this which focus on one specific industry are also known as Vortals, or Vertical Industry Portals.

PRESENTING A CV ON THE WEB

As more and more recruitment is done online, it is increasingly important for potential employers to be able to access your CV on the Web. Many designers, whether freelance or employed, have an online portfolio of their work to showcase their skills. Often the About Me page is a CV, highlighting what work experience they have.

One of the great advantages of putting your CV on the Web is that it can be easily updated whenever there is something significant to add. It can also reflect your personality and style, in ways a standard CV never can. Some CVs are set out like FAQs, listing everything from the designer's favourite drink to their regular bedtime; others are more like web-logs, detailing current passions, while standard CVs concentrate on work-based achievements and skills. This example focuses on putting a traditional CV online.

Before you start, it is best to get the content up to

scratch. As it reflects your professionalism, you want something that is smart, snappy and intriguing enough to make employers want to find out more about you. Generally recruitment consultants advise that your CV should:

• Start with a 30-word summary that sums you up and is your personal 'mission statement'.
• Have a clear and uncluttered layout.
• Be chronological – that is set out your employment starting with your current job and working back to previous ones. It should also begin with your employment and go into other details, such as education, technology skills, contact information, etc.
• Use active words rather than passive ones, avoid jargon, be concise and be free of spelling and
• grammatical mistakes.

Simply putting the text on a web page and uploading it to your site is not going to leave much of an impression. Here we are going to set up a three-column table to bring some contrast to the layout and to break up the information into easily read chunks. (For the purpose of this exercise, we're assuming that this page is just one of several on the web site and will have all the standard navigation features.)

The left-hand column will contain the main CV information, while the right-hand column will hold related information – such as thumbnails of some of the sites worked on, or a list of publications where your work has appeared, etc. The middle column uses a spacer GIF to create some white space between the two other columns (act like a gutter). The spacer GIF gets around the problem that tables adjust their width and height according to the longest object in the row or column and is a 1 pixel by 1 pixel image whch is either transparent, or has the same background colour as the table. Using the width attribute this can then be resized to the dimension you want and will keep the table from collapsing in on itself (e.g. <IMG SRC="spacer.gif" width="17" height="1">).

In the left-hand table we nest a new two-column table, with cellpadding set to 5 so that the text does not go up to the edge of the table. For our 'mission statement' box, we want to span both columns so use the attribute colspan="2" within the <td> tag. Set out your statement and format the text as desired.

Insert a new table row <tr> and table cell with a non-breaking space to create some white space before the main heading e.g:
<tr>
<td colspan="2">&nbs;</td>
</tr>
Insert a new row and cell for the heading Experience and change the background colour (using the bgcolor attribute) to give it some impact. Under this heading we want the left-hand column to show the dates we held a particular job and then the right-hand box to give details of the company and the position we held, e.g:
<tr>
<td width="18%" valign="top" bgcolor="#CCCCCC"

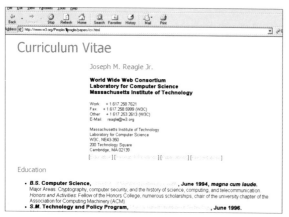

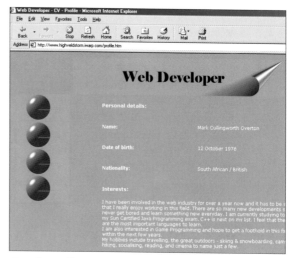

class="cvtext">2002-present</td>
<td width="82%" class="cvtext" bgcolor="FFFFCC">
Designer, Bloggs and Co…etc…</td>
</tr>

Again, the columns are differentiated by having different background colours, but they are light enough to ensure the text is legible. Here cascading style sheets are used to apply the text formatting.

There are a number of ways the content can be emphasized, besides the headings themselves. To enable employers to scan read your achievements in each job it is best to set them out as bullet points. Using the <UL>…</UL> container tag for unordered lists the bullets are added automatically for each list item, marked with the <LI> tag. You can change the default bullet type to a circle <UL TYPE="circle"> or a square <UL TYPE="square"> or can create your own icons. Company names or the titles of jobs you held can be highlighted in one colour and the URLs of web sites you have been involved with can be marked in another.

While this is a fairly simple table design, the possibilities online are virtually endless. You can set up the CV as an image map that takes you to different pages for each section; or include disjointed rollovers, so that high-lighting a URL swaps the image on view, or use Flash to create animated timelines.

➡ **Bullets, Content, Eye Flow, Readability, Site Layout, Uploading a Web Site**

PROGRESSIVE RENDERING
AND INTERLACING

Having to wait for a large image to download completely, especially over a dial-up connection, can test readers' patience and may even cause them to leave your site. If you use very large images, perhaps as online photo galleries or graphic design portfolios, you can give the impression that a picture is downloading faster by using progressive rendering or interlacing techniques.

When regular JPEGs, GIFs or PNGs load into a web page, they do so line-by-line, filling up the allocated space gradually from top to bottom. When they are saved as interlaced or progressive graphics, the image appears almost immediately, but in a low, blocky resolution. As more of the image is downloaded, the resolution improves until the file is complete. This gradual display makes the image recognizable from the beginning, and keeps the reader's attention as the 'focus' improves, rather than tempting them into quitting the site.

All three major web image formats can be rendered progressively using good graphics software like Fireworks and Photoshop. You should be able to set GIF files to Interlaced during the export process of most graphics packages, while options to set JPEGs and PNGs to Progressive are rarer outside the leading programs.

➡ *File Size, Image Compression, Page Loading Time*

PROMOTING A WEB SITE

Marketing your pages. The most expensive way to promote your site is through advertising, but there are cheaper ways to encourage others to visit your site, such as by trading links and ensuring your site is picked up by search engines.

However bizarre, fantastic or sensational your site, it still has to compete for attention with millions of others. Advertising your URL, online as well as off is effective, but you need deep pockets to make it work for you. For most on the Web, it is more cost-effective to promote yourself through association. The majority of people will arrive at your site either by following a link from another site or as the result of a search. To increase the chances of them getting through it's best to set up reciprocal links with as many relevant sites as possible. You can do this by joining a web circle/web ring (where sites on similar

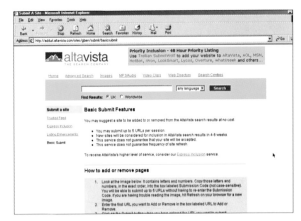

topics link to each other) or by contacting individual sites that cover similar areas and trading links.

To see what sites are linked to yours go to AltaVista (www.altavista.com) and in the Search box enter link: followed by yourdomain.com (e.g. link:amazon.co.uk). Up comes a list of pages that have links to the URL you entered.

You should also promote your web site online and off. The web address should be printed on all office stationery and used in any brochures, ads or promotions you run; when sending email it should have your website details, particularly if you are posting to newsgroups; if you have something newsworthy it is also worth trying for a mention in local magazines, newspapers or newsletters.

For your site to be picked up in a search, it is important to be registered with as many of the top engines as possible. If you don't want the bother of submitting your URL to lots of individual search tools there are a number of Web services that will do it for you (for a fee).

If your site operates in a specialist area it is worth registering with one of the specialized search engines that may cover that topic. To see if there is one go to: www.search.com, which covers more than 800 special interest search engines around the Web.

Search engines operate in different ways, but many use spiders that find pages and then index the content from the information in the keywords and phrases inserted as meta tags at the head of each HTML page.

➠ *Banner, Meta Tag, Search Engine*

PROPORTIONING PRINCIPLES

Because screen real estate is at a premium, graphics and illustrations on the Web will naturally be smaller than they are in print publications. But while this lack of detail may disappoint designers, how these graphics are used in relation to each other and to other elements of a web page carries much more importance.

By combining smaller and larger elements on the same page, a clear relationship is created between the items. The user's eye is naturally drawn to a larger element and correctly perceives it to be the more important. This means that the space taken up by more important stories should be larger than for others, and that image-based links to the latest features should be larger than less important links.

Bearing this in mind, do not use a large graphic simply for illustration. It is a waste of screen space and, given the conventions of the Web, a reader may spend time wiping

their cursor over it looking for the phantom link. Instead, consider using the image as a background, although make sure it contrasts suitably with the text or other foreground elements. One solution could be to use the large image as a washed out background with the smaller image in front. This is often used to create eye-catching visual effects in banner advertising.

➠ *Eye Flow, Distortion Techniques, Illustration, Image Use*

ABOVE: *Screen real estate is in high demand and is therefore expensive.*

RASTER

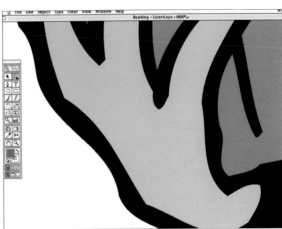

Graphics format; pixel-based images that are used on the Web in the form of GIFs or JPEGs. The raster is the area of the monitor that is used to display images; as such it is slightly smaller than the size of the screen itself. Its size also alters with the resolution set by the computer's video adapter. So a resolution of 800 x 600 on a 15-in monitor has a different raster to 1,024 x 768. Fortunately, most monitors are auto-sizing and calculate all this for themselves.

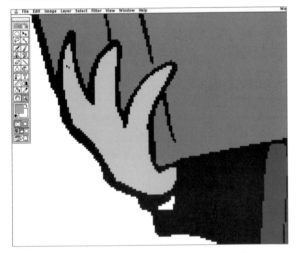

Raster graphics are pixel-based. They are also known as bitmaps. With bitmapped images, the picture is made up of thousands or millions of small dots, or pixels, like a mosaic. Each image pixel has data that describes the colour and brightness of that particular area of the picture. To show this on screen the computer reads the image data and maps this to the screen pixels. As these files contain information about each pixel in the image, raster file sizes are much larger than vector graphics, where the lines and filled areas are all described by geometric formulas.

In general vector graphics are created by drawing programs, like Illustrator or Freehand, while raster graphics are produced by Paint applications, such as Photoshop or Paint Shop Pro. With these raster programs you can edit the individual pixels, or change them as a group to create special effects such as a drop shadow or blurred edge. However, unlike vector graphics – where changes can be effected simply by adjusting the formula –

bitmapped images cannot be resized significantly without looking blurred and pixelated.

There are several file formats for raster graphics, such as .bmp which is the standard uncompressed format for image files in Windows. The two main formats specifically used for the Web are GIF and JPEG. A third, PNG, combines the best of both, but is only supported by later version browsers, so is not yet widely used. All three use compression to reduce the file size and enable images to be downloaded more quickly.

GIF is still the main format for online graphics, particularly where images are made up of a few solid blocks of colour. For pictures where there are lots of different shades and colours it is best to use JPEG, which can support 24-bit color (that is some 16.7 million colours) against the 8-bit (256 colours) support offered by GIFs. However they start, all images on the Web usually end up as bitmaps. Most drawing programs, like Illustrator and Freehand, now include their own tools to rasterize illustrations, that is convert them to bitmaps.

➡ *Bitmap, GIF, Image Resolution, JPEG, Pixel, TIFF*

READABILITY

You can create the best-looking pages on the Web, but if the text content is poor quality, the result could be a visitor-losing embarrassment to your company and yourself. There are several points to remember.

1. As designers have mastered the standard HTML language, the standards of the English language appear to

have gone out the window, and the kind of errors that would never reach a printing press are commonplace on the Web. In fact, checking spelling and grammar is as important as checking valid hyperlinks and image

references. Always create content in a word processor and get someone else to proofread it before publication.

2. Keep text blocks narrow. Long lines of text are difficult to read and each line should include no more than 12 words. Use a fixed-width design to keep the width of paragraphs to 400 pixels at most.

3. Long paragraphs are a turn-off, and six lines is a realistic maximum. HTML paragraphing inserts line breaks to add white space to a page, and this spacing can

be increased – and readability enhanced – by using bold or coloured cross-heads every few paragraphs.

4. Don't use too many typefaces on a page. Use one font for paragraph text and one for headings. Research shows that large blocks of text are easier to read if set in a serif face like Times; sans-serif faces like Helvetica or Arial are suited to smaller chunks of text like headlines or captions, although they are often favoured for body text.

5. Setting the wrong paragraph alignment can render text difficult to follow. Left-aligned text is the only option for paragraphs as it gives the reader a constant starting point when they return to the start of the next line. Centred text is fine for single lines like headlines, while right-aligned text works if it is anchored to a sharp-edge such as when used for a picture caption or section header.

6. Make sure the text contrasts with the background. Black on white is best for paragraphs, and if you must use light text on dark colour, embolden the text to make it more readable.

7. When creating text as a graphic for small buttons or section headers, switch off anti-aliasing in your graphics package as smaller blocks of text can blur to the point of illegibility when it is applied. For larger blocks of image-based text, use anti-aliasing to avoid it becoming blocky and equally unreadable.

➽ *Content, Font, Type*

RESIZING IMAGES

Image manipulation techniques. The smaller an image, the fewer the pixels and the quicker it will download. This advantage comes at a price, though: the fewer the pixels the less detail shown in the picture. Trying to get the balance right, between an interesting graphic and a file size that's small enough to be downloaded in a reasonable time, is a constant battle for the designer.

Some software programs help take the strain. In Macromedia Fireworks, for example, you can specify the ideal file size for an image, and the program creates the best possible graphic, automatically selecting the most suitable file format. More typically, however, it is the designer who will be resizing the image. There are basically two ways to resize an image: by changing the resolution, which alters the number of pixels per inch; or to add or remove the total number of pixels. Normally, you can resize the image by selecting a new measurement in pixels, by specifying a percentage increase or decrease from the original, or by entering the actual/print size, which also enables you to alter the resolution.

Simply altering the resolution without resampling the image doesn't lose any data. The same data is used so that either fewer or more pixels fit into a given space.

If you downsample an image, i.e. take away pixels to make the image smaller, then quality will be affected because you are losing data to resize the image. This is particularly obvious if you drastically resize a graphic, from a postcard-sized image to a thumbnail, for example. The image will become very blurred. If you do have to do it, it is best to do it in a number of steps, checking the quality at each stage.

If you are resampling the picture to make it bigger, quality is also affected because you are adding pixels. Different techniques are used to try and match these to the original picture, but with varying success. Generally, it is advisable not to upsize low resolution images. However you alter the size of the image the quality can be improved by using the Sharpen filter after resizing.

The resize command in most picture editors is different to changing the canvas size. Canvas size alters the dimensions of an image by adding or taking away pixels around the edge of an image, while the resize command pushes the whole image into a larger or smaller area.

➡ *Graphic Design Package, Image Manipulation, Image Resolution, Retouching Images*

RESPONSE-O-MATIC
(www.response-o-matic.com)

Online form-processing services like Response-O-Matic enable you to add interactive forms to your site without doing any programming.

Despite the vintage look to the site, Response-O-Matic is offering a service that's as modern as any. It lets you add feedback forms to your site without having to do any programming in Perl, Java or something equally complex. The basic forms for your site are designed in HTML. The questions can be what you like and the forms can use any combination you wish of check boxes, radio buttons and

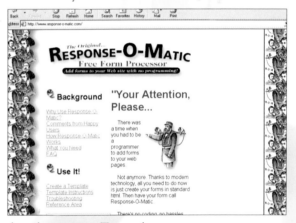

drop down menus. To ease the process you can create a form template, using the Form Wizard, and then just modify the questions to the ones you want.

When the visitor fills in the form and clicks on the submit button the information is sent to Response-O-Matic for processing (rather than having to go to a special program on your own server that you would have to set up). A 'Thank You' page is displayed for the visitor who has filled in the form together with the details they entered. At the same time the information from the form is emailed to you. It can be formatted in such a way that it can be cut-and-pasted into a spreadsheet or database program.

➡ *Feedback Form, Free Web Extras*

RETOUCHING IMAGES

Selective image correction. If an entire image requires enhancement, tweaking the brightness, contrast, tone and colour balance can transform its appearance, but such global correction will not clear up blemishes such as dust, hair or cracks, or enliven faded areas. Instead, you can use the selection of tools provided by graphics editing packages to touch up as much, or as little, of the image as you like.

These tools are effectively a combination of distortion filters and brush tools, letting the user edit areas of photos by freehand rather than by applying marquees and masks. Some even share the same names – the blur and sharpen tools, for instance, are fairly self-explanatory, the former blurring the area you paint, the latter increasing the contrast of the selected areas.

You may also come across the smudge tool, which blends pixels as you drag the cursor, simulating the action of dragging a finger through wet paint. Smudge is rarely used for image correction, however, and should be used sparingly even when distorting images.

Some tools have inherited their names and their actions from traditional darkroom photography, but are easy to understand. Dodge lightens the pixels of the area you paint, burn darkens pixels, while the sponge tool changes the saturation of a selected area. Dodge and burn can be set to edit the highlights, midtones and shadows of a selected part of an image, which will bring out the details if an image is too dark or too light. You can also set the exposure levels of these tools, which, unless you want to create the impression of dramatic over-exposure, should always be below 20 per cent. The sponge tool can be set to saturate or desaturate faded or excessively vivid areas of an image.

Small scratches can be hidden using the blur tool, but larger blemishes might call for the rubber stamp, a cloning tool applied by first clicking on the area you want to copy, and then painting where you want the image duplicated. While this tool can be used to create dramatic effects – adding an extra eye to someone's forehead, for instance – it is best used for small areas when retouching, as large sweeps of copied pixels will tend to show up dramatically.

Some photo-specific graphics packages include tools like red-eye reduction and scratch removal filters, which are easy to use and can correct common problems quickly and easily.

➡ *Distortion Techniques, Graphic Design Package, Image Enhancement Techniques, Photography, Scanning*

ABOVE: There are various editing tools available that can be used to retouch or correct an image. The blur and sharpen tools can be used to great effect, as shown here.

RGB

Red, Green, Blue. As these are the three base colours from which all others are created on a monitor, they are also the basis for specifying colours on the Web. For each pixel on-screen, computers create the

colours you see by combining three coloured lights: red, green and blue. The amount of light in each colour channel is given a value from 0 (weakest) to 255 (full intensity). When the three channels are all at the most intense you have white. Any colour seen on screen can be described by these three values. So a medium blue colour

could be made up of R:128 G:128 B:255. In most image-editing programs you can find out the RGB value of any colour by hovering the eye dropper tool over it.

On a web page, though, the RGB colours are shown by their hexadecimal value, with a base-16 numbering system using 0-9 and A-F (to represent 10-15) instead of the more usual decimal system. To have a background colour on a Web page we insert the tag <bgcolor="#RRGGBB"> in the HTML, where RR is the Red value in hexadecimal, GG the green value etc. For the medium blue colour that would represent <bgcolor="#8080FF">.

➠ *Colour, Dithering, Hex Code, Pixel, Web Palette*

ROLLOVERS

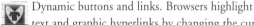

Dynamic buttons and links. Browsers highlight text and graphic hyperlinks by changing the cursor from a conventional pointer to a hand symbol, but if you want links and buttons to be absolutely clear to readers, visual triggers are key, and changing the state of a graphical or text hyperlink is simple and effective.

Cascading style sheets (CSS) offer an easy way of highlighting text hyperlinks. Each CSS style you create has a property called 'hover', which is activated when the user places a cursor over a link.

Alongside the definition of a style (at the top of an HTML page or in a separate .css file), add a property called A.stylename:hover (where stylename is the name of the style in question). Then specify the character traits you want changed when the cursor hovers. For instance, if you wanted text in the stylename to become red and lose its underline when the cursor appears, add A.stylename:hover {color: red; text-decoration: none} to your stylesheet.

A common mistake when using this method is to change the size of or embolden the link. Avoid this, as the transitory increase in size will effect the positioning of all the text in the same line or paragraph as the link.

While CSS hover-based rollovers are simple to set up, graphical rollovers are far more effective. Although there are Java rollover applets available, these can take a while to load, and small JavaScript can do the same job much more quickly.

There are three main types of rollover: button rollovers, where an image changes as the cursor hovers over it; distance rollovers, where a remote image changes as you hover over a series of buttons; and one-to-many rollovers, a combination of the two. Button rollovers are the most common, and are usually used for menu items and hyperlinks. Distance and one-to-many rollovers are widely used on homepages, where the user might hover over a menu item and see a written explanation of that section of the site elsewhere on-screen.

The leading web graphics packages come with utilities to help create rollovers, and Fireworks even has preset bevel effects, changing the edges and shade of your original button so that it looks as though it is physically raised, inset or inverted. All should export the relevant section of HTML and JavaScript as well as the set of graphics required.

JavaScript uses the onMouse controls to change the image, and as onMouse has four states, so you could include four button states. OnMouseOver controls the state of the button when the cursor hovers over it, while OnMouseOut is usually used to revert back to the default button when the cursor moves away. OnMouseDown changes the button state if the mouse is clicked on a button, while onMouseUp specifies the image that remains after the mouse button is lifted.

These controls can be incorporated into a regular A HREF hyperlink tag, and the default image is also given a NAME attribute referred to by the onMouse

controls, as in this HTML code (note that different utilities create rollover code differently. This is one of the simplest examples):

```
<A HREF="destination_page.html"
onMouseOver="{button.src='highlighted.gif'; return
true}"
onMouseOut=" {button.src='default.gif'; return true}">
onMouseDown=" {button.src='clicked.gif'; return true}">
onMouseUp=" {button.src='default.gif'; return true}">
<IMG SRC="default.gif" BORDER="0"
NAME="button"></A>
```

Rollovers effectively represent several images loading in the place of one, so keep file sizes small and avoid animated GIFs or the effect will be lost. If a distance rollover requires a small section of a larger image to change, use a good graphics package to split the image up into manageable chunks before starting work on the rollover process itself.

➡ *Fireworks (Macromedia), JavaScript, Navigation*

TOP LEFT: *The RGB value of any colour is determined by the combination of the three coloured lights: Red, Green and Blue.*

ROTATION

Rotating an image can not only tidy up a scanned picture it can also offer a different perspective on the world. Rather than look at an image square on, it can take on a different perspective by rotating it a few degrees. With most photo editors there are several ways of achieving this. The first is to select the object and use the rotate handle to turn the image to the position you want.

Alternatively, you may be able to select a custom rotate dialog box where you can enter any angle you want to rotate the image by. Most photo editors also have a number of preset angles (e.g. 90 left, 90 right, 180) that you can apply. Equally, you can flip the image around its horizontal or vertical axis.

Sometimes rather than rotate the image, it is easier to rotate the canvas it lies on. Many of the same features you can apply to the image itself can be used on the background canvas. For example, you can rotate the canvas through a set number of degrees, etc. Occasionally, particularly if the image has been scanned in, the original photo may be slightly skewed. Some programs will automatically straighten the image and even crop off any white space around it.

➡ *Graphic Design Package, Image Manipulation*

SAVING IMAGES FROM THE WEB

Sometimes there may be a striking image on a web page that you want to save to your hard drive – as long as it is not copyright-protected of course. Downloading such images is best done through the browser, but remember that the technique is slightly different depending on which type of browser you have and the platform on which you are using it.

On a PC, using Internet Explorer, right-click the image, select the 'Save picture as' option and select the folder where you want to save it. The right click gives other options if you want to save the picture as a background or email to a friend. If using Netscape Navigator on the PC right click the graphic and select 'Save image'.

On a Macintosh using Internet Explorer, click and hold the mouse button over the image and select 'Download image to disk' from the pop-up menu. For Netscape, hold down the mouse button and select 'Copy image' when the menu appears. Similar methods are

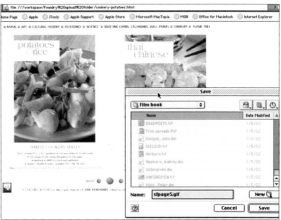

needed for downloading free images and clip art, although some graphics sites save storage space by compressing the images and saving them as zip files.

➡ *Clip Art, File Type, Stock Photo Suppliers*

SCANNING IMAGES

There are plenty of ways to acquire images. There is an abundance of graphics available on the Web, and the increasing use of digital cameras makes it easy to capture the picture you want. Even so, there are still times when you will have to scan something in – whether it's flat art or a three-dimensional object.

It is best to roughly size an image you are using to the dimensions it will take up on the web page. Remember that on the Web you need only one image pixel for each screen pixel. So, a graphic that is 200 x 150 pixels will take up roughly a quarter of the screen if the monitor resolution is 800 x 600.

At the end of the day the final resolution of the image will be 72 dpi. If you don't plan to do any work on the image then it is easiest just to scan at that resolution. However, if the image needs retouching or changing in some way, it is best to scan it in at a higher resolution – somewhere between 100 and 150 dpi – so you have more pixels to play with. If you scan at much higher resolutions you can use an image-editing program to remove the extra pixels, but image quality will suffer. If you do need a higher resolution scan for a print version of the same image it is as well to do two different scans. If your scanner has a menu of fixed resolutions, chose one of those. If you can select your own, go for 144 dpi, which is double the resolution of the final graphic.

If you are going to work on a black-and-white image it is better to scan it in greyscale (8-bit mode) rather than as the simple 2-bit black-and-white. This way you get a wider range of tones which can be altered before converting the image back to black-and-white as the final step.

Although the images will eventually be saved as GIFs or JPEGs it is best to save the scanned files in the TIFF file format, which was originally developed by scanner manufacturers and is very colour-accurate.

When scanning an image from a printed page, the dot pattern created as part of the printing process will show through. To remove this, apply a slight blur to the image, make it slightly smaller and then apply a sharpening filter.

➠ *Clip Enhancement Techniques, Image Resolution*

ABOVE: When scanning a black and white image, it is best to scan it as a greyscale (8-bit mode).

SCREEN RESOLUTION

The screen resolution is the total number of pixels available. This will depend not only on the physical size of the monitor (15-in, 19-in etc.), but also on the capabilities of the video card which is driving it. For instance on a 17-in monitor you could have several settings ranging from 800 x 600 (800 dots, or pixels, on each of 600 lines) to 1,280 x 1,024. As you increase the number of pixels, the pixels will get smaller as you are packing more into the same available space. This means that your images and other on-screen elements will appear smaller. As a result more can be seen on the screen.

To cope with the different screen resolutions, web browsers effectively ignore it. In a browser, one image pixel equals one screen pixel. If your graphic is 300 pixels wide and 200 pixels tall it is displayed on exactly the same number of pixels on-screen. So, if the screen resolution is set higher that number of pixels will take up a smaller area and the picture will appear smaller. The converse is true if the resolution is set lower.

Consequently, in designing elements of your web page you will not know exactly how big or small they will be viewed by your visitors, but you will see how they measure up in proportion to each other.

➡ *Designing for Different Resolutions,*
Proportioning Principles

SCRIPT

The distinction between programs and scripts is increasingly blurred. They both issue commands to tell the server (or browser) what to do. However, traditional programs are written in a heavyweight programming language like C++, Java or Visual Basic, while scripts are written in the more specialized scripting languages such as Perl or JavaScript. The scripts are run line by line through a script 'interpreter', which actions the commands. By contrast, programs, which tend to be more complex, have to be compiled into machine code which can be handled directly by the computer's processor. Scripting languages also tend to be more focused on the area in which they are used. So, for example with JavaScript, which is purely designed for use on the Web, instructions centre on refining what the browser does, checking for plug-ins, browser versions etc.

As they are usually designed for a specific task, scripting languages are fairly easy to understand, even for complete novices. There are also many ready-made scripts freely available to download from the Web at sites like www.scriptsearch.com. These cover both client-side scripting, such as JavaScript and Server-side scripts like Perl and CGI.

➡ *Applet, CGI, JavaScript, Perl*

SEARCH ENGINES

Information search tool; programs that search the Web for pages that correspond to the keywords or phrases requested. Although there are hundreds – if not thousands – of search engines on the Web, there are only a few key sites that are used for the majority of searches; these include Alta Vista, Yahoo, Google, AlltheWeb, AskJeeves and MSN. Typing in a keyword or phrase will return a list of sites, along with a brief description, a link and, in some search engines, a rating of how likely it is to match the information requested. If you want your site to be noticed, therefore, it is important you register your site

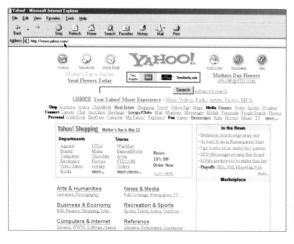

with these search engines.

Most search engines work by sending out a spider that crawls the web to find as many pages as possible which are then indexed and categorized. Consequently, you can improve the chances of your site being returned on a relevant search by filling in the information in the Meta Tags. This is used by some search engines for automatic indexing of web pages and for the descriptions alongside the entries.

There are some search engines, more typically referred to as directories, such as About.com that use human editors to describe and rate the sites discovered.

➡ *Meta Tag, Promoting a Web Site*

SERVER

There are many different types of server which, on a local area network, are computers that manage different resources. Often servers have a dedicated purpose; for example, a file server and linked storage devices are only used for storing files, while a print server manages traffic to and from printers. Similarly, a network server controls the administration and security of network traffic.

In a client/server architecture, such as the Internet, the server is a computer, or program, that responds to commands from a client. For example, a mail server collects and distributes messages to an email client program such as Outlook Express. On the Web, every site sits on a server, or host computer. The operating system used can be one of several types, such as UNIX, Windows or Macintosh. These all have the same function – to control communications over the Internet. In addition there is a software program, the web server itself, which sits on the host computer and delivers the web pages requested by the client software, in this case the browser. The web server will also carry out other browser requests, such as searching a database and returning the results together with the web page to the browser.

➡ *Browser, Client, FTP, Uploading a Web Site, Web Hosting*

FAR LEFT: Search engines use 'spiders' to crawl the web and gather all the relevant pages available.

SERVER-SIDE

Programs run on the server. In general, web programs are either client-side (meaning they are run by the browser) or server-side. Server-side programs, such as CGI scripts, run as their name suggests – on the server. They handle jobs that need access to data which is not found on the client PC. In the past, all processing was server-side, such as database-driven content where the browser handed the request to the server which sorted it out and sent back the information with the web page.

Given that users operate on a range of different platforms, there needs to be a uniform way in which the browser can pass on user input and ask the server to run the correct program. This is done using the common gateway interface (CGI), a standard way of handling requests for programs. The CGI scripts themselves can be written in a number of languages, of which the most common is Perl (Practical Extraction and Report Language). There are many sites which offer scripts for anything from hit counters to online stores. A second way is to link the programs into the web server and database software by an API (application programming interface). This is faster, because it does not require a new program to be started at every request. However, different APIs support different servers and different programming languages.

➠ *Client-Side*

SHADOWS

Special graphic effects. A shadow effect added to text, a background, photo or button, can give the impression of depth. Most photo editors work in similar ways: select the graphic and apply the shadow effect. Under the controls you can select the positioning of the shadow (left, right, behind, etc.) and how close the shadow is to its object. You can also change the shadow colour and set its transparency level. There is also a soften control to provide more or less contrast at the edges.

When adding a shadow to block of colour, such as a background or sidebar, it is easier to draw a line along the edge of the object and apply the shadow to that rather than to apply it directly. This makes it easier to control the width of the shadow. By increasing or decreasing the line width, you can change the shadow size.

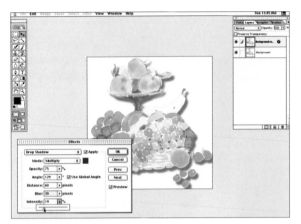

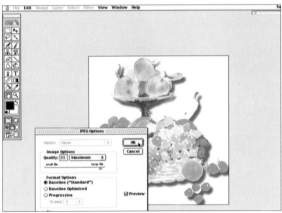

If you save a graphic as a GIF with a transparent background and put it on a coloured or textured background, the shadow looks very hard. The same is true if you apply a drop shadow to text and save it with a transparent background: the edges don't show up at all well. To solve this problem, place the graphic on a white background. If the web page has a coloured or textured background, create a background for the graphic that matches. To do this, create a new layer and fill it with the exact colour or texture of the web page. Ensure all three layers of the graphic are visible – the illustration layer, the shadow layer and the background layer – and export the image as a GIF89a file. While it is possible to do this for most background patterns, it is virtually impossible to match regularly repeated patterns such as stripes.

Alternatively, with a soft shadow it may be better to save the graphic as a JPEG rather than a GIF. A softer shadow has a greater number of intermediate colours than a hard-edged shadow and can be achieved more easily in the JPEG format, which supports more colours than a GIF can. The only limitation is that a JPEG will not let you keep part of the graphic transparent.

➡ *Graphic Design Package, Image Enhancement Techniques*

SIMULATING HTML TEXT WITH GRAPHICS

HTML and CSS let web designers specify which fonts appear in their pages. But while designers can specify several fonts in case the viewer's PC lacks the desired typeface, it is not inconceivable that the reader has none of the fonts, rendering the design process worthless. What can be worse is if fonts and font spacing differ slightly across browsers and operation systems. Photoshop sometimes has problems with irregular spacing (kerning) when mock HTML is produced. The solution is to code the text in HTML, print the screen and then crop the "text graphic" to size.

However, you can get the fonts you want on your page, regardless of who is reading it, by saving headlines and small blocks of text as graphics. All graphics packages let you type and shade text, and the best give control over spacing between lines and allow horizontal and vertical scaling. Simply export a tightly-cropped text block as a GIF file and drop it into your page as you would any graphic. Even drop capitals can be added this way.

When creating headline graphics with a large typeface, turn anti-aliasing on for a smooth appearance, but switch it off if you use smaller fonts, or black type will become grey. Effects like drop shadows, glows and bevels can be added, and you can fill bold text with a pattern or a

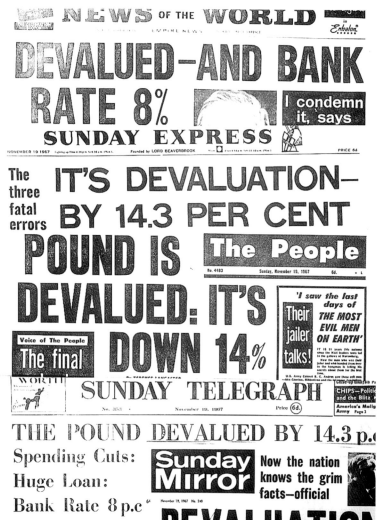

graduated tint. Use such effects with caution though, and stick to your site's colour scheme. And despite this new-found font freedom, remember the design principle of not mixing too many fonts on a single page – three or four will suffice.

➡ *Font, Graphic Design Package, Readability*

ABOVE: Avoid font difficulties and incompatibility by saving headlines and small blocks of text as graphics.

SITE LAYOUT

Using tables for design in HTML. Tables can be both a great aid and a great nuisance. They offer a good way to clearly structure the page layout and are useful to control alignment, but the HTML can be very confusing when tables are nested within each other. It can also be a headache to remember which table elements are controlled at the table level and which at the cell level.

For the overall page structure, tables can be used to create the major sections. For instance a left-hand column could house the navigation buttons while the main column has the content. The width of the table can either be fixed (each column is a precise number of pixels) or relative (where they are resized relative to the width of the window). To achieve this the table width is set to 100 per cent and each column is a percentage of this. Tables can also be a combination of fixed and relative values. For example, the left-hand navigation is set to a fixed pixel width while the main content section varies as the window is resized.

Tables are made up from the <table>...</table> tag with rows inside <tr>...</tr>. Inside each row are the table cells <td>...</td> marked td for table data. These are where the content – either text or graphics – goes. There are no column tags, the number of columns is measured by the number of <td> tags within each row.

To avoid a rigid block design you can stretch cells so that they span a number of rows or columns. Spanning is controlled by the rowspan and colspan attributes. For example, in a two column table you could stretch the top row of cells across one column to create space for a heading (e.g. <td colspan="2">Heading</td>).

Aside from using the table to format the page there are attributes which also let you format the appearance of the table. Elements you control at the table level (that is with the <table> tag) are the width and height of the table, the spacing between cells (cellspacing attribute), the padding within cells (cellpadding attribute), the border thickness (border) and background colour (bgcolor). While you are constructing the table it's easiest to set the border to 1 so it is visible. At the cell level you can alter the width and height of cells, the background colour and the alignment of objects it contains.

➡ *Design Basics, HTML Tags, Page Layout, Spacing*

SITE MAP

Overview of site structure; designed to help users find their way around your web site. Not only does a site map provide an overall view of your site's structure, it should also have direct links to each of the main content sections.

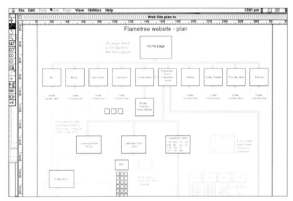

The common analogy to a site map is a table of contents in a book. Without having to leaf through all the pages in the book a table of contents shows the chapter headings and the main information they contain. Similarly, the site map does not list all the pages, but it gives a hierarchical view of the main sections and content.

To save on download time it is usually easier to use a text-based site map rather than a graphical one. Setting it within a table makes it easier to format. Small sites probably don't need a site map, but for larger sites it not only helps navigation but it can also aid search engine placement as it makes it easier for the search engine spider to discover all the site's pages.

➡ *File Organization*

Contents

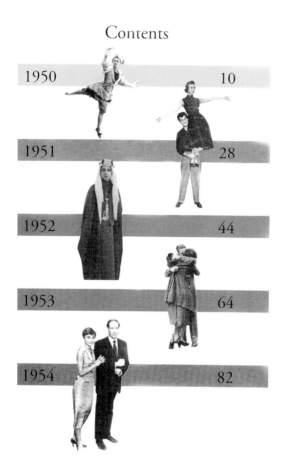

SMARTSAVER PRO (ULEAD)

Image optimization utility. SmartSaver Pro is dedicated to optimizing web graphics so that they download faster and look as good as possible. It isn't a graphic design package, in that it does not let you create your own images, but it will help construct animated GIFs and rollovers from imported images through a straightforward dialog box-based interface.

SmartSaver's image compression tools allow two-up comparison of files exported to JPEG, GIF and PNG formats. Custom colour palettes can be created for GIFs to reduce file sizes as much as possible. In the compression process, areas of some graphics degrade more than others, and SmartSaver lets the user specify areas where image quality should be preserved as much as possibly. Image slicing can be custom or automatic.

Masks can be imported from other packages to act as frames or backgrounds for images, and layered images can be converted to animations – SmartSaver lets you set frame delay and loop settings.

Imported graphics can easily be converted into rollovers using SmartSaver's dialog box-based system. The software can create basic rollovers, where the graphic hovered over changes, and remote rollovers, where a second graphic changes when you move the mouse over a button. Audio clips can also be incorporated into rollovers. A 15-day trial of SmartSaver is available at www.ulead.com.

➡ *Image Compression, Optimizing Graphics, Rollovers*

ABOVE: A site map works in the same way as a book's contents page; it gives an overview of the main sections and contents.

SPACING

How you use white space in web design is as important as how you use colour. Spacing between page elements can add extra emphasis to the content and helps guide the reader's eye around the page. While reading, the eye strays towards white space; if all it can see is a solid block of text or tightly packed images, it will skirt over the content looking for the space.

However, this does not mean you should overload a site with white space at the expense of content, and getting the balance right is essential. If your page is organized into a three-column grid, for example, separate the columns slightly using the cellpadding or cellspacing table attributes. This gives a clear definition between the columns, but apply a padding of no more than 25 pixels or the columns will be too far apart and will lose their connection. Similarly, you can use the cellpadding attributes to put a small white 'border' around the most important blocks of text.

Images should also be set as islands of white space. The vspace and hspace attributes place additional space around two sides of an image, or you can use the single-pixel GIF trick to add space to just one side of the image, and preserve alignment with other elements.

➡ *Eye Flow, Spacing Using the Single-Pixel GIF*

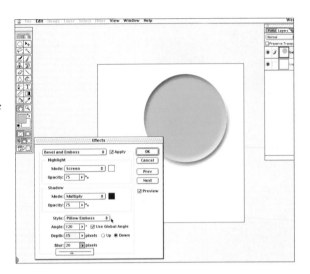

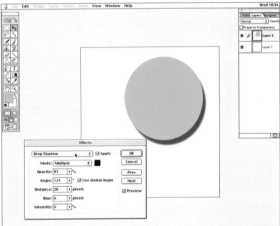

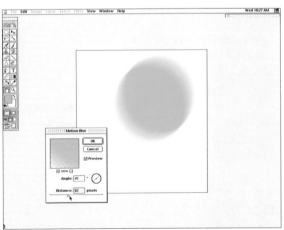

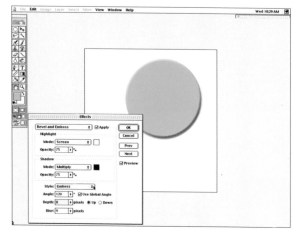

SPACING USING THE SINGLE-PIXEL GIF

Transparent single-pixel spacer GIF, resized to create space on a page and help align the elements.

HTML is better for markup than it is for layout. It is most noticeable when you try and align objects on the page. With HTML alone it is very difficult, but there are workarounds, such as the single-pixel transparent GIF. This is good for creating white space on the page. As the spacer image is cached it does not need to be constantly downloaded. As a result it can be reused dozens or hundreds of times within a site without affecting performance.

As the GIF is transparent it is in effect invisible. The size of the single-pixel GIF can be changed by altering the width and height values. This can be used in tables to keep a table cell a certain width or height. It can also be used at the start of a paragraph to create an indent (e.g. <img width="25" height="5" src="spacer.gif">). Alternatively you can create the same effect without resizing the spacer GIF by using the horizontal space and vertical space attributes (e.g. <img hspace="25" src="spacer.gif">). Because these attributes add space either side of the image (the spacer GIF) it effectively doubles the space compared with just changing the width.
➧ *Alignment, Spacing*

SPECIAL EFFECTS FOR IMAGES

Most graphics editors come with their own set of special effects you can use to spice up your images.

In addition, there are third-party plug-ins you can buy to add even more effects. Spicing up your pictures is easy to do with all the graphics programs available today. Although each package may vary in the effects that are available, there is a core group common to most programs, whether its Adobe's Photoshop, Macromedia's Fireworks or Jasc's Paint Shop Pro. The effects can be quite subtle, such as a gentle blurring in a picture, or quite dramatic, such as adding a bevel effect to a button to give a 3D look.

While most graphics editors have their own built-in filters to add special effects, some also support third-party plug-ins, such as Kai's Power Tools or Alien Skin Software's Eye Candy collection. The plug-in effects can be used in much the same way as those shipped with the program. Generally, you apply the effect to an object and a new set of controls appears that lets you adjust specific elements of that effect. For example, you can apply a glow effect which adds a colour around the edge of an object. Using the controls you can set the colour of the glow, its width, its opacity (the degree of transparency it has) and an offset value that enables you to add space between the object and the glow.

Nor do you have to stop at one effect. Most graphics editors will let you apply as many effects as you want and alter the order in which they are applied to the image. This can make a big difference. For example, if you create a button and add a bevel effect after a drop shadow, it is a lot flatter than if you apply the bevel effect before adding the drop shadow. As well as bevel, emboss, and glow effects, quite subtle or striking effects can be used by applying the blur or sharpen effect. The blur effect softens details in an image by averaging the pixel colours to alter the contrast around the edges. If you choose the Gaussian Blur effect you can control the amount of blur added. Alternatively, if the picture is too soft, or looks a little out of focus, you can apply the Sharpening effects to enhance the edges of an image by increasing the contrast.
➧ *Bevel and Emboss, Filter, Graphic Design Package, Image Enhancement Techniques, Shadows*

FAR LEFT: Using special effects techniques, you can add a 'glow' to an image by surrounding it with a different colour.

SPECIAL TEXT CHARACTERS

Not all characters have keyboard equivalents, so they need to be inserted into the text by their special name or number. The ASCII characters used on web pages have the letters and numbers needed, but only a few basic symbols; there needs to be a special way to show special characters, such as a trademark symbol or copyright mark. This is done in HTML by using a special name or specific number. For example, to mark the copyright on your web page there is no keyboard equivalent. To insert the symbol © you need to put © in the code, or the equivalent number which is ©. However, the one you are likely to use most is the text string that marks a non-breaking space. This gets round the fact that browsers ignore any extra character spaces in HTML documents. When you do want to add a character space, insert   in the code or the number

There are a host of other special characters you can use, ranging from the symbol for the pound (£ – £) to the Yen (¥ – ¥). Note that some characters, such as curly quotes (left – &147; and right – &148;) do not have a name you can use, they are always specified by giving their number.

➠ *Font, HTML, Type*

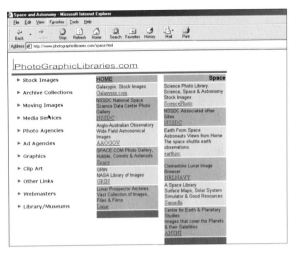

SPLASH PAGE

Introductory page of a web site. In the early days of the Internet, most sites had a splash page that was the entry point to the site. Rather like the name plate on a door, with a welcome mat underneath, it did little more than let you know you were in the right place. Then came Flash, which lived up to its name and brought some glitter to the Web, but at a cost in bandwidth and annoyance to users. Flash proved to be a distraction rather than something fundamental to the appeal of the site. This is changing, however, and rather than just being a chance for designers to show off, it is often used to create memorable effects and to reinforce brands.

Even so, there are a number of factors to consider before deploying a splash page, particularly the purpose it is intended to serve. Does it, for example, give the user a choice between a Flash or Frame version of the site or one without? Does it offer different viewing options, or is

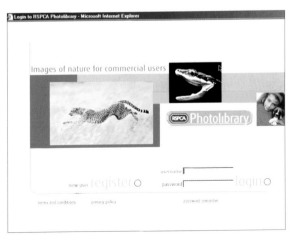

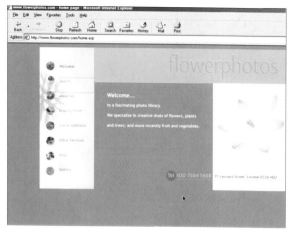

it a required disclaimer for financial services sites or sites where there are minimum age requirements?

In terms of the content, the splash page should have full details of the site with contact links and an idea of its purpose. Most importantly, so as not to frustrate repeat visitors, it should offer a 'skip intro' link so that the intro animation does not have to be viewed each time visitors return.

➠ *Introduction Page*

STOCK PHOTO SUPPLIERS

Online image libraries. A picture can add a lot to a web page, no matter that it's low resolution and small size to speed up download time, but sourcing them can often prove problematic. There are several sites that offer free stock photo images online, such as at the aptly named www.freeimages.co.uk. However, most free images are tasters to photographic collections that have to be purchased.

Most of the big image libraries have sites online (for a listing see www.photographiclibraries.com). Almost all have a search function to enable you to look through the archive for the type of image you want. You can then download low-resolution copies. Licensing rights for these photographs can be expensive but some, like Gettyworks.com (www.gettyworks.com) or Corbis (www.corbis.com) offer low-price collections or individually priced photos for web use.

Whatever source the image comes from, be sure you are clear on the licensing terms permitted. It will tend to be either rights-managed – which is one fee, one use – or royalty free, where one fee is charged for unlimited use. However, royalty free images may carry other restrictions, such as not permitting the photographs to be used for particular commercial or promotional purposes, so be aware of the licensing rules before you use any image.

➠ *Corbis Images, GettyOne Images, Image Licensing, Photodisc,*

LEFT: Macromedia's Flash brought glitter and glamour to the entire web, but particularly to splash pages.

STORYBOARD

Plan of site structure. Storyboards are a helpful way to present, test and define the structure of the site before going ahead with building the pages. The structure of a large site can often be complicated, yet it is essential that everyone involved with its development is clear how it works. Once detailed content is included – whether it's text, graphics or multimedia – the room for confusion is immense. One way around this problem is to lay out the structure of the site in a storyboard.

The term is borrowed from the movie industry where every frame is planned out on a storyboard before any footage is shot. Similarly, on the Web, storyboarding gives you a chance to work through the structure of the site before committing to the expense in time and resources of building the pages. It is an essential step for agencies who need to present the concept of the site, together with its look and feel, in order to get the client's approval before they proceed.

The storyboard itself, also called a branching diagram, can be built using the site map within web-authoring tools such as Dreamweaver. It should show what pages will be included in the site, together with the kinds of information each page will contain.

➡ *Site Map, Web-Site Structure*

SYSTEM FONT

Font used for system display. The system font is the typeface used on the Macintosh and some PC applications, in all its menus, titles and windows. It is also used to describe the base set of font combinations that come with each computer, across different platforms.

The advantage becomes clear when you specify a typeface that you want to use on your web site. Not every user is going to have every font. Similarly, fonts from the same family may have different names (such as Arial and Helvetica) or be called something different on different platforms (for example, Times New Roman on a Windows PC is roughly the same as Times on a Mac).

For this reason, HTML editors such as Dreamweaver have preset combinations of fonts. These are made up of system fonts commonly found on most of the new computers now sold. If the user does not have the first font installed, the browser will use the second or third one specified. For example, a common combination would be <font face="Verdana, Arial, Helvetica, sans-serif">...</font>. By including a generic font family (serif, sans-serif) the browser will use one of that style if it cannot find any of the other fonts you have named.

➡ *Font, Technical Limitation*

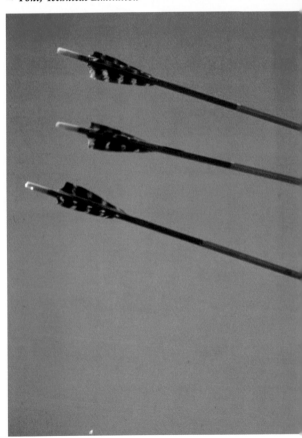

```
<!DOCTYPE HTML PUBLIC "-//W3C//DTD HTML 4.0 Transitional//EN">
<HTML><HEAD><TITLE>Untitled</TITLE><META NAME="GENERATOR" CONTENT="Freeway
3.1"><STYLE TYPE="text/css"> <!-- .style17 { font-size: 36px; } .style19 {
font-size: 60px; } .style20 { font-size: 60px; letter-spacing: -0.6px; } .styl
{ font-size: 53px; } --> </STYLE> </HEAD><BODY TOPMARGIN=0 LEFTMARGIN=0
MARGINHEIGHT=0 MARGINWIDTH=0 BGCOLOR="#ffffff"><TABLE BORDER=0 CELLSPACING=0
CELLPADDING=0 WIDTH=537><TR VALIGN=TOP><TD COLSPAN=2></TD><TD
HEIGHT=19></TD></TR><TR VALIGN=TOP><TD></TD><TD><P><B><FONT
FACE="Arial,Helvetica,sans-serif" SIZE=7><SPAN CLASS="style17">Simple Text
Faces</SPAN></FONT></B></P><P><B><FONT
FACE="Arial,Helvetica,sans-serif"> </FONT></B></P><P><FONT
FACE="Arial,Helvetica,sans-serif" SIZE=7><SPAN CLASS="style19">This is a sans
serif <BR>font </SPAN></FONT><FONT FACE="Arial,Helvetica,sans-serif" SIZE=7><
CLASS="style20">commonly used <BR>in Windows and Mac
computers.</SPAN></FONT><FONT FACE="Arial,Helvetica,sans-serif" SIZE=7><SPAN
CLASS="style16"></SPAN></FONT></P><P><FONT
FACE="Arial,Helvetica,sans-serif"> </FONT></P><P><FONT
FACE="Arial,Helvetica,sans-serif"> </FONT></P><TD
HEIGHT=405></TD></TR><TR><TD WIDTH=13><IMG SRC="Resources/_clear.gif" BORDER=0
WIDTH=13 HEIGHT=1 ALT=""></TD><TD WIDTH=522><IMG SRC="Resources/_clear.gif"
```

TARGETS

The target attribute is used to specify where linked documents should be displayed. When a web site uses frames there has to be a way of specifying where linked documents should load. By default this will actually be in the same window as the link. However, this is not ideal if, for example, you have a navigation panel in the left frame and want to display the linked content in the main frame. A solution to this is to give the anchor tag a target attribute and to name the frame in which you want the content to load. So, for example, you click on a link and want the content to load in the frame "main" the code would be <a href="linkedcontent.html" target="main">...</a>. Besides a specifically named frame there are several other reserved target names.

A link with target="_blank" opens a linked document in a new browser window (it does so with any link, not just when set in frames). Target="_self" is the default for

BELOW: A target, in web terms, ensures that a link document is displayed in the correct place.

anchor tags and loads the new document in the same frame or window as the source of the link. As it is the default, it does not need to be specified with the <a> tags. With target="_top" the linked document will display outside the frames directly in the browser window.
→ *Anchor, Frame, Links*

TECHNICAL LIMITATIONS

The Web is not like other media; unlike print publishing, when you build a site, you do not know how it is going to appear on the reader's system. A high-spec system will be able to display all the streaming video clips you want, but users of older PCs will miss out on such cutting-edge content. Good web design is all about catering for the realistic lowest common denominator. The current lowest acceptable screen size is 640 x 480-pixels, and you can meet this limitation by designing to a fixed width of 600 pixels. Such a user might have a depth of only 256 colours, and adhering to the web-safe palette of 216 colours is always good practice.

Consider the user's access speeds. While offices have faster, leased-line access, only a small percentage of home users have broadband connections, and most rely on 56 Kbps modems. To shorten download times, make sure you do not overload a page with graphics and keep the size of both page and images reasonably small.

Not all users will be equipped with the latest browsers, so check your page on older browsers and try not to use standards that are only supported by certain browsers. Also avoid using non-standard technologies that require new plug-ins: users would rather not wait to see content, however inspiring.
→ *Cross-Browser Compatibility, Fixed-Width Page Design, Web-Safe Colours*

TESTING

Although it is often left to a last-minute rush, testing is a vital part of web-site development, and should cover all areas.

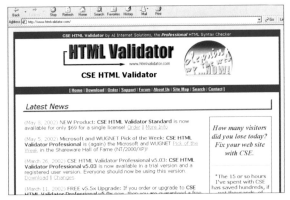

The first area for testing, especially for designers, is the look and feel. Check every page to make sure they are consistent in layout, colour and style. Also check the coding. W3C have an online validation service but most web-authoring tools have built-in HTML checkers. For more advanced proofing there are special programs such as CSE HTML Validator (www.htmlvalidator.com).

Most validators will also perform basic functional checks, such as verifying every link in the site. But beyond testing the structure of the site it is also important to check it matches its purpose with some form of user testing. This does not necessarily mean a full usability test, but it is worth working through the main tasks likely to be carried out on site, to ensure they work smoothly and efficiently.

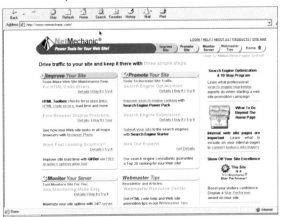

You must also ensure your site will work with different systems and browsers. Most of us can't keep a bank of computers available for testing, but there are online services like NetMechanic (www.netmechanic.com) which do and will send a snapshot of your pages taken from different combinations of browser and platform.

➡ *Maintaining a Web Site*

TEXTURE

A basic background or button can be transformed by adding a texture effect to it. The web page can become a brick wall, stained glass or canvas backdrop. Images on site can be given a tiled effect or have a grain, paint, or glass look added.

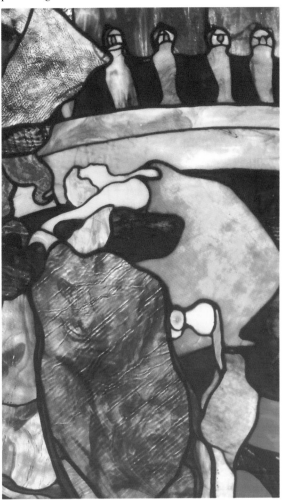

For the background, the texture just needs to be applied to a small image. This is then tiled – repeated – as many times as is needed to fill the background. It is a good way of creating a layered effect as text, graphics and links can go over the top of the tiled background. However, you need to make sure there is sufficient contrast between the textured background and any text or images used on top of it, or the site will be unreadable. You also need to be careful with some textured fills you use that an ugly seam does not appear where the tiles meet.

An alternative to using the textured tiles is to create a false background, i.e. use your graphics editor to create a rectangular image that fills the required space and then add a texturizer special effect to fill the rectangle with the look you want.

➡ *Graphic Design Package, Image Enhancement Techniques*

THUMBNAILS

Small versions of images, often linked to a larger or full-size version of the same image; used to speed up download time and ease navigation around a web site.

Thumbnails are particularly useful for online catalogues or galleries where visitors can browse the 'thumbnail-sized' versions of the product or graphic. When they see one that interests them they can click on it and are taken to another page where a larger version of the same image is downloaded.

By keeping the thumbnails to a reasonable size – both in dimensions and file size – the download time of the 'gallery' page is kept as low as possible. This page should

make it clear that users can click on any link to get a larger view. Consequently, it is only those that do who need wait for the larger picture to download.

The page with the full-size view should have the same navigation – or identification – as the rest of the site with links back to the previous page. It should also have more detailed, or different, information to that available on the gallery page so that visitors feel they have got some added value by following the link.

➡ *File Size, Image Resizing, Image Resolution*

TIFF

Tag Image File Format; graphics file format. The TIFF format is widely used for saving scanned images before being converted into other file types more convenient for the Web.

TIFF is one of the most widely used file formats for bitmapped images, particularly in the print world, as it is cross-platform and supported on many operating systems including Windows, UNIX and the Macintosh. Files in the TIFF format have .tif as the extension.

It was originally developed by scanner manufacturers looking for a standard file format for desktop publishing. Consequently, it is very colour accurate and many designers prefer to save scanned images as TIFF files, before converting them into other formats like GIF, JPEG, or PNG for the Web.

The TIFF format compresses files using the same lossless compression technique adopted in GIF files. The LZW compression method looks for pixels or image elements of the same colour that can be described as a unit.

However, on the Web, PNG is more of a substitute for TIFF files. PNG can support 48-bit colour storage (compared to 8-bit for GIFs) while still compressing files substantially. Generally PNG files are around a third smaller than the comparable TIFF files, while still maintaining image quality.

➡ *File Type*

CENTRE LEFT: Stained glass is just one of the effects which can liven up a button or a basic background.

TILING BACKGROUND IMAGE

Adding a background image to your page can have a very decorative effect – and you only need one tile. The way tiling works is for a single small image ('tile') to be downloaded, which can be repeated infinitely, however big the page. This process is also a good way of creating a layered effect on the Web, as text, graphics and links can go over the top of the tiled background.

However, it is important to keep an eye on the contrast between the text and the image underneath. If you have a light background use dark type, or light type if you have a dark background. The background tiles should also be consistently dark or light. Otherwise, if you have a mixture, neither the dark or light type is going to show up reliably.

The code to add a background tile is <BODY BACKGROUND="tile.gif">. But like the debutante at the ball, you do need to decide if you want to show the seams. A tile with seams has a wallpaper style effect. It has an obvious border. To create seamless tiles is a lot trickier, but graphics tools, such as Adobe's ImageReady do make the process easier.

➡ *Background Image, HTML*

TRANSPARENT IMAGES

Images with a see-through area. There are several methods to add transparent areas to web graphics in order to let the background show through and to create more interesting shapes.

One of the best features of GIFs is that they allow part of the image to be transparent. As a result, the background colour or image on a web page can show through and much more interesting design possibilities open up. By removing the typical rectangular box from around the image you reveal much more fascinating shapes.

The simplest way to create a transparent image is through index transparency. In most graphics programs you use the transparency pointer or eyedropper tool to select the specific colour pixel you want to be see-through. Be careful though, as this is an all-or-nothing approach: all instances of the colour you have selected will turn transparent. So if you have a red background and a red dot in the centre, the dot will also become transparent.

This can be avoided in some web graphics packages by using the Matte colour tool, which is also a useful tool to prevent the 'halo' effect seen on some web graphics, where the edge of the image does not blend into the background, as a result of using anti-aliasing.

Some graphics editors, such as Photoshop, include a much more advanced system for creating transparent areas, called Alpha transparency. Under this system a map of the transparent areas is saved as a separate channel – the Alpha Channel. The transparency of the pixels can be turned on or off, regardless of what colour they are. This alpha channel is then superimposed over the image to enable the background to show through the transparent areas. It is rather tricky and something for the specialist.

The same result can be achieved more simply using the PNG format. This supports variable levels of transparency

that enable you to create special effects, such as glows and drop shadows. As with traditional GIFs, the PNG files can also use the simple transparency technique in which one colour is either transparent or not. JPEGs do not have the transparency features that GIF or PNG do, but there is a way to get a similar effect if your web page background is a solid colour. You can create the illusion that the JPEG is on a transparent layer by making the canvas the same colour as the page background before you save it.

➡ **GIF, Graphic Design Package, Image Manipulation**

TRIAL SOFTWARE

Try-before-you-buy programs are a useful way of evaluating which software is best for you.

There is no shortage of software to help you build web sites, but it can be difficult to work out which is best for you. It would be a very expensive process if you had to buy each program you were interested in. Happily, there is a solution – trial software. This is becoming increasingly popular with vendors who realize that with so many rival products and the high cost of software, users do want to try before they buy. In fact there are tryout versions of most of the major HTML editors and web-authoring programs, such as Macromedia's HomeSite, Dreamweaver, and Fireworks or Adobe's GoLive and Photoshop.

Trialware will be restricted in different ways. Some products are fully-functioning, but only for a certain time period (typically 30 days) after which they cease to operate. Sometimes the program can be restored by inputting the license number of the purchased product, otherwise the trial version needs to be replaced by a full version. In other programs the try out version may not have all the functions working or certain options are restricted, for example printouts may have 'trial version' marked all over them.

➡ **Dreamweaver (Macromedia), Fireworks (Macromedia), Flash (Macromedia), Freehand (Macromedia), Homesite (Macromedia)**

LEFT: A tiled background with seams creates a wallpaper effect, like the decorative William Morris tiles shown here.

TRIPOD (www.tripod.com)

Web-hosting service. As with any homepage hosting service, Tripod offer a range of schemes, from the ad-supported basic free site to a subscription-based service minus the banner ads. Part of the giant Lycos network, the monthly paid-for web-hosting services enable you to add more disk space and bandwidth. This could be especially useful if you plan to use bandwidth-hungry services such as digital video on site.

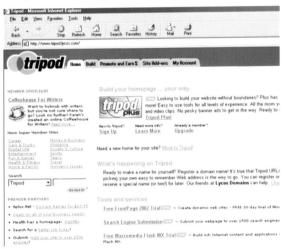

As Tripod supports FrontPage you can construct your site using Microsoft's web-authoring tool and simply FTP the pages online. Alternatively, Tripod offers its own Site Builder software, based on a product by Trellix, which lets you easily create online sites with web galleries, guestbooks, maps etc. While it is a visual editor, you can use HTML if you prefer to have more personal control over the code.

If you want to add further functionality there are a number of add-ons. Tripod have their own scripting tool for writing CGI and JavaScripts. They also offer free images and animations, on-site polling, and feedback mechanisms that won't reveal your email address.

➡ *Angelfire, Geocities, Free Web Hosting*

TUTORIALS

Learning online. Thanks to the open nature of the Web, it is not necessary to learn how to craft your web site alone. Whether it is a simple course in HTML or the technical merits of DHTML versus Flash for

animation, then there will be a tutorial to help. Put a simple search query for web design tutorials to Google and there are nearly three quarters of a million responses.

If you are using a web-authoring tool, the first place to check out is the publisher's web site, as many have technical solutions areas where expert users offer the benefit of their experience. Among those that do are Macromedia for Homesite, Dreamweaver and Fireworks amongst others, and Adobe for Photoshop and InDesign.

One of the pioneers of web advice was HTML

LEFT: Tutorials on web design are now available online so you don't have to study alone.

TYPE

On-screen characters. The type, or appearance of characters on-screen, can greatly help visitors navigate through text and aids the appeal of a site. The style of type used on a computer is known as a font. It is often thought of as the typeface. This is usually one of two types: serif, which has little strokes or curls at the end of a character; and sans-serif which does not. The most common serif font on the Web is Times with Arial as a standard non-serif font.

These are both proportional fonts, one of two basic types of font with which you will work in designing for the Web. Most text uses proportional fonts (called variable width fonts in Netscape) where the different letters can take up a different amount of space (e.g. 'm' spreads out while 'i' breathes in).

There are also fixed-width fonts (also called monospace), such as Courier, that give equal space to each character. They are only used with a few HTML tags such as the <pre> tag for preformatted text where each line is displayed exactly as it is written including extra spaces or <tt> for typewriter text.

➡ **Font, Typography**

Goodies (www.htmlgoodies.com) with 'how to' guides, code libraries and tag reference guides. Whether a beginner or advanced, W3 Schools online (www.w3schools.com) can give you the run-down on all the development technologies from HTML to XML and JavaScript, while WebReference.com (www.webreference.com/) pronounces itself as the reference source for webmasters and webmasters in training.

➡ *HTML Goodies, Webreference.com*

TYPOGRAPHY

The rules for specifying fonts for the web are similar to print publishing, except that you cannot be sure what fonts are installed on the destination system. Fortunately, cascading style sheets (CSS) are giving the designer more control.

1. The small proportions of the browser window mean the dramatic differences in font size in print publishing are non-existent. Rather than using a 50–100-point difference between headline and body fonts, web designers only have a maximum headline size of around 36 points, so colour must be used to make the headline stand out.

2. On high-resolution screens, line lengths can be too long to follow comfortably across the page. The BLOCKQUOTE tag sets a narrow paragraph width but it is better to set the text in a fixed-width table or specify where each line ends using the <BR> line break tab at the end of each line.

3. Font sizes in HTML are relative (3 being the standard, 7 the largest) but users can choose larger or smaller fonts according to their own taste. Use cascading style sheets to set precise sizes. CSS lets you specify font and line spacing sizes in pixels, points, ems and metric measures.

4. Because the type size tends to be larger on the Web, the print convention of using serif fonts for body text and sans-serif fonts for headlines and other one-line page furniture does not apply online, and most sites now use a sans-serif font throughout.

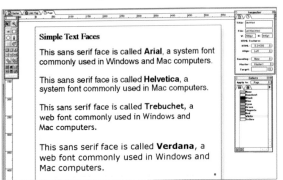

Simple Text Faces

This sans serif face is called **Arial**, a system font commonly used in Windows and Mac computers.

This sans serif face is called **Helvetica**, a system font commonly used in Mac computers.

This sans serif face is called **Trebuchet**, a web font commonly used in Windows and Mac computers.

This sans serif face is called **Verdana**, a web font commonly used in Windows and Mac computers.

5. Print rules regarding upper and lower case still apply, and you should use mixed case as much as possible. All upper case stands out too much and on the Web is seen as the written form of shouting, while all lower case in body text and headlines looks like grammatical ineptitude.

6. Arial (Windows) and Helvetica (Mac) are the most popular sans-serif fonts online because they are installed on most PCs, but consider using a typeface designed especially for the Web like Verdana or Trebuchet MS. Do not italicize fonts as the square pixel grid will create a jagged effect.

7. To specify a font in HTML or CSS, list a group of fonts and the browser will display the first one that is installed on the PC. If you have a rare display font in mind, name that first, then put the standard alternatives at the end of the list. If a display font is essential for a headline, create it as a graphic instead.

➡ *Font, Readability, Simulating HTML Text with Graphics, Type*

UPLOADING A WEB SITE

Transferring web pages. Once finished, the web site has to be published and made available to its audience. This provides the designer with their most regular link to the web server – uploading the finished pages. The standard way to transfer these files (the HTML documents, graphics and other files) between computers on the Internet is by FTP (File Transfer Protocol).

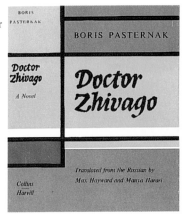

BORIS PASTERNAK

BORIS PASTERNAK

Doctor Zhivago
A Novel

Doctor Zhivago

Translated from the Russian by Max Hayward and Manya Harari

Collins Harvill

There are a number of programs that make this whole procedure drag and drop simple, such as CuteFTP and LapLink FTP for the PC and the aptly-named Fetch on the Macintosh. Additionally, FTP functions for uploading the pages and synchronizing them are built in to many of

the web-authoring tools, such as Macromedia's Dreamweaver, Adobe's GoLive and Microsoft's FrontPage.

Whichever tool you use, the process is similar. You first need to connect to the ISP's Web server where your site is being hosted. For security reasons it is unlikely that your personal web directory will be accessible by anonymous users. So you will also need a user name and password to log on to the directory where you'll place the HTML pages and any graphic files that go with it.

These details, together with the exact name of your server need to be entered into the FTP program you are using. Once connected find the directory on the server where you want to copy your files. It may be you need to create this directory or remove files and folders that are already there.

Depending on your program you may need to specify whether the data should be sent as plain text files (ASCII

mode) as with HTML documents, or in binary mode, such as the graphics or multimedia files. Some programs will determine this for you and by selecting the Auto option it's possible to transfer the whole site including files of both types in the one session. However, it is not always 100 per cent reliable.

Instead of the well understood terms downloading and uploading, most programs will stick to the traditional FTP terminology of getting and putting. The Put command uploads files, that is, sends them from your PC to the Web server. The Get command downloads the pages, so files are transferred from the web server to the PC.

➡ *Anonymous FTP, CuteFTP, FTP, LaplinkFTP, Server*

LEFT: Just like a book, upon completion a web site is published and made available to its audience.

URL

 Uniform Resource Locator; web site address. A URL gives not only the location of a site but also the protocol needed to access it.

http: // www.garden of stars.com

Hyper Text Transfer Protocol | World Wide Web | Domain Name | Top Level Domain

The URL of a site is its address on the World Wide Web. All web sites have URLs, which not only describe the location of a page or file, but also how to access it.

They are made up of two parts. The first part describes what protocol to use to access the file, such as HTTP (Hyper Text Transfer Protocol) if it is for a web page, or FTP (File Transfer Program) if it is for a program file.

The second part gives the domain name, or IP address, where the server is located, such as the site for the publishers of this book, www.foundry.co.uk. Consequently, you could have different URLs pointing to different files at the same domain.

ftp://www.companydomainname.com/program.exe would be a program downloaded using the FTP protocol, whereas http://www.companydomainname.com/index.html would load the Homepage for the site, using the HTTP protocol.

As you delve further down into the site the URLs are going to get longer and more difficult to remember. Consequently, most browsers have a facility to let you store URLs you want to visit again as bookmarks, as they are known in Netscape, or Favorites, as they are called in Internet Explorer.

➡ *Domain Name, HTTP*

USABILITY

Creating a user-friendly interface. A guaranteed way to drive visitors away from your site is to create an unfriendly, slow-loading interface. But usability does not have to mean bland, image-free pages, it is just a case of understanding about how users will find their way around the site.

Don't waste everyone's time on splash pages and unnecessary animated graphics. Splash screens say very little that placing your company logo in a prominent position can't, and anything that delays a user's entry to the site could well turn them away for good. Site-wide consistency is vital. The basic page structure should be the same, and the navigation menu should be in the same place on every page, with ALT tags for each menu button.

Web conventions must be adhered to. Don't underline text, especially in blue, as users will mistake it for a hyperlink, and conversely make the links stand out to the reader. Try and avoid making a page too wide, as few users enjoy having to scroll horizontally. When preparing a site, watch as colleagues have a look around the pages and gauge how easily they navigate through. When the site is live, get more user feedback to increase usability and attract more visitors.

➡ *Readability, User Interface*

USER INTERFACE

Whether using an image-based metaphor, or traditional text-based links, it is important that the user interface is consistent and clear. To help understand the mass of information available on site, some designers use a metaphor to represent the way the web pages are structured. Instead of a largely text-based Homepage the interface is shown as a town or a room, such as a doctor's surgery. Then each section is represented by some object – such as pills for medicines, a scalpel or other instruments for surgery, books for reference, etc.

Such imagery does have drawbacks: it is graphics heavy, which can slow download time and not everything may fit the metaphor neatly, particularly as a site expands. However, limited use, such as with particular tools, can work well. The classic example is the shopping cart. Everyone knows it from the real world and the same metaphor fits the virtual store.

Consistency and clarity also help make a user interface, user friendly. For instance, navigational tools should be placed consistently through the site, not moved around. Sections should be called the same throughout and labels should make it clear what they are about. Links should look like links. Text links should be coloured the same throughout the site. Traditionally this has been blue and underlined. However, using HTML and cascading style sheets it is possible to have different styles for links, mouse overs and visited links etc. Whatever you choose, it should be the same throughout the site and it should stand out from the rest of the text.

➡ *Usability*

LEFT: It is crucial that the user interface is consistent and clear. To help achieve this, navigational tools should appear throughout the site.

UTILIZING JAVASCRIPT

Incorporating JavaScript is one of the easiest ways to add interactive and dynamic features to a web site. The Netscape-developed script language excels at enhancing navigation and making quick calculations and communications that put very little load on the server.

JavaScript is difficult for the web newcomer to learn, but there are thousands of scripts available for download that can be pasted into HTML pages and tweaked to suit a site's own needs. You will find large JavaScript libraries containing everything from the mildly entertaining to the thoroughly productive at JavaScript World (www.jsworld.com), the JavaScript Source (http://javascript.internet.com) and HotScripts (www.hotscripts.com).

The simplest JavaScript routines consist of no more than one line that places a rich text description of a hyperlink's destination page on the browser's status bar when a user hovers over the link. Rollovers and pop-up windows are JavaScript favourites, while the arrival of the Euro has prompted some developers to create conversion calculators that you can incorporate into your site.

Less cosmetic uses for JavaScript include form verification tools (which ensure that data is entered in a correct format before processing) and password utilities, ad banner rotation routines or shopping cart scripts. Such scripts link to an external database files and CGI or ASP form handlers after converting the received data into a suitable format.

When you write or copy a script, make sure it is supported by the browsers you intend to support. The latest version, JavaScript 5.0, is only supported by versions 6.0 of Netscape Navigator and Internet Explorer. Version 1.2, however, is supported by Navigator and IE 4.0, regarded as the current entry-level browser. If you find a script written for version 1.3+ that you must use, try and find a version 1.2 equivalent and including them both in the page – the browser will recognize the most suitable version.

➡ *Functionality, JavaScript, Rollover*

VBSCRIPT

Scripting language. VBScript is short for Visual Basic Script Edition. It is a client-side scripting language, similar to JavaScript and it is embedded in the HTML file that uses it. By being inserted in the <HEAD> of the document, the script is loaded into the memory while the rest of the page is downloading. The script will run as it is read – if, for example, it is checking which version of a browser is being used – or on some event, such as a click of the mouse or a rollover.

VBScript is based on Microsoft's Visual Basic programming language, although it is simpler to use. It allows web designers to provide dynamic content to their pages, including interactive navigational controls. VBScript is supported by Microsoft's Internet Explorer browser, but not by Netscape. Similarly, most modern browsers' users can turn off scripting support as a security measure. Because there are no guarantees that the client-side scripting is supported it is advisable to provide alternative content between the <NOSCRIPT> and </NOSCRIPT> tags. One way round this is to use VBScript as a server-side scripting language and it is the default language for ASP (Active Server Pages).

➡ *Functionality, JavaScript, ASP*

VECTOR

Graphics format. Software for creating or editing graphics comes in two basic types – drawing programs or painting programs. Drawing programs, such as Adobe Illustrator, create pictures using simple lines and curves (vectors) that are described by mathematical formulas. By contrast, painting programs use screen pixels to represent the image, rather like tiles in a mosaic.

Drawing programs are great for logos, simple line drawings or text banners. They can be resized easily without affecting the quality of the image, by simply adjusting the formula. As they are not mapped to the individual pixel you don't get the lumpy, blurred effect that happens when you enlarge a bitmap.

Vector graphics are also generally smaller in file size than their bitmapped equivalents. Great for the Web, except that most browsers only view bitmap files, like JPEGs and GIFs directly.

As a result you have to rasterize the vector graphic, that is convert it into a bitmap. Because most images created in a drawing program have solid blocks of colours they are best saved as GIF files. Previously, to do this you would have had to save the graphic in your drawing program and then import it into a paint program such as Photoshop to handle the conversion. Now, however, there are some hybrid programs, like Microsoft's PhotoDraw, that let you create files of both types. Many drawing programs, such

as Freehand and Illustrator, also let you save files directly as GIFs (although they are not always as good at optimizing file size as the paint programs).

Vector-graphics are also the basis of Flash, Macromedia's multimedia format. Flash is great for the Web as you can produce full-screen animation with integrated sound within a small file size. Flash movies can be put on a web page, or actually be the web page itself, and they are increasingly used for splash pages, interactive games, zooming in to maps and diagrams, even music videos. However, they do need to be viewed through a Flash player or plug-in, though these are now widely available on the Net.

Eventually your image will be seen on screen, or in print. Yet, practically all output devices, such as printers and screen monitors, are raster devices that have to translate the vector graphics into bitmaps so that they can be displayed.

➡ *Adobe Illustrator, File Size, Flash (Macromedia), Freehand (Macromedia), Pixel, Raster*

LEFT: Make sure the script you use can be interpreted successfully!

W3C

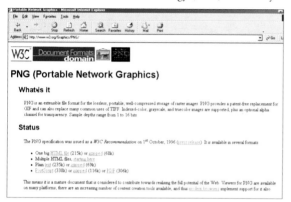

Web standards body. The World Wide Web Consortium (W3C) oversees the development of the Web. It is a volunteer organization based at the Massachusetts Institute of Technology (MIT) and led by Tim Berners-Lee, the Englishman who first proposed HTML back in 1989, while working at the European Laboratory for Particle Physics (CERN). He wanted a simple document structure that could incorporate a 'hypertext' process to link related documents over a network. Initially, it was intended as a way for scientists to be able to share and manage large amounts of information.

Since its inception in 1994 W3C has set the standards for HTML and set recommended practices in order to try and ensure the openness of the Web. W3C is also a forum for new developments. A lot of information can be found at their web site www.w3.org. Not only does it cover the history and future of the Web it also enables you to test the validity of your code and to look up definitions for various tags and attributes. As well as HTML, it covers XML, CSS and other new developments.

➡ *Web Standards*

W3SCHOOLS (www.w3schools.com)

Web tutorials. Novice or expert, there's something for everyone at W3Schools, whether it's a reference guide, online validation or a step-by-step.

W3Schools.com comes with the motto 'the best things in life ARE free'. It certainly packs a great deal of information into a relatively short space. It caters for both the learner and the master class. Even skilled web developers should turn up for school it says, rather grandly, as 'you might find some points of view a little different from your existing experience and you will be much better prepared for the future'.

If you can get over the schoolmaster-type tone there are many quick-and-easy tutorials covering everything

from XHTML to SOAP. Helpfully, there are also thousands of cut-and-paste examples and with the online HTML editor they supply you can play around with the examples and customize them to suit your needs.

If you have done your lessons right your code should be well-formed. To check if it is, the site has a series of links to online validators run by the Web standards body W3C and others. Simply enter the URL for your page, click the validate button and up comes your test results.

➡ *ASP, CSS, HTML, JavaScript*

WATERMARK

Traditionally a watermark has been used on special printed paper to authenticate its origins and attest to its quality. It is most noticeably seen with currency,

where watermarks are added to help prevent counterfeiting. In the same way, designers, writers and publishers are looking to protect the copyright in their creations using digital watermarks. The watermark can hold all sorts of information, such as who owns the copyright, the audience for which it is intended, and whether it is royalty free or restricted in its use. The watermarks are only visible in software that can read it – currently possible with Digimarc, the PictureMarc plug-in for Adobe Photoshop and for Adobe Acrobat PDF files.

A background image can also be used as a watermark on a web page. This differs from usual backgrounds in that the watermark does not move when you scroll the page. It means taking some care in the design of your page to make sure the watermark doesn't obscure any content that scrolls over it. It's also a feature that doesn't have universal browser support.

➡ **Background Image**

ABOVE: Just as watermarks prevent the counterfeiting of bank notes, designers, writers and publishers are using digital watermarks to protect their work.

WEB DESIGN PROCESS

A web site can take some time to get from the drawing board to the Internet, but the process can be made a lot easier by taking one stage at a time:

1. Identify the purpose of the proposed web site. Decide who it is aimed at and what subject matter will be broached. Search the web for sites covering the same topics or business rivals, and decide how your site will be different. These decisions will help decide the tone of the site's overall design.

2. Create a basic section structure, drawing up a list of the primary sections and subdirectories that the site will be split into. Create a storyboard – a flowchart showing how the pages will connect to the parent pages and to each other. Decide the content of each page and assign filenames.

3. Choose a colour scheme and typefaces. The choice depends on the site's focus and target audience. If it is a business site, choose formal styles, serif fonts and cool shades; hobbyist or personal sites might go for a lighter feel with brighter colours and less austere typefaces.

4. Decide whether you are going to design the page to a fixed width, and if so, which width should you choose? An 800 x 600-pixel window will display on most monitors without any horizontal scroll, but will you want to risk alienating users of 640 x 480-pixel screens?

5. Create the basic template, first sketching it out, then transferring your ideas to a web editor (possibly after creating an outline in a graphics design package). Create the static graphics – the banner complete with your logo and some basic navigation buttons, for instance, and add them to the template. Transfer the directory structure from the storyboard to the site management section of your web editor.

6. Decide which additional functionality you want to use such as JavaScript or Flash and write or download the necessary scripts. Add any over graphics and apply relative links to your navigation menu.

7. Write the content for all the pages in a word processor so you can spellcheck it before publication. Get a colleague to proofread your work.

8. Feed the new content into the templates and save the pages into the directory structure defined in the original storyboard.

9. When all the pages are ready, proof locally or on a closed server for errors. Ask colleagues to check the site's usability. Run an HTML verification tool like Web Site Garage to check the validity of your code.

10. Upload the site to a server and announce its arrival through web directories and search engines.
➠ *Site Map, Storyboard*

WEB HOSTING

Web server services. Having completed your web site you need to find someone to host it. For personal sites and small 'brochure-style' sites it may be

sufficient to use the free web space most ISPs offer their customers. They do have drawbacks though. Space is limited, usually the ISP's domain name is part of the URL, access speeds may be slow because many members share the same server, and with free services there might be adverts on the site.

Professional web-hosting packages are more flexible as they offer solutions to fit different size web sites – but they come at a price. First you need to check the host uses compatible technologies (For example, UNIX-based servers won't support FrontPage extensions).

Different packages offer variable amounts of web space. If your site has hundreds of pages, or lots of graphics or audio and video files, you're going to need one of the top-end solutions. Equally, you might be better to go with a service offering unlimited data transfer rather than the typical offering of 5–10 gigabytes (GB) per month.

Web hosting services also differ considerably in the special features they offer – such as free scripts and database support, all the way through to secure e-commerce facilities and streaming audio servers.
➠ *Domain Name*

ABOVE LEFT: The final stage of the web design process is announcing the new site's arrival.

WEB PALETTE

Browser-safe colour range; web-safe colours provide a consistent view from low spec machines to the highest, but impose other limitations. The web palette is a selection of 216 colours that will not dither on PCs or Macs. It is built into all the main system and browser palettes. If you designed a GIF with non web-safe colours it would appear with some shifting and dithering on an 8-bit monitor. That is because the browser compensates for the lack of colours the monitor can display by blending (dithering) other colours together to approximate the ones it needs. By using web-safe colours in the graphics you design you can be sure they will look as good on 8-bit monitors as any others. As most images will display properly on 16- and 24-bit monitors it is really only an issue for 8-bit resolution monitors (that can only display 256 colours). It also doesn't affect photographic images or JPEG files the same.

The benefit of using the web palette (also referred to as Web216, Browser-safe and non-dithering) in your designs is that they will have a consistent look for all users across platforms. However, the colour selection isn't the greatest and does have its limitations.

➡ *Browser, Dithering, Pixel, RGB, Web-Safe Colours*

WEB-SAFE COLOURS

Universal colour palette. Because of differences in the specifications of PCs and Macintosh systems, and in a bid to meet the realistic lowest common denominator of 256-colour graphics subsystems, only 216 colours can be certain of appearing identically on all computer systems. Web editors and graphics design programs can be locked to use web-safe colours, and you should use only web-safe colours where possible.

The palette size of 216 colours is a result of accident rather than design. The first colour PCs and Macintosh systems only had 8-bit graphics subsystems with a limited amount of memory, and so could display only 256 colours at most. All other colours would have to be created by combinations of these 256 using a technology called dithering. When choosing which 256 colours should be displayed without dithering, however, the major computer platform developers disagreed slightly, and only 216 colours remained common to the basic palettes of PCs and Macs.

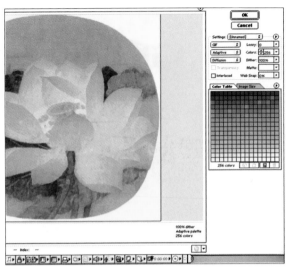

Web-safe palette charts can be viewed online at sites such as www.web-source.net/216_color_chart.htm, and one look at the hex codes of each colour will give a clue as to how the palette was created. The web-safe palette only contains RGB values of 0, 20 per cent, 40 per cent, 60 per cent, 80 per cent and 100 per cent of 255, that is to

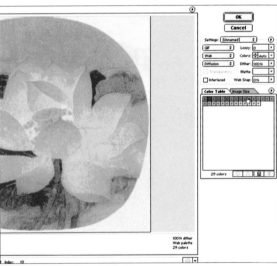

say only red, green and blue values of 0 (00 in hex), 51 (33), 102 (66), 153 (99), 204 (CC) and 255 (FF) are used. If you are entering hex codes manually, colours based on values outside these six will not be web-safe.

It is not necessary to use web-safe colours at all times. Photographs saved as JPEGs, for instance, will degrade when a web-safe palette is applied, and the dithering involved will probably push the file size up as well.

Simple GIFs should always be created from the web-safe palette, especially where expanses of one or two colours are concerned – what looks like a sea of red on your Macintosh screen could become a swamp of brown when the page is opened on a PC.

Small blocks of text – saved as GIFs or generated by HTML – should be web safe, as dithering could render the type unreadable on older monitors. The three or four main components of your site's colour scheme should always be referred to by their web safe hex codes to ensure consistency.

➡ *Dithering, Hex Code, RGB, Web Palette*

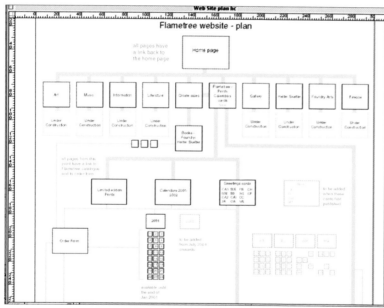

WEB SITE STRUCTURE

The first step in designing a web site is to set out its structure. This governs the site's directory structure, and determines the nature of the navigation system that readers will ultimately see on every page.

Beyond small sites in which all the files sit in one root directory, there are three main types of site structure in widespread use – hierarchical, sequential, and grid.

The hierarchical structure is based on a series of nested directories, all of which stem from the index page in the root directory. The index or homepage links to several section index pages, each of which sits in its own directory and links to a set of topic pages or to third-level directories containing further subsection indexes. The whole structure resembles an inverted family tree, with the branches meeting at the homepage.

The hierarchic structure's navigation system links every page to its parent and, if applicable, its child page. The main, second-level sections and the homepage should also be accessible from every page.

A typical example of the hierarchic structure is a news site that is divided into topics and subtopics.

In a sequential structure, pages flow out from the homepage to form a linear narrative. It is usually suited to extended features and tutorials. It is impossible to read page 5, for instance, without having opened pages 1 to 4. The navigation structure of each page merely takes the reader to 'Previous' and 'Next' pages, as well as back Home.

Pages can have additional single pages breaking out from them (to illustrate a tutorial, for instance), but these should form an online cul-de-sac where the only direction is back to the referring page. In such a case, opening a second browser window for these side pages is a neat solution.

The grid structure is different in that all pages have equal weight and all link to each other. The user can follow any route through the pages, so the content of such a structure has to be well conceived so that each page can stand independent of the others. The grid structure is best used in academic sites where the reader will already have a basic knowledge of a subject.

When you have decided on a structure, sketch a storyboard showing the links between directories and pages and base your site and navigation system around it. A firm structure is the first step towards offering readers an intuitive, usable web site.

➡ *Navigation, Site Map, Storyboard*

WEB STANDARDS

 Conforming to W3C recommendations. HTML standards are recommended by the World Wide Web Consortium (W3C) for browser developers, web software companies and developers to follow. W3C now recommends standards for HTML, XHTML, CSS and XML as well as a host of less important web technologies.

W3C makes its recommendations after a lengthy consultation process that begins when one of the organization's members – which include the computer industry's biggest corporations – makes a submission for a new standard. W3C's working group then produces a series of drafts until the final version is recommended to the industry.

Web standards are designed to be both backwards-compatible and forwards-compatible. Pages conforming to older recommendations should appear error-free on future browsers, while sites based on future standards should at least display their core content on older browsers.

Many of the W3C's recommendations have yet to reach the desktop, and while the XHTML 1.1 standard was ratified in May 2001, versions 6.0 of Netscape Navigator and Microsoft Internet Explorer (IE) both conform to HTML 4.0, recommended back in 1998. This in itself was an achievement, as versions 4.0 of Navigator and IE appeared at a time of heightened competition and attempted to outdo each other with proprietary tags called 'extensions'.

Now that the browser makers are conforming to the standards, it is down to the designers to comply. It makes sense to write to the recommendations. By conforming to HTML 3.2 for instance, you know that your site will be compatible with most currently installed browsers. If you do not conform, you might have to write two separate sites, one for each major

Other standards in development at the W3C are cascading style sheets (CSS1 and CSS2 are already recommended, a compact CSS3 is in draft), XML and XSL.

Even if you intend writing to a W3C standard, your web editing software might not be (FrontPage, for example, favours some IE extensions) so have a copy of the HTML standards to hand and run a site through an HTML checker such as Web Site Garage (http://websitegarage.netscape.com) or Doctor HTML (www2.imagiware.com/RxHTML/) to trace any non-standard elements.

➡ *Cross-Browser Compatibility, W3C*

WEBREFERENCE.COM *(www.webreference.com)*

Site-building tutorials. A reference site mainly for those with some experience of web design and development, Webreference.com does have links that are useful for everyone. This site is more for the intermediate to expert designer or developer. Its tutorials and articles deal with the latest cutting edge technology, rather than basic 'how to' guides. The site covers a lot of ground. The expert comment covers 3D, Graphics and Design, HTML, DHTML and JavaScript as well as Perl and XML.

As a reference site it has a colour reference chart to help you pick colours for web charts – either as names or numbers – and it has a guide to HTML characters and XML. It also has a number of forums where you can pick the brains of your fellow designers. In fact, you can link through to any of the discussion groups run by Internet.com, the company that owns the web site and many others (including HTML Goodies).

Just so it's not all work and no play the site does have its own license plate Internet gallery. If you have what the Americans call a 'vanity plate' that's linked in some way to the Internet, then you are in. The car license plates that have made it so far include INTRNET, DOT COM and BYTE LAW.

➡ *CSS, DHTML, HTML, JavaScript, Perl, XML*

CENTRE: Webreference.com provides a wealth of information on web design and development.

browser – a certain waste of resources.

In the future, standards compliance will be even more important. The XHTML standard, which has replaced HTML as the recommended markup language, is a stepping stone to a standard that will allow developers to create content for desktop PC, mobile PDAs and mobile phones, all in one file.

WINZIP FILE

Compressed file. To save space and download time many files on the Internet are saved as ZIP files. This is particular so on FTP sites or shareware sites where a large number of programs are being stored. ZIP files have .zip as the file extension. Once downloaded the compressed file needs to be unzipped before it can work. WinZip is one of the most popular programs for handling these ZIP files in Windows (StuffIt Expander for the Mac can also decompress these files).

When WinZip unzips the file it opens the ZIP archive, extracts all the files in it, decompresses them and stores them in separate new files. The program also has an Internet Browser Support add-on. This works as a helper application to both Internet Explorer and Netscape. It automates the downloading of compressed files to a Downloads folder on the user's hard drive. It will then (optionally) open them.

To protect against any nasty viruses lurking in the ZIP file, WinZip can link up to most virus scanners and can create archives, in order to keep related files together, while compressing them to save space. A trial version of Winzip can be downloaded from www.winzip.com.

➥ *File Size*

WYSIWYG

What you see is what you get; web-page layout. There are many ways to create HTML pages, but for the beginner the easiest is with WYSIWYG (what you see is what you get) programs. Web-authoring tools such as Macromedia's Dreamweaver and Microsoft's FrontPage are fast becoming the Web equivalent of page layout tools like QuarkXPress.

As WYSIWYG HTML editors they let you build and view the pages graphically, just as they will appear in the browser. You can draw tables, add images and set up text styles without ever looking at the HTML code or typing in a tag.

In practice, if you want to get beyond a fairly simple page you do need to have a basic understanding of the code behind. To make it easier Dreamweaver lets you split the page view so you have the graphical page view below and the code for it above.

One note of caution though. While your page may look good in the preview browser of your WYSIWYG HTML editor it's no guarantee it's going to look the same for your visitors who will be accessing your site through a variety of browsers viewed on desktops of different resolutions.

➥ *Dreamweaver (Macromedia), FrontPage (Microsoft)*

XML

Extensible Markup Language. Although this is similar to HTML in syntax, it operates differently. While HTML controls how documents are displayed, XML simply looks at the structure. It separates the content on a page from the way it is presented. As a markup language HTML uses a fixed number of tags.

It also specifies exactly what each one means and how it will look in the browser. XML only uses the tags to separate pieces of data. Thus, <p> in an XML file is not necessarily a paragraph mark, but can be anything – such as price or person – according to the application that reads it.

With XML, users create their own tags for special kinds of documents, such as a medical chart or a transcript of a play; hence it is extensible. XML-capable browsers then lay out the document following instructions supplied in the associated style sheets.

The advantage of separating style from structure is that you can take the same content and deliver it in different ways – such as in HTML for a web site or via WAP for a mobile phone – without having to produce different pages for each device.

➡ *Functionality, Webreference.com*

XHTML

Markup Language. As the next generation of HTML, XHTML is a much tougher task master specifically designed for smaller handheld devices. As demands on browsers are becoming more complicated, so the software gets bigger. This means they are not always suitable for smaller devices, such as handhelds. EXtensible Hypertext Markup Language (XHTML) aims to cut HTML down in size by simplifying the rules and being much stricter about applying them. It also introduces a new idea of profiles, by which not all devices support all tags. With Modularized XHTML, devices like PDAs can say what tags they do or do not support (e.g. not colour) while web sites let them know what tags are needed.

XHTML is often seen as the next generation of HTML. It is based on the latest HTML standard, version 4.01 and is designed to be used with XML. While it might not always seem so, HTML is generally forgiving if you make a mistake, such as improperly nesting a tag.

Among the several changes introduced with XHTML are that all attributes, events and tags must be in lower case; all elements must be closed and correctly nested; values for attributes must go in quote marks; and there must be a DOCTYPE declaration.

➡ *Functionality*

LEFT: XML enables information to be delivered in different ways, for example via WAP to a mobile phone.

THE TOP 10 RULES OF USER-FRIENDLY WEB DESIGN

Anyone can create a web site; the difficulty is building a good one, in which form and function work together. It is easy to be seduced by all the flashy gimmicks and cool extras you can add to your site. With animated GIFs, looping sound tracks, flashing banners, rotating pictures and ticker tape style text, it is not difficult to create a site that has all the sophistication of a pair of Elton John's spectacles. But, at the end of the day, no amount of glitter is going to keep people at a site that has nothing of interest to them.

The minimalist look is definitely in when it comes to web design. The philosophy is very much less is more, as we'll see in some of the rules listed below. These 'rules' are drawn from dozens of usability studies carried out on thousands of sites across the World Wide Web. They are guidelines drawn from the experience of users around the Web on what they do and don't like.

With these, as with all rules, the temptation is to break them. After all, the Web is a public space, there for you to make of it what you will. But before ignoring the tried and tested experience of others it's as well to have some notion of why these rules exist in the first place and whether, in particular cases, it may be safe to ignore them.

1. LIKE HANNIBAL, HAVE A PLAN

Just like in a professional football game, most of the work in a web site comes in the training. Before you start laying out the pages you need a clear idea of what information will be available on the site and how it is to be structured, so that it is easy and logical to navigate.

The first stage of that process is to decide what to call the different categories and sections you intend to have on the site. These need to make sense to the user and help them find what they want, rather than fit in with any arcane naming conventions your company or organization may have. You may know that FXG is the name of your wonderful line of notebooks, but your users won't. Nor can you rely on them to search for the information. Studies show that most users rely on category names to locate information, rather than doing a site search.

It is also essential to plan out the navigation elements and the basic design (look and feel) of the site rather than having to lose time later revising pages that you thought you had finished.

2. GO FOR THE CONTENTED LOOK

Ultimately, it is the content of a site that draws people back, so unless that is right, you haven't got an audience. On bigger sites, the process of getting the content right – making sure that it sells its message, sets the right tone and

is both jargon-free and relevant to the audience – will need the help of professional writers. But there are ways in which design can be used to make the content more accessible and readable.

The quality of the content is less important than its presentation. Most content on the Web isn't read, it is scanned (only when something of interest is noted is it read fully), so the information needs to be presented in a way which helps to smooth out this scan reading.

Your message just won't get through if it is presented as one long expanse of text. It needs to be broken up into logical units, each with its own heading or series of headings, sub-heads, introductions, break-out quotes and links to other relevant items.

Stories also have to live up to their billing. News should be just that – new. There's nothing more likely to turn a visitor away than a 'latest news' section carrying out-of-date stories or events. Also annoying for readers are undated items, which leave them to guess which are the recent articles and which aren't.

3. LINK YOUR WAY HOME

Research has shown that where there are strong visual clues to links, users will find information up to seven times faster. These visual clues include the traditional blue, underlined text used on many sites for hyperlinks; although perhaps not the most aesthetically pleasing combination, it is now well embedded in the user's psyche with the idea of links (NB. as blue is associated with a link it shouldn't be used for non-link text as it will only confuse users).

Users also expect the link to change colour when clicked so as to prevent the frustration of inadvertently following the same link several times and bouncing backwards and forwards between the same pages.

Well signposted links can also ease navigation. On some sites this is the only way for the visitors to reorient themselves. To escape the frustration of ending up down some virtual blind alley there should be a clear link to get back Home from every page.

4. BE CONSISTENT

Users like the familiar and consistency on several fronts – design, navigation and technology – is important in helping your visitors feel in control of what they're doing. When a web site behaves how the visitors expect it to, it is reassuring for them. It also makes the site easier to use.

This consistency isn't just with reference to your site, but also to how it differs from, or is similar to, other sites. After all, your users will spend much of their time online at other peoples' sites. Their expectations of how to use your site are built on their experiences elsewhere.

There is a clear advantage in making sure that certain common elements, such as logos, navigation bars, links, page footnotes, etc. are consistently placed and styled throughout the site.

Users also build up expectations of what will follow certain actions, so elements should act as expected. For example, with radio buttons; when these are selected, users prefer to be asked to confirm the action (as normally happens) rather than see it triggered automatically.

5. AVOID DEATH BY FORM-FILLING

The Web is a form-filler's paradise. From registration to email subscriptions to online purchases, there are few sites that don't try to grab information from you. Yet studies show that most users regard forms as a necessary (often unnecessary) evil. In the balance between finding out more about your visitors and keeping them, it is better to make your forms as short and automated as possible. However curious you are, users should only be asked for essential data (any additional information requested should be clearly optional and separate). Make sure the language used is easily understood, friendly and as straightforward as possible. Where possible, information should be autofilled (such as entering the billing address details in the delivery address box).

Users also prefer to know what they are letting themselves in for, so they should be given some idea of how long the process will take (e.g. This three step process …).

6. AUTOMATE REPETITIVE TASKS

Where possible, let the site do the work. It makes it easier for visitors to use your site and to find what they want. Ultimately, that will increase their satisfaction and responsiveness. The entry 'barriers' that need to be automated include saving and recalling user names and passwords. Similarly, more functional elements can be automated, such as saving past search results, calculating delivery costs or using registration information to auto-complete other forms.

7. WATCH OUT FOR THE BONSAI TREE EFFECT

In the effort to create a clear, cool interface some sites end up as the web equivalent of a Bonsai tree – small, but perfectly formed. Unfortunately, this doesn't help your user. As everything is in proportion, the font size is also small, which makes your pages difficult to read. There is also little space for navigational aids, pictures etc.

8. DON'T OVERUSE TECHNOLOGY

It is easy to be seduced by web technology. Technological advances come fast and furious, but not all of them remain popular with users. At one stage, Push technology was all the rage, but now has largely disappeared. What dictates success or failure is user acceptance and users, as a group, are generally conservative.

Users dislike distractions. Perhaps because of the original 'open' values of the Web they are particularly suspicious of anything that attempts to blur the distinction between advertisements and web page content. In fact, studies have found that users can deliberately screen out distractions, such as animations and blinking or flashing text, which they associate with adverts. So be careful if you put content in shapes, styles or positions normally used in advertising.

Similarly, pop-up windows, long a favourite with advertisers, are being used for follow-on or linked content. Research suggests that users find pop-ups irritating and consider them to be more frustrating than useful.

For similar reasons, be wary of splash screens (for splash read Flash). They might look nice and provide a great opportunity to be creative, but do they add anything to the user's experience? To avoid irritating and delaying regular visitors, splash screens should come with a Skip Intro button. But the very fact that they need to come equipped with their own escape device perhaps suggests just how essential they are.

Even more annoying are sites where you have to click on the final splash page image to enter the site – although there is no text to inform the user and it doesn't happen automatically. From the close of the intro, the site should always load directly to the Home page.

9. OPTIMIZE GRAPHICS

Like Michael Schumacher meeting the Grand Prix tailenders, most web users are impatient. They won't wait for slow sites to download. In fact, research has found that users are unlikely to wait more than 10 seconds for a page to load. The ideal load time should be less than half that.

Generally, a slow download time is due to graphics – either too many on the page or too big – or slow server speed. Graphics are relatively easy to fix, as most image editors today have special tools for optimizing pictures for the Web.

10. CHECK THE SITE FOR ERRORS

Just when you think you've finished – start checking. There are plenty of tools to help you, but it is mostly a question of going through the site page by page and building your own bug list. You should attempt to view your pages through as many different browsers as possible and use an HTML validation program. Not only will this check the code is right, but most will also check that the various links are working. A 'page not found' message, a missing link, a runtime error … all of these things can damage the image of a site and put off visitors.

SOFTWARE TOOLS

HTML EDITORS

HomeSite
PC only

www.macromedia.com

HomeSite is for those who like to hand-code their HTML, although it does have its own drag-and-drop window for laying out visual elements. It is particularly strong in the manual coding tools it offers, including clear colour-coding for a variety of script types, from CSS to JavaScript, and a useful Tag inspector.

BBEdit
Mac only

www.barebones.com

BBEdit is the equivalent hand-coder's tool for the Macintosh. It is rich in features, including colour-coded HTML syntax, support for more than a dozen programming languages, multiple file search and replace, built-in FTP function and an HTML checker. (There is a freeware edition – BBEdit Lite – with fewer features available from www.barebones.com)

WYSIWYG WEB AUTHORING TOOLS

Dreamweaver
PC/Mac

www.macromedia.com

Dreamweaver is a good balance of easy-to-navigate interface with heavy-duty features behind and is the tool of choice for many professionals. Its increasing integration with the other Macromedia products – HomeSite, Flash, Fireworks, and Director – makes it essential for the serious web designer. Particularly useful when troubleshooting pages is the way it enables you to switch between the Design and Code view, or see both simultaneously. One of the most fully featured tools on the market, it has an advantage over its rivals in that it is less likely to add proprietary code, or change code that you have written.

Dreamweaver UltraDev
PC/Mac

www.macromedia.com

Sometimes referred to as Dreamweaver on steroids. It has all the features of the basic WYSIWYG authoring tool together with a whole set of scripts and wizards to enable you to link up your site to a database. Although more complicated to learn, it's great for those who want database-driven content.

GoLive
PC/Mac

www.adobe.com

Adobe's version of drag-and-drop web authoring is well integrated with the company's graphics applications, such as Photoshop and Illustrator. As a result, GoLive has been viewed as a product for the more advanced designer. In fact, GoLive has a lot of features to make web authoring easier. It is particularly good for site management and has a very useful set of table-editing tools. It also has the Smart Objects function, which makes adding files to the page – whether images, animation or video – drag-and-drop simple. One drawback though, with lots of palettes, windows and menus, your desktop can soon get in a muddle.

FrontPage
PC only
www.microsoft.com

A step up from using Word to produce web pages, FrontPage offers the Microsoft treatment of wizards, themes and templates to make web site creation easy for beginners or people in a hurry. It has suffered in the past from a reputation for bloating the code. Some of the extra features it includes, such as adding a counter to your page, need FrontPage extensions to run. If you do use these, make sure that your ISP supports the extensions.

HoTMetaL Pro
PC only
www.hotmetalpro.com

Hot metal Pro's traditional strength as a heavy duty HTML text editor still shines through, in much the same way that HTML is pushed in the name of the product. Now owned by Corel, it is a full drag-and-drop authoring tool that comes with a much lower price tag than some of its meatier rivals. One useful touch is the Asset Manager, which provides an easy way to add counters and scrolling text. It also comes with an FTP program for transferring the finished site and provides remote editing facilities.

IMAGE EDITORS

Adobe Photoshop/ImageReady
PC/Mac
www.adobe.com

The professional's tool of choice, Photoshop has become the de facto standard in image-editing. There is a steep learning curve to master all that it offers, but it is worth it, provided your equipment is up to it. It does require

a lot of memory to work effectively. Photoshop was originally designed to edit images for print. A separate program, ImageReady, was available for web optimization and editing. Now, however, it is integrated into Photoshop itself, so you can work on images from print to online screen. ImageReady is handy for slicing images, producing rollovers, basic animation and making it easier to add transparency to GIFs.

Photoshop Elements
PC/Mac
www.adobe.com

For those trembling at Photoshop's industry standard price tag there is Photoshop Elements. This slim cousin to the main program is aimed at the home market. It is much easier to learn – and to use – despite which it still has a number of special effects and filters to add to images.

Paint Shop Pro
PC only
www.jasc.com

A good starting point for the novice. As feature-rich as most of the more expensive image editors, it is easier to learn. It has a comprehensive set of filters that can be added to images, with the chance to preview them before applying them. It also has a buttonize option, which simplifies creating web page buttons. Included with the program is its own fully-fledged animation application – Animation Shop.

Fireworks
PC/Mac
www.macromedia.com

Fireworks is specifically designed for working with web images and integrating with its sister products, Dreamweaver and Flash. It can bring bitmaps, vectors and animations down in size. Particularly useful when optimizing graphics is the preview window, where you can try images in different formats and see the effect it has on file size and download time. Other useful features include the pop-up menu creator for a quick and easy way to create dropdown menus and rollovers that are drag-and-drop simple. It also includes a number of features to help with the batch-processing of images.

Serif PhotoPlus
PC only
www.serif.com

At the budget end of the market, Serif's PhotoPlus has a surprising number of high-end capabilities. It can do many of the things that its more expensive rivals do, such as Photoshop-style options for creating bevels, drop-shadows, etc. It also has an automatic image extraction aid and can provide some funky effects using its Warp tool.

DRAWING APPLICATIONS

Illustrator
PC/Mac
www.adobe.com

The industry standard for vector graphics, Illustrator is a good all-round drawing program, suitable for both print and web-based projects. It has a number of features designed to speed up the design process. There are symbol

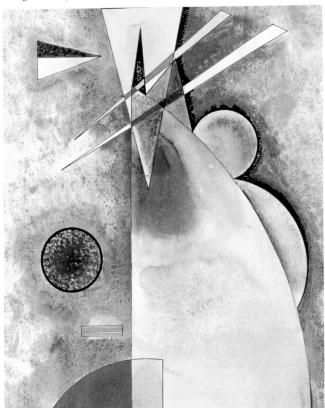

tools to easily create repeating graphics and keep file size down. There are features to optimize slicing, support for Flash and anti-aliasing to make small text easier to read. It also offers scripting support to automate those tedious, repetitive tasks.

Freehand
PC/Mac
www.macromedia.com

Freehand is Macromedia's rival to Illustrator as the drawing program of choice. It provides the tools to create sophisticated vector-based illustrations, which can then be repurposed across different mediums, such as the Web or print. Master Pages enable users to set attributes which can be shared by a range of pages in a document. Editable symbol libraries mean graphics can be updated instantly. Illustrations used for Flash movies can also be tested right inside Freehand using the Flash Navigation Panel.

Expression 2
PC/Mac
www.creaturehouse.com

Whatever your style – bold, messy or simple – you can express it here. Expression 2 allows users to take pictures and use them to create their own types of brush strokes. They are saved as skeletal strokes. These can then be applied like any paintbrush, with the added advantage of being both scaleable and editable. The finished artwork can be exported to a variety of formats including Flash SWF.

CorelDraw Graphics Suite
PC/Mac
www.corel.com

The Graphics Suite is actually several programs in one package. CorelDraw is the vector graphics editor, Photo-Paint is the image editor, and R.A.V.E. a powerful animation tool. Graphics can be saved in a variety of formats including support for SVG and Macromedia's SWF format. Files can be published in HTML, or output to PDF, Flash or print. CorelDraw is particularly strong on the range of texture-fill effects it offers.

MULTIMEDIA/ANIMATION APPLICATIONS

Flash MX
PC/Mac
www.macromedia.com

Once the scourge of bandwidth and wasteful exhibitionism, Flash now has a mainstream role. For the designer, it can be used to create simple animations or user-interfaces. For the developer, it is at the heart of new interactive content, thanks in part to its support for standard video files. The clips can be compressed and fitted into the Timeline so that they can be controlled by ActionScript and treated like any other object. The Actions Editor has a useful reference panel, with information on every command available. Hints also appear when you enter code manually. Templates can be generated from any Flash movie to speed up work on repetitive projects. In fact, the whole design process can be short-circuited by using the pre-defined files that come with the program.

LiveMotion
PC/Mac
www.adobe.com

Adobe's answer to the ever-present Flash. The LiveMotion software has full ActionScript support, so it can be used to create interactive content in a variety of formats including the same SWF format used by Flash. Using the Script Editor, you can generate Automation scripts – snippets of code that can be reused to speed up the whole creation process. As an Adobe product, it is also tightly integrated with their other design tools. Indeed, Photoshop users can import images with layers and automatically convert these layers into an animated sequence.

Director
PC/Mac
www.macromedia.com

This is a heavyweight product, at a heavyweight price. But what you get for your money is not only a superb animation tool but also a sophisticated product for creating fantastic multimedia presentations, whether for the Web or CD-ROM/DVD. In particular, Director includes Web 3D which enables you to import 3D models and alter them by applying the appropriate behaviour or script. The knowledgeable can add these 'behaviours' using Director's native scripting language Lingo, or from the range of 3D behaviours and triggers available in Director's Library palette. It's possible to add movement and special effects to virtually any model. What's more, these animations are played through the 3D-enhanced Shockwave player. As Shockwave 3D is scaleable, content can still be viewed by users with relatively low-spec PCs.

Toon Boom Studio
PC/Mac
www.toonboomstudio.com

If by animation you really mean cartoons, then Toon Boom Studio is the tool for you. Its claim to fame (or otherwise) is that it was used to create The Rugrats. The whole process is split into several different modes – the Exposure Sheet for organizing files; the Animate mode for drawing and testing the animation; and Paint for colouring. The Sound Element Editor is a real time saver as it not only lets you edit the audio tracks, but also analyses the voice track and suggests the sequence of mouth shapes needed to produce it. Another handy element is the 3D scene-planning mode, which helps you to plan and arrange background elements according to different 'camera' angles. Each animation can then be output as either a SWF or QuickTime file.

SWiSH
PC
www.swishzone.com

At the budget end of the market, SwiSH lets you create Flash …without Flash. It enables you to create simple Flash effects for your web site without having to go through the steep learning curve demanded by the other, more sophisticated products. In fact, SWiSH comes with more than 150 built-in effects (although some of them are a little corny), including text animations, rollover buttons, intro movies and interactive presentations. It also includes SWF optimization tools to keep file sizes down. What it doesn't have is the advanced scripting features of Flash, but for a budget SWF-generating package SWiSH is hard to beat.

DV/STREAMING VIDEO

After Effects
PC/Mac
www.adobe.com

Software that lets you add visual effects to film, multimedia, video and the Web. It covers both 2D and 3D effects and comes with a whole host of special filters. For example, the Light Transmission property for 3D layers can be used to create a stained glass window effect, or to cast a coloured shadow. Multiple views can be used to alter a composition according to different perspectives.

There are also tools to control anti-aliasing and motion blur. Finished files can be exported as SWF format, RealMedia, QuickTime or Windows Media and, as always with Adobe, there is close integration between After Effects and the company's other products, such as Photoshop and Premiere.

Cleaner
PC/Mac
www.discreet.com

Cleaner will import virtually any kind of movie file and package it for streaming on the Web, whether for RealVideo, QuickTime or Windows Media. A settings wizard makes it easy to set up clear streaming video, so you can add interactive content such as Buy Me! Links or hot spots. As it is a cross-platform encoding tool (and works with many of the main design and editing tools including GoLive, Dreamweaver, Flash, and Premiere), it is rapidly becoming a standard solution for streaming media over the Internet.

Premiere
PC/Mac
www.adobe.com

Want to be the Spielberg of the Web? Premiere is the all-in-one video-editing application that enables you to capture, edit and format video for the Internet. Using your PC's FireWire or i.Link port, Premiere can usually capture video from your camcorder without the need for additional hardware, such as a video capture card. It has the whole suite of professional editing tools – the audio mixer, a storyboard window for visualizing the layout of clips, the Timeline window for editing together the video project and adding transitions or effects, and a customizable workspace so that you can arrange the windows and palettes on screen as you want them.

MISCELLANEOUS

HTML Shrinker Pro
PC only
www.thepluginsite.com
The housekeeper of the HTML world. It tidies up your code, but leaves any comments or SSI commands alone. What it will remove are excess spacing, unnecessary tags and odd line breaks. It not only scours the HTML, it will also strip clean JavaScript, PHP, VBScript and Perl. The Light version is freeware (more accurately linkware, if you use it you place a link on your site to the Home page of HTML Shrinker). The Pro version, available at a modest cost, has more features and works faster.

CSE HTML Validator Pro
PC only
www.htmlvalidator.com/
If you want to check your HTML for problems then CSE HTML Validator Lite will whizz through and spotlight any major errors. It also has the great price tag of being free (not only free of charge but free of ads as well). However, the serious designer/developer will probably want the commercial Pro version, which includes link checking, a more powerful HTML/text editor and a wider-ranging syntax checker that also covers CSS and WML.

TopStyle Pro
PC only
www.bradsoft.com/topstyle/
By the original creator of HomeSite, this program aims to bring the same ease-of-use to creating flexible cross-browser style sheets. It does so by using wizards to help set them up. It includes colour coding, to clearly separate different elements and mark off invalid names, and also

offers context-sensitive links to the appropriate Help item. Perhaps equally importantly, it aids you through the minefield of cross-browser support by showing which browsers support the current style property and which properties or values are invalid or unsupported.

Adobe Acrobat
PC/Mac
www.adobe.com
Acrobat creates PDF files that enable documents to be seen just as they were originally presented, regardless of the type of computer or platform they are viewed on. Documents will have the same layout, images, fonts, links, etc., even if the person viewing them does not have them on his system. For the PDF documents to be viewed, all that is needed is the Acrobat Reader, free from www.adobe.com. As many vendors deliver their help files in PDF format, most users will have this already installed. Additionally, Acrobat has a number of navigation features, which makes it easier to read through long documents. It's also possible to comment on, or digitally sign, PDF files from within a web browser.

GLOSSARY

Accessibility

Initiatives to make web sites more easily available and readable by people with disabilities, particularly those with sight or hearing impairments.

ADSL

Asymmetric Digital Subscriber Line is part of the broadband revolution as it provides a fast, 'always on' connection to the Internet, over existing phone lines. Download speeds are up to 10 times faster than over the quickest traditional dial-up connection.

Alternative text

Text used to describe an image that will display in the browser window. It is specified by using the ALT attribute within the <IMG> tag.

ASCII

Short for the American Standard Code for Information Exchange. ASCII files are just made up of alphanumeric characters. Sometimes referred to as plain text files.

Attribute

Comes within the HTML tag to provide extra information about how to treat the tagged item.

Avatar

A character or figure used to represent people in graphics-based chat rooms.

AVI

Audio Video Interleaved. A standard file format for mixed digital video and audio files that ensures smoother playback.

Binary files

Files made up of compiled data, such as images, programs, or movies. Binaries are also sometimes referred to as raw or image data.

Bit depth

In design, the number of bits used to record each pixel of information for an image file. The more bits, the greater the number of colours that can be displayed. For instance, 8-bit can represent 256 colours, or shades of grey, while 24-bit can show 16.7 million colours.

Block element

In HTML, this applies to a chunk, or block, of text that automatically has space inserted above and below it.

Cache

An area where frequently used data is kept. The information can be accessed more quickly from the cache than it can from other areas, such as the hard drive. Web pages can also be cached, so that when you want to look at them again they are loaded speedily from the computer, rather than being downloaded again from the Internet.

Capture

In Windows, pressing the Print Screen key enables you to save, or 'capture', the current screen as an image. The image can then be pasted into a document or graphics editor. To capture just the active window and not the whole screen press Alt and Print Screen.

Case-sensitive

Software may distinguish between lowercase (small) and uppercase (capital) letters. For example, most passwords are case-sensitive, so writing 'George543' as the password will not be the same as 'george543'.

Child

A small window displayed inside a main window, often used to display options.

Container tag

In HTML, a tag that has both an opening and a closing (e.g. <h2>...</h2>).

Data transfer rate

The data transfer rate is the speed at which data – which can be anything the computer processes such as numbers, words, or images – can be read from the hard disk and transferred to the processor.

Deprecated

To match the old-fashioned sound of the word, deprecated tags are those in HTML that are viewed as out of date. Designers are discouraged from using them in favour of newer specifications (more often than not, style sheets).

Design spec

The blueprint that sets out how each area of the site is to be laid out.

Dialog box

A message window that expects some form of response (such as pressing a button). It is a dialog in the sense that it's the closest there is to a conversation between the computer and the user.

Domain name

The domain name is part of the site name (or URL) and ends with the TLD (top-level domain) category. Some of

the newer TLDs being introduced to compensate for the shortage of available names are .info and biz. The Domain name is a lot easier for people to remember than the 12-digit IP address that it corresponds to. It is the numerical IP address that is actually used to locate the site on the Web.

DPI

Dots per inch. This is the resolution of a printed image. It is the number of dots that a printer can print on an inch of paper. It is also often (but wrongly) used to represent the screen resolution of web graphics. The correct way to measure this is by the number of pixels per inch (ppi).

DTD

Document Type Definition. A file that defines the tags in an XML or SGML document and specifies how they should be interpreted and displayed.

Dynamic

Generally, it is used to mean something that changes immediately it is needed, such as a web page where the information is updated in real-time. Dynamic HTML is a set of technologies, among them CSS and JavaScript, that can help add animation and interaction to web pages.

Emoticon
Emotional Icons, better known as 'smileys'. Made by pressing keyboard keys, they look like faces displaying some particular emotion. Often used in chat rooms to speed up conversation.

End tag
Optional with some tags in HTML, the end tag is often the same as the start tag but with a slash character (/) before it.

Event handler
An action that is triggered when a certain event happens. That event can be interactive – such as the user clicking a button, or it can simply be the page loading.

Ezine
You'll find a few in your inbox. Short for electronic magazine, an ezine is a magazine or newsletter that's available via the Web or email, usually for free.

FAQ
A handy standby for any web site. While many users will feel humiliated to click on the Help button they will quite happily read through a list of Frequently Asked Questions.

Firewall
While firewalls can protect networks (and individual PCs) from outside threats such as hackers, they can also interfere with some of your site's best features. Instant messaging is particularly prone to being blocked by corporate firewalls.

Flame
Red-hot passions can be aroused by messages in email forums or other online chats. To flame is to send rude or insulting emails to someone whose opinion you don't agree with. Those who do are called flamers. When setting up your bulletin boards or forums you need to decide if they will be moderated and how you will deal with any abuses.

Forum
As in Roman days, a public space where people can meet and talk with each other. In virtual forums it is by posting messages that can be read and replied to.

Frames
A way of splitting the browser window into separate areas each of which can hold and display a different HTML page.

FTP
File Transfer Protocol is a system for moving files between computers on the Internet. It is a client/server system where one PC must be running as an FTP server, while the other has an FTP client.

Gamma
Marks the overall brightness of a computer monitor's display.

GUI
Graphical User Interface (pronounced gooey). The designer's friend. A way of representing files, functions and folders with images (icons). The same visual shorthand is often applied to navigation elements on web pages.

Hacker
This term has lost its original meaning as someone who loved messing around with computers and is now synonymous with people who try to break into computer systems illegally.

Helper Applications
Programs, such as sound or movie players that are launched by the browser to play content downloaded from the Web that it can't play itself. They are different from plug-ins, as they are not part of the browser and can be run as stand-alone programs (e.g. RealPlayer).

Hierarchical File System
A way of storing and organizing files so that each file or folder is within other folders on a disk. The main directory (folder) for the disk is called the root. The 'route' to get from there to a particular file or folder is called the path.

Hit
The original way to measure traffic to a web site has now been superseded. While the number of hits was an indication of how popular a site was, it would take several hits to download a full page. Now the number of visits (that is individual users) to a web page is used as a better measure of how busy a site is.

Home page
The Home page can be the first page you see when you log on to the Internet or the start page of any web site.

Hotspot
An area of an image that does something if you move the mouse pointer over it and click. Normally, you can tell where the hotspot is, as the mouse pointer changes shape from an arrow to a hand.

Host
Another term for the server. Web-hosting services are provided by companies that offer server space for web sites.

Indexed colour
A graphics editing option that enables you to map an image to a different, usually restricted, palette of colours.

Information Architect
With complex sites, there is the difficulty of information overload. The information architect is responsible for deciding how information should be organized on the web pages and how users can access it.

Inheritance
Used in cascading style sheets to determine the properties that elements will inherit from other elements, unless some other property is specifically attributed to them.

Interstitials
While-you-wait advertisements. Interstitial ads are shown in between the web pages loading.

IP/IP Address
The numeric address used to locate and identify computers on a network. The IP address is made up of four numbers from 0 to 255, separated by dots (.).

IRC
Internet Relay Chat – chat for short – is the protocol that enables real-time messaging between users.

ISDN
Integrated Services Digital Network. A way of transmitting digital data over a telephone network at high speed – much faster than normal modems. Now superseded by DSL technologies.

ISP

Internet Service Provider. A company that offers users a connection to the Internet, whether dial-up or, increasingly, broadband. The Internet Service Provider has high-speed connections to the backbone of the Internet.

Java virtual machine

The layer within the software that acts as a sandbox to execute the Java code. It is because the code runs in the virtual machine that Java can work with different operating systems across different platforms.

Keyword

The word that is most relevant or important. Often used in searches where any document found must have the keywords in them. You can increase the chances of your pages being returned by search engines by specifying the relevant keywords in the <META> tag at the top of your HTML page.

Load balancing

Only likely if your site becomes very popular. Load balancing splits the site data between servers (or mirrors the same data to several servers) so users can get the information they want from the server that is least busy or most accessible.

Lossless compression

Graphics are compressed using a system where all the original information stored in the image is kept intact.

Lossy compression

Offers a smaller file size but during compression some of the data is lost or approximated.

Media Player

A utility program supplied free with Windows, which allows you to run multimedia files including sound or video files.

Mailto:

With this hyperlink the user's email client opens automatically with certain details, such as the address it is being sent to, already filled in.

MIME

Multipurpose Internet Mail Extensions. Used with browsers and email software to specify the format of a file so that the operating system opens the correct application to use it.

Monospaced

Fonts in which every character takes up an equal amount of space, helpful for aligning text very accurately. The most common monospaced font is Courier.

MP3

Very popular file format for storing music files. Uses MPEG compression to reduce file size dramatically while maintaining near CD-ROM quality.

MPEG

Moving Pictures Expert Group. A set of standards for compressing audio and video files.

Multi-homing

Not pigeons returning to their lofts, but web servers that host more than one domain.

Nesting

In HTML, placing one set of tags within another, such as the list tags.

Netiquette

NETwork ETIQUETTE. Netiquette describes the rules of polite, online society. If you don't behave you could be flamed or kicked out of the particular newsgroup or forum. Like all rules of etiquette, what constitutes bad behaviour will vary according to different fashions and groups, but it generally includes posting large amounts of irrelevant material, insulting other people, and posting offensive material.

Palette

A restricted set of colours available to use in a graphic.

Pathname

The route to a file, where the directory, folders sub-folders and filenames are separated by slashes (/).

Perl

Practical Extraction and Report Language. A common programming language for server-side scripting.

PHP

Similar to ASP, this is an open source tool for creating dynamically generated web pages.

PPP

Point-to-point protocol. The method by which TCP/IP information packets can be sent over phone lines.

Protocol

A set of codes and signals that determine how information is exchanged between computers, either across a network or via a modem. Several protocols are used on the Web, including HTTP and FTP.

QuickTime

A highly compressed video format originally used on Apple computers but also available for PCs. It is often used for interactive multimedia software such as encyclopedias. A QuickTime plug-in is needed on PCs.

Refresh rate

To maintain a constant flicker-free image the screen has to be regularly refreshed. This happens many times a second and the frequency is referred to as the refresh rate.

The way it works is that the image is made up of tiny dots of phosphor that shine. As the glow only lasts a few tenths of a second, the dots are fired by an electron picture beam to get them to glow again. This process is repeated up to 70 times or more per second.

Rendering

The process by which the computer takes a 3D model with its data, viewpoints and effects and converts it into a flat screen image that can also be printed out.

Resolution

Measure of the number of pixels that are displayed on your screen. The more pixels per inch (ppi) the sharper the image and the higher the resolution. In print the resolution is measured in dots per inch.

Rich text format (RTF)

A document format that includes all the commands describing the page, type, font and formatting. Because it is supported by most word processors it is a good way to enable formatted documents to be exchanged across different platforms.

Script

Tells the software what to do. Unlike fully fledged programs which are compiled into fast running machine code, scripts are interpreted (read) like any document – line-by-line. Because they aren't turned into machine code they are easier to read and consequently change.

Service

An application that's running all the time on a computer. Sometimes called a daemon.

SGML

Standard Generalized Markup Language. The big daddy of HTML. SGML is a metalanguage, mostly used by government and educational institutions, which provides a set of rules for marking up the structure of text documents and data. HTML is just a subset of SGML itself.

Shareware

Software which is available free for you to sample. If you keep it, you are expected to pay a fee to the writer. Often confused with public-domain software, which is completely free.

Shockwave

A programming language designed to bring animation to web pages. To view its effects you need a plug-in, available free from www.macromedia.com. It enables you to view Director, Authorware, Flash or Freehand multimedia content through your browser.

Staging server

A server that is set up and organized with the same software and pages as the server that is being used to publish the finished site. The staging server can be used to test pages and allow client access before the site is publicly launched.

Standalone tag
In HTML a tag that has no closing tag, such as the <IMG> tag.

Status bar
A line at the bottom of the browser window, which can include various information about the task currently being worked on, such as the file name, the number of items to download, etc.

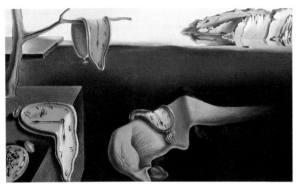

Streaming
A technology that allows media players to start playback before a file has been fully downloaded.

TCP/IP
Stands for transmission control protocol/internet protocol. This is the network protocol used to send information over the Internet. It describes how information must be packaged and addressed so that it reaches the right destination and the computer can understand it.

Telnet
A protocol that allows you to run programs stored on another computer. Often used for administrating web services remotely, such as changing file and directory permissions.

TWAIN
Likely to be mentioned in association with your scanner. TWAIN stands for Technology Without An Interesting Name. It is the standard way for scanners to communicate with a PC. All scanners come with a

TWAIN driver, which makes them compatible with any TWAIN-supporting software (such as most image editing programs).

Validate
In SGML and XML, to check that the document's content matches the rules specified in the document type definition (DTD).

VRML
Virtual Reality Modelling Language. The scripting language used to define 3D shapes on the Web. VRML 3D environments are often called 'Worlds' to differentiate them from the flat 2D image of 'pages' normally associated with the Web.

WAP
Wireless application protocol. WAP-enabled mobile phones can view simple web pages to look at email, check share prices, or get the latest news.

WAIS
Wide Area information Service. This is the protocol used by search engines to build indexes of text pages, such as web pages, so that they can be rapidly searched for information.

WHOIS
A way of checking if a domain name is taken. If it is you can see WHOIS the owner.

WML
Wireless Markup Language. Part of WAP, this is an XML-based language for creating applications for wireless devices.

XML
Extensible Markup Language. A developing standard for marking up documents and data. Although, like HTML, it is based on SGML, XML is more flexible and extensible.

XSL
Extensible Style Language. A style sheet language for use with XML.

BIBLIOGRAPHY

Alexander, Ric, (ed.), *Cyber-Killers*, Orion, UK, 1997

Anuff, Joey, Ana Marie Cox and Terry Colon, *Suck: Worst Case Scenarios*, Wired Books Inc, 1997

Ater, Mark P. and Betty Ater, *Internet User's Handbook 2001*, McFarland & Company, 2001

Baron, Chris and Bob Weil, *Drag 'n' Drop CGI: Enhance Your Web Site Without Programming*, Addison-Wesley, US, 1999

Barron, Bill and Jill Elsworth, *The Internet Unleashed*, SAMS, 1999

Bates, Alan, *Advanced Web Skills*, Dorling Kindersley, 2000

Baumgardt, Michael, *Adobe Photoshop 7 Web Design*, Adobe Press, 2002

Bellinaso, Marco and Kevin Hoffman, *ASP.NET Website Programming: Problem – Design – Solution*, Wrox Press Inc, 2002

Berners-Lee, Tim et al, *Weaving the Web*, Harper, San Francisco, 1999

Besley, Kris et al, *Foundation Macromedia Flash MX*, friends of Ed. 2002

Black, Roger and Steve Krug, *Don't Make Me Think: A Common Sense Approach to Web Usability*, Que, 2000

Bradley, Phil, *The Advanced Internet Searcher's Handbook*, Library Association Publishing, 2001

Buyens, Jim, *Microsoft FrontPage Version 2002 Inside Out*, Microsoft Press, 2001

Castells, Manuel, *The Internet Galaxy*, Oxford University Press, 2001

Castro, Elizabeth, *HTML 4 For the World Wide Web, Fourth Edition: Visual Quick Start Guide*, Peachpit Press, 1999

Collin, Simon, *The Virgin Guide to the Internet*, Ted Smart, 1999

Comer, Douglas and Ralph Droms, *Computer Networks and Internets*, Prentice Hall, 2001

Cooper, Brian, Annalisa Milner and Tim Worsley, *Essential Internet Guide*, UK, 2000

Cotler, Emily and Kelly Goto, *Web Redesign: Workflow That Works*, New Riders Publishing, Indianapolis, 2001

Davis, Ziff, *How to Use Netscape Navigator*, Ziff-Davis Press Development Group, 1997

Downing, Thomas A. and Michael A. Covington, *Dictionary of Computer and Internet Terms*, Barron's, New York, 1998

England, Janice, *Practical Computing for Beginners*, Roper Penberthy Publishing, 2001

Engst, Adam, *The Internet Starter Kit*, Hayden, San Francisco, 1999

Flanders, Vincent and Michael Willis, *Web Pages That Suck*, Sybex, US, 1999

Freedman, Alan, *The Computer Glossary*, American Management Association, New York, 1998

Freidlein, Ashley, *Web Project Management: Delivering Successful Commercial Web Sites*, Morgan Kaufmann Publishers, 2002

Gaskill, Dennis, *Web Site Design Made Easy*, Morton Pub Co, 2001

Gentry, Lorna, Kelli Brookes and Jill Bond, *New Rider's Official Internet and World Wide Web Yellow Pages*, New Riders Publishing, Indianapolis, 1999

Graham, Ian S., *HTML 4.0 Sourcebook*, John Wiley & Sons, US, 1999

Hackos, Joann T., *Content Management for Dynamic Web Delivery*, John Wiley & Sons, US, 2002

Hale, Constance, *WiredStyle*, HardWired, US, 1999

Harn, Harley, *Internet and Web Yellow Pages*, McGraw-Hill, US, 1999

Harris, G., *Internet for Beginners*, Paragon Publishing Ltd., UK, 2000

Herber, Norbert and Ethan Watrall, *Flash MX Savvy with CD-ROM*, Sybex, 2002

Homer, Alex et al, *Professional Active Server Pages 3.0*, Wrox Press Inc, 1999

Hughes, Lisa and Tim Benton, *The Internet*, Hodder, UK, 1999

Hurwitz, Dan & Jesse Liberty, *Programming ASP.NET (O'Reilly Windows)*, O'Reilly & Associates, Sebastopol, CA, 2002

Hyman, Michael, *PC Roadkill*, IDG, US, 1999

Ingham, Linda, *Grandma's Guide to the Internet*, Willow Island Editions, 2000

Internet Users' Reference: 2002 Edition, Addison Wesley, 2000

James, Jeff, *The Internet and Multiplayer and Gaming Bible*, St Martin's Press, US, 1999

Johnson, Steven, *Interface Culture: How New Technology Transforms the Way We Create and Communicate*, Harper, San Francisco, 1997

Junor, Bill, *Internet: The User's Guide for Everyone*, Branden Publishing Co., 1995

Kalbag, Asha, *World Wide Web for Beginners*, Usborne Publishing Ltd., UK, 1997

Kennedy, Angus, *The Mini Rough Guide Website Directory*, Rough Guides, London, 2001

Kennedy, Angus, *The Rough Guide to the Internet*, Rough Guides, London, 2001

Koman, Richard and Jennifer Niederst, *Learning Web Design: A Beginner's Guide to HTML, Graphics, and Beyond*, O'Reilly & Associates, Sebastopol, CA 2001

Lewis, Chris, *101 Essential Tips Using the Internet*, Dorling Kindersley, UK, 1997

Levine, John R., *The Internet for Dummies*, Hungry Minds Inc., 2000

Littman, Jonathan, *The Fugitive Game*, Little Brown, US, 1999

Lowery, Joseph W., *Dreamweaver MX Bible with CD-ROM*, John Wiley & Sons, US, 2002

Mandel, Thomas and Gerard Van der Leun, *Rules of the Net*, Hyperion, US, 1999

McLaughlin, Brett, *Java & XML, 2nd Edition: Solutions to Real-world Problems*, O'Reilly & Associates, Sebastopol, CA, 2001

Meyer, Eric A., *Cascading Style Sheets: The Definitive Guide*, O'Reilly & Associates, Sebastopol, CA, 2000

Meyer, Eric S., *Eric Meyer on CSS: Mastering the Language of Web Design*, New Riders Publishing, Indianapolis, 2002

Miller, Michael, *Absolute Beginner's Guide to Computers and the Internet*, Que, 2002

Morris, Kenneth M., *User's Guide to the Information Age*, Light Bulb Press, 1999

Mueller, Scott, *Upgrading and Repairing PCs*, Que, US, 1999

Multi-Media, Dorling Kindersley, UK, 1996

Musciano, Chuck and Bill Kennedy, *HTML & XHTML: The Definitive Guide, 4th Edition*, O'Reilly & Associates, Sebastopol, CA, 2002

Naughton, John, *A Brief History of the Future*, Orion Paperbacks, 2000

Negroponte, Nicholas, *Being Digital*, Knopf, US, 1999

Neilsen, Jakob and Marie Tahir, *Homepage Usability: 50 Websites Deconstructed*, New Riders Publishing, Indianapolis, 2001

Neilsen, Jakob, *Designing Web Usability: The Practice of Simplicity*, New Riders Publishing, Indianapolis, 1999

Newcomer, Eric, *Understanding Web Services: XML, WSDL, SOAP, and UDDI*, Addison Wesley Professional, 2002

Niederst, Jennifer, *Web Design in a Nutshell*, O'Reilly & Associates, Sebastopol, CA, 2001

Phillips, Lee Anne and Rick Darnell, *Practical HTML 4.0*, Simon & Schuster, New York, 1999

Platt, Charles, *Anarchy Online: Net Sex Net CrimeU*, Harper Prism, US, 1999

Randall, Neil, *The Soul of the Internet*, Thomson, US, 1999

Raymond, Eric, *New Hacker's Dictionary, 3rd Edition*, MIT Press, Cambridge, MA, 1996

Reader's Digest Beginner's Guide to Home Computing, The Reader's Digest Association Limited, UK, 1998

Rosenfeld, Louis and Peter Morville, *Information Architecture for the World Wide Web*, O'Reilly & Associates, Sebastopol, CA, 1998

Selkirk, Errol, *Computers for Beginners*, Writers and Readers, 1995

Sellers, Don, *Getting Hits*, Peachpit Press, Berkeley, CA, 1997

Shelly, Gary B., Steven G. Forsythe, and Thomas J. Cashman, *Netscape Navigator 6*, Course Technology, 2001

Siebel, Thomas M. and Pat House, *Cyber Rules*, Doubleday, New York, 1999

Siegel, David, *Creating Killer Web Sites*, Hayden, San Francisco, 1996

Simpson, Paul, *The Rough Guide to Shopping Online*, Rough Guides, 2001

Steinmetz, Ralf and Nahrstedt, *Multimedia*, Prentice Hall, 2002

Thatcher, Jim et al, *Constructing Accessible Web Sites*, Glasshaus, 2002

Treays, R., *Computers for Beginners*, Usborne Publishing Ltd., 1997

Walther, Stephen, *ASP.NET Unleashed*, Sams, 2001

Weinman, Lynda, *Designing Web Graphics.3*, New Riders Publishing, Indianapolis, 1999

Williams, Hugh E. and David Lane, *Web Database Applications with PHP & MySQL*, O'Reilly & Associates, Sebastopol, CA, 2002

Wingate, Philippa and Asha Kolbag, *The Usborne Complete Book of the Internet and World Wide Web*, EDC Publishing, Tulsa, OK, 1999

Wolf, Michael *Burn Rate*, Simon & Schuster, New York, 1999

Wong, Thomas, *101 Ways to Boost Your Web Traffic, Internet Promotion Made Easier*, 2nd Edition, Intesync, 2002

Zeff, Robbin and Brad Aronson, *Advertising on the Internet*, John Wiley & Sons, US, 1999

ACKNOWLEDGEMENTS

AUTHOR BIOGRAPHIES

ROGER LAING

Author

Writer and journalist Roger Laing has edited several online publications, including sites backed by major I.T. companies such as Lotus and Microsoft. He has also written and edited various books and magazines covering PCs, the Internet, web design and information technology. He has an M.A. in Experimental Psychology from Oxford University.

RHYS LEWIS

Author

During his ten years in IT journalism Rhys Lewis has written for PC Magazine, Computer Shopper, MacUser and PC Direct where he was online editor and wrote a monthly column on how to design, maintain and market a web site. He has worked on sites for Reed, Dennis and ZDNet.

PRIYA RAVEENDRAN

Consultant Editor

Priya is from London and has worked in the new media industry for four years. She has spent the last two years working for e-commerce company lastminute.com as a web designer and is now the Lead Creative Producer, focussing on the design and development of the company's website and their partner pages.

PICTURE CREDITS

Adobe Systems Incorporated: 56
Allsport: 89, 93 (l), 163 (t).
Anglepoise Ltd of Redditch: 62.
Associated Press: 120.
Christie's Images: 60, 140, 180.
Dennis Hardley: 66.
Dorling Kindersley: 130, 152.
Foundry Arts: 14, 18, 25 (tl), 50, 72, 114, 143 (tr), 151, 156 (m), 174, 186.
Foundry Arts/Graham Stride: 52, 190.
Greg Evans: 26 (t), 68 (r), 101, 106, 148, 177 (bl).
Impact: Ansar, M :22, Cavendish, P: 11 (t); Moyse, C: 95 (b); Shepheard, S: 82.
Niall McInerney: 38.
Mary Evans: 111.
Pictorial Press Ltd: 58.
Still Pictures: 30, Heuclin, D: 104, 164 (t)
Topham: 13, 16, 21, 33(l), 34, 37, 40, 44, 47, 48, 64(r), 74, 76, 80, 91, 97, 99, 102, 116 (b), 118 (l), 123 (t), 127 (t), 128, 132, 134, 136 (tl), 139 (r), 144 (t), 154, 159, 167, 168, 171, 173, 179, 184, 186, 189, 195 (t), 198, 201.
V&A Picture Library: 182.
Bridgeman Art Library: Cartier Bresson, H: 42, Mondrian: 146.

INDEX